RED ROAD FROM STALINGRAD

RED ROAD FROM STALINGRAD

Recollections of a Soviet Infantryman

MANSUR ABDULIN

Editor: Artem Drabkin
Translator: Denis Fedosov
Research Articles: Alexei Isaev
English text: Christopher Summerville

Pen & Sword
MILITARY

First published in Great Britain in 2004 by
Pen & Sword Military
An imprint of Pen & Sword Books Ltd
47 Church Street
Barnsley
South Yorkshire
S70 2AS

Maps: Max Bohdanowski

Publication made possible by the I Remember website
(www.iremember.ru/index_e.htm) and its director, Artem Drabkin

ISBN 1 84415 145 X

Typeset in Sabon by Phoenix Typesetting, Auldgirth, Dumfriesshire
Printed and bound in England by CPI UK.

Pen & Sword Ltd incorporates the Imprints of Pen & Sword Aviation, Pen
& Sword Maritime, Pen & Sword Military, Wharncliffe Local History,
Pen & Sword Select, Pen & Sword Military Classics and Leo Cooper.

For a complete list of Pen & Sword titles please contact
PEN & SWORD BOOKS LTD
47 Church Street, Barnsley, South Yorkshire, S70 2AS, England
E-mail: enquiries@pen-and-sword.co.uk
Website: www.pen-and-sword.co.uk

Contents

Editorial Preface

'This must never happen again!' Such was the slogan proclaimed after the Great Victory, which became an important principle in Soviet domestic and foreign policy. Winning, together with its allies, the bloodiest war in history, the country suffered enormous losses. Almost 27 million people perished (almost 15 per cent of the peacetime population). Millions of my compatriots were killed in action, ended their lives in German concentration camps, starved or froze to death in besieged Leningrad or in evacuation. The 'scorched earth' policy, which both armies pursued during retreat, resulted in the total destruction of the lands which before the war counted a population of 88 million and had produced up to 40 per cent of GDP. Millions of people lost their homes and were forced to live in abominable conditions. The fear that such a catastrophe might repeat itself haunted the nation. It was one of the reasons that the country's leadership adopted an enormous defense budget, which became a terrible strain for the economy. Because of this very real fear, ordinary people used to store a certain amount of 'strategic products' – salt, matches, sugar, canned goods . . . I remember as kid how my grand mother – who had lived through the famine of war – kept trying all the time to give me something to eat, and was very distressed when I refused! We children, born some thirty years after the war, continued to refight it in our play, in the streets. We divided into groups of 'our men' and 'Germans' and the first German words we learned were 'Hände hoch,' 'Nicht schiessen,' and 'Hitler Kaputt.' In almost every house one could see some reminder of the war. I still have my father's decorations and a German case for gas mask filters standing in the corridor of my flat – it's a good thing to sit on when you're tying your shoelaces!

A desire to forget the horrors of the war as fast as possible, to heal its wounds–as well as to conceal the mistakes of the country's leadership and military chiefs–led to a propaganda campaign based on the image of a faceless Soviet soldier, 'bearing on his shoulders the full weight of the struggle with German fascism,' while praising the 'heroism of the Soviet people.' This attitude meant propagating a simplified, strictly official interpretation of what really happened. As a result, those memoirs published in the Soviet era were strongly affected by both external and internal censorship. Only in the late eighties could the full truth about the war come to light.

That was the decade Mansur Abdulin's book was published. Last year, when I saw it for the first time, I realized that here I held a true confession of the 'heroic Soviet people', written by a highly original man. What makes these memoirs absolutely unique is that Abdulin was involved in front line action for a whole year, while statistics tell us that on average, a Red Army infantryman survived the battlefield for only a fortnight, after which he was either killed or wounded. This period of time allowed Mansur to gain a wealth of experience, which he relates in this book. Being a gifted story-teller, Abdulin, in a frank and straightforward way, describes his life in the trenches. He was perfectly aware that the carnage, which he was forced to be a part of, left him practically no chance of survival. His main goal was to sell his life as dearly as possible, which meant killing others, killing as many enemy soldiers as he was able. The war on the Eastern Front was marked by an amazing degree of hatred and violence, connected largely with the German intentions of totally annihilating the USSR and enslaving its population. The Western reader has already had an opportunity to learn of the experiences of the German side, by reading the books of such veterans as Guy Sajer or Günter K. Koschorrek, while memoirs of Soviet soldiers were almost totally inaccessible. This is why I instantly felt enthusiastic about an English edition.

But how could I find the author? The book was published thirteen years ago and Abdulin must be no less than eighty by now. Was he alive? How could I reach him? It was mentioned in the accompanying text that Mansur Abdulin resides in Novotroitsk, in the Orenburg Region. I called the information office of this small town situated in the Southern Urals. The girl at the other end of the line misspelled the surname at first, and answered that she didn't have such a man on her list. My heart sank! 'What did you say the name was?' 'Abdulin.'

'Sorry, I was looking for "Abdullin". Just a moment . . . Yes, we have an Abdulin M.G.' I immediately phoned Mansur and introduced myself: 'How would you feel about preparing an English edition of your book?' 'Why not? Let's give it a try . . .'

Artem Drabkin,
Moscow 2004

Maps

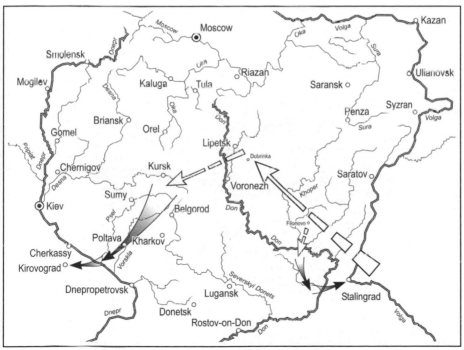

The Eastern Front showing Mansur Abdulin's route

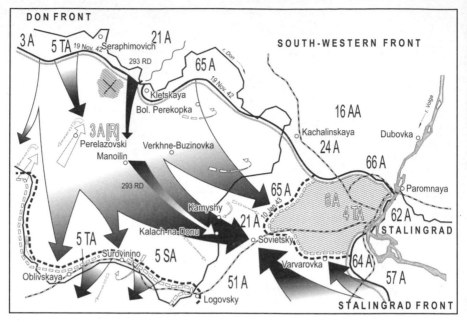

'Operation Uranium': encirclement of the Sixth Army in Stalingrad

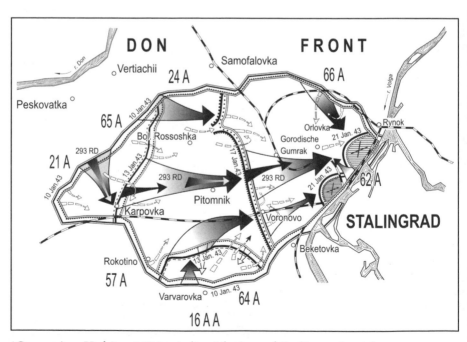

'Operation Kol 'tso' (Ring): liquidation of Stalingrad pocket

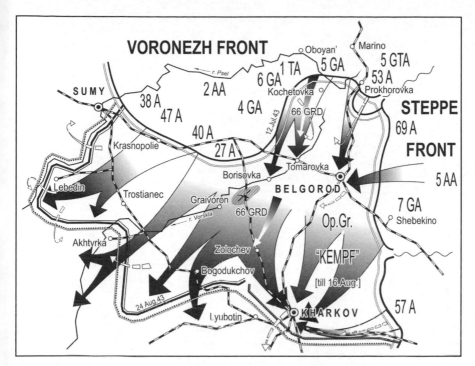

Belgorod-Kharkov: the 'Rumiantsev' strategic offensive

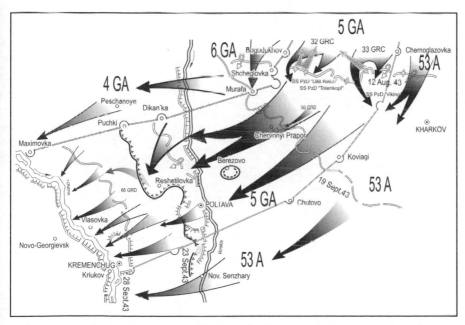

Advance to the Dnieper: operations of 5th Guards Army in the Ukraine campaign

CHAPTER ONE

The Front

The war, the front, means shooting. Mortars, machine- and sub-machine guns, artillery. I made my first shot in action on 6 November 1942, on the South-Western Front, from an autoloading SVT rifle. This is how it was . . .

A couple of days before the attack, every company held solemn meetings, 'dedicated to the 25th Anniversary of our Soviet State.' We took an oath to carry out the order of the Motherland – 'No retreat!' – then we crossed the Don. The river was quiet, the passage went well, and at a rapid pace, we entered a ravine high on the right bank.

'Watch your step!' We keep hearing this warning, and for us mortarmen, it has an important and specific meaning. Mortarmen are loaded with gun carriages, barrels and base-plates: if you are moving fast, and fall or flounder, the equipment – because of the momentum – can crush the back of your skull. I have seen many lightly wounded soldiers stumble, only to be finished off by their heavy load.

We are advancing over a kind of waste ground. We seem to be stepping on old sacks and clumps of grass: in the dark we can't see what's beneath our feet. What bothers us is some stinking smell. We run away from it, forward, forward! A violet flare appears in the sky, and in its light we see the faces of the dead. Both Germans and our own men.

More flares. I furtively look at my comrades: do they see them? Yes, they do. But everyone seems calm. No one makes a fuss. Not even a swear word. War is war. This is how it is. And what can be more natural! I have just turned nineteen and I know that the others are about the same age. Everyone has had a similar experience: a quick course of practice shoots at the Tashkent Infantry School.

I jump over dead bodies, and in my mind flashes a thought: how quickly men become accustomed to things which, at one time, they would have found impossible to imagine. Another thought – and a strange one in such circumstances – I am satisfied with myself. If a comrade glanced at me, he would see nothing but a common expression of concentration. At the front, being like everyone else – that is, no worse than the others – means being assured of one's value. A very important thing for self-respect. However startled I was by the sickening scene illuminated by the flare (the true face of war, its essence, when notices like 'Died a valiant death' are issued), I, nevertheless, am doing all the necessary things, just like the other men: trying not to stumble, ducking down when the whistling bullets fly.

We run the final few metres bent double. The ravine is becoming shallower: now the bullets whizz very low. Eventually I jump into the trench: alive, no bruises, my knapsack and gun right here. A few minutes to catch my breath and I'm ready to fire whenever the order comes.

'What took you so long?' We hear harsh voices, some foul language, then the front line soldiers vanish from the trenches, like ghosts into thin air. Loaded with their mortars and machine-guns, they march past us into the ravine from which we have just emerged. I had anticipated a different reception, and the instant disappearance of the trenches' preceding inhabitants leaves an unpleasant impression. Probably I expected the 'old men' to stay with us a while, to show us what to do. How to fight . . .

'You're making me laugh!' chuckles Pavel Suvorov, our crew leader. 'They must also cross the Don while it's dark, and need time to get to the rear without the Nazis spotting them.' Suvorov's good-humoured crowing convinces me of one thing: the moment we jumped down here we became front line soldiers. And whatever happens in the time to come, no one will remember, or take into consideration, the fact that we are just former cadets fresh from an infantry school.

It is surprising how the instinct of self-preservation works in a man. It seems that everyone else experienced the same feelings as I did: but we can already hear the signallers calling, 'This is "Breech-block", can you hear me? Over!' while battalion artillerymen drag cases of ammunition towards their cannon; and on the breastwork, machine-gunners install their Maxims. In our company the mortars are also ready for combat, and Fuat Khudaibergenov, along with myself (in

Suvorov's gun crew he is the charger and I, the gun-layer), have neatly arranged the shells next to our mortar. Since we have a war, everyone should try to be an efficient cog in the entire fighting mechanism. That's the most important thing.

So now that the hands have done all the necessary stuff, one might have a look around. The trenches seem old, with battered edges: 'This means that we have been here a long time,' explains Nikolai Makarov from the neighbouring gun crew. All the gun crews in our company were formed in the military school. 'Or they were taken from the Germans,' objects Victor Kozlov. Both speak calmly, as though they have been fighting for ages. German flares keep darting into the sky, lighting the bottom of the trench, while machine-guns fire incessantly.

'Afraid of our night attack?' smiles Ivan Konski, and in his eyes, which shine for a moment in the pallid light, I catch an expression of confidence, which finally calms me down. Senior Lieutenant Buteiko, our company commander, has already sent someone to the observation post, and warns me that I should be ready to replace the man on duty at dawn.

'Well, Mansur, are you hot now?' asks the deputy commander of the company, Junior Political Instructor Fatkulla Khismatullin, in Tartar. He has come up to us along with the CO. Before the war Khismatullin was a history teacher, and he used to ask us to explain in detail where we were born and what we wanted to do in life. This was for a future book he planned to write. He translates his question into Russian, so Buteiko and the rest of the men can understand: 'I'm asking him whether he is hot now!' Everyone has a big laugh. The thing is, I was born in Siberia, and during the practice shoots collapsed several times in the Tashkent heat. I was even afraid they would discharge me. We remember how in the school, because of the salt and sweat, we had to wash our blouses daily, and they would tear at the seams every fortnight. How we dreamed: 'Wish I was at the front!'

'Here we are at the front!' concludes Buteiko, looking at his watch. 'Now don't forget what you were taught . . .' The experienced company commander, who was in this war right from the start, taught us, among other things, to use additional charges as often as possible in order to clean our mortar barrels of gunpowder remains. If a barrel is not clean, the shell inside moves more slowly and if, during a barrage, a shell is inserted before the preceding one is fired, it can cause an explosion inside the tube . . .

'You can have a rest now,' said Buteiko, and he and Khismatullin, bending down, move further along the trench. Sergei Lopunov immediately asks Fuat to give him a needle and a piece of string, while Victor Kozhevnikov demands a pencil and some paper. We know that our charger always has in his kit whatever one might need: needles, string, shoe-laces, buttons, scissors, a razor, Vaseline, soap, shoe-polish, a brush, iodine, bandages, etc. Fuat always likes to have everything in excellent order. And he is never idle. Even now, while we are busy remembering the past, he uses the spare time to repair the torn lining of his greatcoat, and examines the broken heel of Nikolai Makarov's boot. He is an expert tailor, shoemaker, cook; and when necessary, a smith and a carpenter. As to bread, sugar or *makhorka* [a type of cheap tobacco – editor's note], we never divide it like they do in some platoons, where one man, taking a portion of the stuff, asks 'Who?' while another turns away and says 'Ivanov', 'Petrov' or 'Sidorov.' Fuat is responsible for dividing the goods, and then everyone takes from his waterproof cape one of the forty portions, being absolutely sure that all of them are the same. Translated from Uzbek, the surname Khudaibergenov means 'Gift of God'. Fuat's father was Tartar and his mother Uzbek. He is my age, a big and strong fellow. He does not talk much, but once he surprised us by inviting everyone in the platoon to visit him after the war, to enjoy some pilaw [a favourite Central Asian rice dish, often including chopped meat, vegetables, oil, spices, and stock – editor's note]. We had to promise to come to his place in Tashkent. I was in a better position than the others to make the promise: sometime before the war my father and our family had moved from Siberia to the Sargardon mine in Central Asia, so my way home passes through Tashkent.

All these events I put down in a letter home. I throw the envelope into the pile of letters, and at this precise moment – about two hours before I am due to go on duty – I am seized with fear. There you see Ivan Konski, sound asleep and probably dreaming about his native Smolensk Region. But in my mind there stubbornly persists a disturbing picture: violet faces of the dead. I try to chase away this image by recalling scenes from my childhood.

I was born into a miner's family on 14 September 1923. We lived in a Tashtagol village called Sukhoi, surrounded by dense, virgin forests. For centuries it was inhabited by native Tashtagol people, free and runaway Tartars, Estonians, Hungarians, Germans, Russian Old

Believers, and also the descendants of Cossacks who had participated in the peasant uprising led by Yemellian Pugachev (1773–1775). Each of them had their own faith, their own god, or some sacred object they worshipped. For example, one family had a hole in the corner of a room, through which they communicated with the Highest Power; another had a young larch in their yard, which they considered sacred, decorating its branches with various rags and praying to it.

These people, having their own gods, rules and principles, lived in peace with each other. They were united by a common superstition: that all were ruled by a Highest Power, which severely punished bad men. The local inhabitants, whatever their faith and nationality, were also united by another mystical notion: that there exists an 'owner' of a forest, river, hill, lake, swamp, or mine, who protects his possessions and riches. If anyone dared do a bad thing, the 'owner' would inevitably crush the man, leaving no trace of him.

My parents were both 'newcomers' and 'outsiders' – 'Party folk' (meaning Communist Party members) – free of any religion. But since they were the only people who could read and write, they were respected by the locals. My father worked as a technician in the mine, and being a Communist Party member, attended the workers' faculty courses. My mother, though poorly educated, taught the people of the neighbourhood to write – even if it was just their name.

I was born after the Russian Autocracy collapsed, and its armed forces crushed in the Civil War [1918–21 – editor's note]. The newborn Soviet state was suffering from a prolonged famine, accompanied by terrible diseases such as smallpox, consumption, cholera, and typhus. Often there was no one to make a grave for the dead. Peasant women buried their children without tears, openly showing their joy at having one less mouth to feed. Many adults – and even children – took their lives in different ways. My mother would sometimes get hysterical from constant starvation and despair, screaming madly: 'I'll hang myself! I'll run away from you (meaning myself, my younger brother and my father) . . . someplace!'

Because of this terrible life, she was not ashamed to admit – in front of me and my brother – that she envied some of her friends: women who had buried all their children. Even though I was only three or four years old at the time, I understood her, and bore no hard feelings. I prayed to the Highest Power (which I already believed existed), asking that He might give good health to my parents, and that the 'owner' of the mine would take care of my father when he was underground. I tried to overcome my painful hunger and not to cry. Once, our medico examined me and said to my mother: 'Your kid is not sick or anything, but he is suffering from anaemia and is therefore weak. The best medicine is proper food!' Since then I was scared to cut my finger. I was frightened I would die, that I would bleed to death, and that mum would be happy to get rid of an 'extra mouth'.

Local inhabitants often visited my parents because they were the only literate people in the area. The guests discussed various important themes: 'Tell us frankly, Comrade Abdulin – you being a party man – is there a God or isn't there?' Then they would wait for his answer, catching their breath. 'Unfortunately, there is no God,' came the reply, 'but since people have always needed a strong, all-knowing, just and retributive benefactor, they invented him, so that everyone in the world would be happy.' After these words the guests' eyes almost jumped out of their sockets, but my father hurried to calm them down: 'But over mankind, instead of God, there is the Highest Power of Reason. It reigns over us and will help its people not to lose their way, and not to perish.' This seemed to reassure everyone and offer hope for a good future. People nodded their enormous beards with satisfaction: 'One might still live in this way – but without Faith, one cannot!' And bowing down to the ground, they would exit the door backwards.

From being a small child I liked to draw, saw and plane, invent and construct different gadgets. And when I was in school, I was quite an expert at making wooden skis and ice-skates. I made bird houses in the form of traditional peasant cottages, and starlings had a great liking for them, squabbling among themselves for their possession. I was an active member of the aircraft modelling and glider hobby groups. At twelve years of age, I already had 'Be Ready for Labour and Defence' and 'Voroshilov Shot' badges [these badges were given to those who successfully passed sporting and shooting norms established by the state – editor's note] and went into the forest with my gun to hunt hazel-grouses. I dreamt of becoming an artist, an actor, a mine technician, a photographer, a pilot, a driver, and a Red Army commander. Once I made a wooden camera [this would appear to have been a kind of pinhole camera or *camera obscura*, a simple device widely used before the advent of the modern photographic camera in the nineteenth century – editor's note], but had nothing for a lens – not even a pair of glasses – so I used a red-hot awl to pierce a hole, and with the help of ashes, made a piece of dim glass. It was a great surprise to me when, some distance away from the lens, one could see on it a pretty clear picture of my wolfhound, which happened to pass by at that moment. But the dog was upside down! The inhabitants of the mine, learning about my new toy, praised me with much enthusiasm: 'Little Mansur Abdulin, that kid is quite something! He made an interesting toy which turns all the girls and women upside down, so their skirts fall over their heads! And then you can look at them! It's easy, them having no pants! Ha-ha!' So the girls and women, seeing me with my toy, shouted in panic, and tried to run away or hide. Eventually they ambushed me, knocked me off my feet, and took away the toy, smashing my nose and almost tearing off my ears . . .

Another time (being perhaps the most talented, and certainly the most persistent, participant in amateur dramatics), I was given the role of a White Army officer [opponent of the Red Army in the Russian Civil War of 1918–21 – editor's note], equipped with a pair of red-hot blacksmith's tongs, with which to torture captured Communists, fighting for the Red Army. But the show was never finished, as some of the lads in the audience rushed on stage, roaring, 'Kill the Whitey!' and gave me a sound beating, as if my acting was for real. My liver suffered a lot: as did my desire to become an actor! I also drew well, and decorated some of the writing-books (always in short supply) with my pictures: my father then 'decorated' my buttocks with his raw leather belt, in such a way that for a whole week I had to lie on my stomach with no pants, exhibiting my naked arse to the cockroaches . . .

I spent my childhood in the Miasski Mines. When I grew up a little, I was busy all through the summer from dawn till dusk – just like the rest of the boys and even some girls – looking for gold: sieving the clayey lumps and sand in a simple metal basin or gold digger's scoop. By this time our life had somewhat improved: there was less hunger and we even found some extra money to buy clothes.

In 1940, in order to get a bread card, I left my school and went to work in the mine, where I was responsible for moving the tubs. Then, on 22 June 1941 war broke out. As a miner I was exempt from service but eventually managed to enlist. There were four of us: Nikolai Koniayev, Ivan Vanshin, Victor Karpov and myself. We all went to the military registration bureau and tried to convince the officer that our experience in mining was not so great as to keep us away from the front, but he kept saying: 'I can't, I'm under orders from the

Defence Committee, I don't have the right!' So – I remember this with a smile – we had to threaten him with breaking into a shop at night: then we would probably be sent to a penal battalion, and in court we'd say that Major Galkin tried to stop us from getting to the front! Well, the major solved the problem. He phoned someone straightaway, got the permission, and soon we found ourselves standing naked before the scrutinising eyes of a commission, responsible for choosing cadets for a flying school. Only two of us made it there: my closest friend Nikolai Koniayev and Victor Karpov. Vanshin and myself went back to the military registration bureau, and that same day he departed for the Chirchiks Tank School, and I to the Tashkent Infantry School (named after V. Lenin). Of course I envied them: but fate had it that only I, an infantryman, would survive the war.

After successfully completing my course at the military school, I was again exempt from active service. As an exemplary student, I was to remain at the school as a teacher. Some of my comrades envied me, while others made spiteful remarks: 'He wanted so much to join the front line forces, but we'll see what happens now!' Nevertheless, I had a plan. I plotted with another honours student, whose surname was Taktzer. He was to eat a piece of laundry soap, end up in a hospital, and thus save himself from the front. He got diarrhoea, and I came to the school commissar with a proposal: 'Leave Taktzer here and include me on the list of those being sent to the front!' All my comrades were happy to see me – not least because I was the best singer – and I was made responsible for our group of 700 fresh junior lieutenants.

When we finally joined our division, my comrades were sent to different regiments and I was left at headquarters, in the reserve. I had no desire to stay behind, however, and begged in vain to be dispatched to a front line regiment: 'In the army there are no such things as "I won't! I can't! I don't know how!"' was the answer.

One day, when I was on duty at HQ, I was summoned by the divisional commander. Without giving me time to report myself, he warmly invited me to sit down, and even pushed a pack of *Kazbek* cigarettes closer to my chair: 'Have a smoke.' I had noticed some time ago how he looked at me: like some gypsy at a fair, contemplating a horse he particularly liked. I did not dare smoke in front of the general and prepared myself for the worse, as I already knew that he was looking for a personal adjutant. As usual, he was tipsy. He stared at me with his bull's eyes and mumbled in a bossy tone, barely able to move his swollen tongue: 'Today I decided to sign an order making you my personal adjutant. I am satisfied with your record and your references, and I expect to hear your consent.'

'I would ask you to dispatch me to Regiment 1034, where my comrades are serving,' I replied.

'I did not expect you to refuse! Don't you realize there's nothing romantic about the front line? It's just a slaughterhouse! Say "yes" and you won't regret it. I'll see to it that you get decorations and a new rank. Think about it. I'll treat you well.'

'No, Comrade General. I don't know how to polish boots, but I know how to fight.'

'But why?' He raised his bushy eyebrows, which were streaked with grey, and kept them hovering in anticipation of my answer.

'I made an oath to my friends to fight together with them.'

'No one among your friends would have refused such an offer!'

So this was how I ended up at the front line with my fellow-cadets. I told my Regimental commissar that I wanted to be a rank and file man, because I felt ashamed of commanding soldiers that in terms of age, might well have been my father; and that I wanted to experience 'the smell of powder'. There were enough lieutenants, so my request was granted.

Did I know that I was about to face death? I did. There was no specific scene in my imagination, like the one I later saw at the bottom of the ravine in the violet light of the flare. But man is so mysterious! If I'd have found myself, just this minute, a thousand kilometres away from the ravine, in the blossoming village of Brichmulla, I would again dash to the military registration bureau, and demand to be sent here. The fact was that I didn't want to die, but similarly, I didn't want to live with a guilty conscience. One thought had tormented me back at the mine: what would I be saying when the war is over? That the rear also needed able men, especially in the mines, to work for the nation's defence? This is true. But you can't explain this to everyone; convince everyone. Even girls are summoned to the front. But I wanted to live so much! How unbearably terrifying to become a corpse in a ravine, lit by the violet flame of the flare . . .

This thought is interrupted by the appearance of Suvorov, who, it seems, also cannot not sleep: 'Well, Mansur, afraid?' I feel like someone has hit me in the stomach, 'come on, don't be ashamed,' he winked, 'everyone's afraid.' I frankly confess that looking at the other boys I see no signs. 'They're trying not to show it,' explains Suvorov in a genial tone, and winks again, as though sharing some secret: 'and don't you show it. Keep your tail up!'

I became interested. Suvorov is seven years older than I, a regular army man, who served in the First Moscow Regiment before the war. He was fighting right from the start, and had already been decorated with the Order of the Red Star. I ask him whether he too was afraid? 'You think I don't want to live?' he smiled. 'But what can we do, little Mansur? "We didn't ask them, but they came." ' (a line from a popular song.) 'They want space. Yours and mine! They're "Übermenschen" – supermen – you see? We're only fit to polish their boots. How do you like that? With such people there's only one way: a fight. A big fight. One can't just stand and look, afraid or not . . .'

It is dawn. German machine-gunners have stopped shooting. There are no more flares. The night has passed. 'Well, let's go, I'll show you the way,' says Suvorov.

The sentry-hole is carefully camouflaged. Suvorov looks into the periscope and then, clearing a space for me, remained standing nearby, sunk in thought: 'They are about 300m [just over 328 yards – editor's note] away,' he says, 'and they're facing the sun.' He wishes me luck and leaves.

They're facing the sun. This means I can freely examine their positions. I have fixed a permanent sight on my self-loading rifle, put a cartridge into the barrel, placed the butt against my shoulder, and felt the gun – everything's OK – so I watch the enemy front trenches closely, while different thoughts cross my mind.

I remember our Siberian forests. I'm still a kid. A fresh notch on a larch serves as a target. A y-shaped birch branch driven into the ground is a prop for a heavy hunting rifle. I'm eight years old, and my father is teaching me to shoot: 'Come up and aim like this!' He showed me how to aim, and I clumsily grab the rifle. The sight and the mark are instantly in line. I'm in a hurry, because in the forest one should shoot fast: the hazel-grouse won't wait, it'll fly away! I'm pulling the trigger but nothing happens. Maybe my finger is too weak? I wish my father would postpone my training until I grow up! Red with tension, I pull the trigger with all my strength. My father urges me on: 'Stop aiming, shoot!' I keep pulling and pulling, feeling myself about to explode with the strain. Suddenly I loose off – not a bullet – but an enormous fart, which makes a loud, loathsome sound, like the tearing of the tarpaulin that they use for making miners' uniforms. This sets my father laughing. He was laughing so hard that he squatted down and raised his head so high that I could see every single one of his strong, white teeth. Later he told me that I was pulling the cramp, not the trigger. Eventually I began to shoot so well, that father barely had time to reload the gun. I was happy, but he even more so.

Was I disturbed by the thought that it was not hazel-grouses I was hunting, but human beings? I had something else on my mind. I remembered how two weeks ago, after our division hurriedly mounted a troop train (Regiment 1034 entrained at a small station called Koltubanka) and began moving towards the front, we were attacked by enemy bombers. Our engine driver would suddenly slow down and then speed ahead. The bombs did not damage the train, but the German planes, flying low, succeeded in hitting some of the cars with their machine-guns. The smoke of TNT and coal, the smell of burned earth, the blood of the dead and wounded, the groans: all this I saw, breathed, and heard, while the front was still hundreds of kilometres away. Many of my comrades perished without being able to kill a single Fritz. Can this happen to me? Will I be killed? Will I die in vain? That's impossible! To die without catching a glimpse of the enemy, after all that effort to get to the front?

The only thing I see is the flat steppe as far as the horizon. Everything is still. Not a sound. Then, suddenly, some movement ahead. My heart beats fast. My rifle is in excellent condition – I can hit a tin can from 100m [almost 110 yards – editor's note]. Suddenly I'm hot. The target is getting larger as it approaches. Germans. They're walking in the trench. How many? They're carrying some straw on their shoulders, fastened with belts. They make a turn, and I can see that there are three of them. Now they are walking down their trench along the front side. I must shoot right now. I decide to aim at the middle one. But what's going on? I can't seem to get the slit, the sight, and the target in line: if I line-up the target and the sight, I lose the slit! If I find the slit, I lose the sight! I'm sweating. It fills my eyes. The gun is shaking in my hands. Already realizing that I'll miss, I pull the trigger. The silence is broken by the report.

The Germans instantly disappear, and I – slowly, as if mortally wounded – sink to the bottom of the sentry-hole. How I hate myself at this moment! What a looser! Such an opportunity missed! I realize that I am so afraid, so nervous, because my death might come without any harm to the enemy. If I could kill just one of them! Just to get even for the future. This thought had made me tremble and shoot in haste, as soon as I saw them within range. I am good for nothing!

All this passes through my brain in a split second. Then, I rise up again and put the butt of my rifle to my shoulder. So, where are my Fritzes? They're gone, of course. No! They're still running in the trench, bending even lower and taking longer intervals. A thought flashed: 'Now it's totally impossible to hit them.' Slit, sight, target. Strange, but now there's no trembling. Everything's in order. I make my mark a couple of centimetres in front of the middle Nazi and smoothly pull the trigger.

The first Fritz – bent double, so that only the bundle of straw is visible from time to time – goes on running, but the second one stops, stands up to his full height, his head unnaturally twitching backwards, and making a spiral movement, tumbles down like a rag-doll. Captivated by the slow turning of my victim, I fail to notice what the third German does. 'None of the lads will believe I killed a Nazi!' is my first thought. Only a minute before I was cursing myself, but now I am bursting with pride: 'If only our boys could see this!'

Suddenly I hear a voice: 'Well done, Abdulin! Well done! Aren't you the *komsorg* [leader of the Komsomol members of the unit; this organisation was officially called the VLKSM, the All-Union Lenin's Communist Union of Youth – editor's note] of your company?' I see Captain Chetkasov, our battalion commissar. He puts down his binoculars and smiles at me: 'You are the first in your battalion to inflict a casualty on the enemy!' It turns out that he heard a shot, crawled up to the sentry-hole, and saw me kill the Fritz. An hour later Chetkasov tells me that I am also the first in the whole regiment to shoot down an enemy soldier, and that I shall receive the medal, 'For Bravery'.

I have to say, that in the time to come, I did more important things – and in more difficult circumstances – than this first successful shot. And for those I got no decorations! But the ideology of war is a relative matter. One should remember that our regiment consisted mainly of inexperienced cadets; that it had just arrived at the front; and that it was essential to adapt us to active service conditions as soon as possible. In each company, political instructors spoke of the current goal that men should achieve: every soldier was to kill at least one enemy in memory of the anniversary of the Socialist Revolution.

The commissar presented me with a notebook. On the first page, inscribed in his own hand, was the following citation: 'On 6 November 1942, at the South-Western Front, near the village of Kletskaia, Lenin's Cadet, Mansur G. Abdulin of the Tashkent Infantry School, was the first among the men of Regiment 1034 to inflict a casualty on the enemy, destroying a Hitlerite in honour of the 25th Anniversary of the Great October Revolution. Battalion Commissar Capt. Chetkasov.' Our commissar was a good man. I remember him liking the song, 'Everyone knows the commissar, he is neither young, nor old . . .' Soon I joined the Communist Party and was elected *partorg* [Communist leader – editor's note] of our company. I described the whole event in a second letter to my father, who was an old Bolshevik [long-time member of the VKP(b), the All-Russian Communist Party (of the Bolsheviks) – editor's note]. He should be proud of his son! I wrote that I had killed one Nazi so that, 'I wouldn't feel regret in case anything happens,' adding: 'It was terrifying on that field . . .'

CHAPTER TWO

First Attack

Upstream, in our rear, lies Kulikovo Field, where almost six centuries ago the Russian army defeated Mamai's Mongol hordes. Ahead of us, across the 300m [328 yards – editor's note] wide neutral zone, stand Hitler's hordes, which we must destroy.

On 14 November 1942, our regiment was ordered to break through the German lines and take control of their defensive installations. Essentially this meant going into combat for reconnaissance purposes: though at the time – as soldiers are not supposed to know the strategic plans of their commanders – we were unaware of this fact. Almost without artillery support, we were to storm the enemy wire, while the Fritzes – in order to check the advance of our regiment – would be forced to fire with all of their guns, thus disclosing their positions. This was essential, if our commanders were to accurately pin-point targets for the coming counter-attack. As it happened, we failed to penetrate the German lines but succeeded in drawing the enemy's fire. We lost most of our men in the action, and when the mission was over, our sector of the front line was essentially manned by a single battalion.

The general picture of that first battle became clear that night, when – the fighting having finished – I went with some survivors to stand watch near the neutral zone. There was a drizzle that evening. The temperature dropped sharply. In the dark we could hear the gentle, glassy sound of breaking ice under our feet. And then a full moon rose, coldly illuminating a composition of several hundred statues: life-size figures of soldiers frozen to ice. Some were lying flat on their backs, others twisted and contorted. Some were sitting lopsided with raised hands, as if urging comrades to continue the attack. Petrified faces with wide open eyes and screaming mouths. Piles of bodies were heaped on the barbed wire, hauling it to the ground with their weight, clearing a way to the Nazi trenches. One's mind could not grasp the scene, failing to accept the frozen composition as a fact of life. It seemed as if someone might suddenly switch the camera back on, and the freeze-frame would start moving.

Then it began to snow. The blizzard hid from our eyes the terrible scenes of battle. By morning, the ground was covered with an enormous white blanket. A shroud. Now all the eye could see was the flat steppe: spotless, still, serene. As if primeval purity eternally reigned here. It would remain quiet until 19 November.

The majority of my fellow-cadets perished in that first battle, preparing the way for our victorious counter-attack in the Stalingrad sector. I wonder whether Khismatullin was able to learn from all of them what they wanted to do in life? He, too, died in the combat.

On the morning of 19 November 1942, large lumps of earth suddenly begin to crumble from the frozen walls of the trenches; the ground beneath our feet shakes like a huge piece of rubber; and the very air vibrates, agitated by some gigantic, unseen force, which threatens to tear our eardrums and lungs. Then, across No Man's Land, the earth explodes, heaving a vast column of spoil high into the air, which falls like a hefty black veil, obscuring the German trenches: the voices of our guns, concentrated into a single murderous roar, heralds the long-awaited counter-attack at Stalingrad.

We want to scream 'Hurrah!' But instead something like 'a-a-a . . . !' comes from our mouths. The sound vibrates! And it is ridiculous to hear myself and the others bleating like this: better we keep silent while the artillery speaks! Meanwhile, the black curtain of debris still hangs over the Nazi front line: 'Isn't that enough?' comes a mean thought, 'our gunners are wasting too many shells, they should save some!' But maybe it's better to overdo it than the other way around.

Then the thunder of the cannon suddenly ceases. That same minute, from the snow behind us, hundreds of tanks appear and rush forward, passing over our trenches. After lying low and waiting for them to pass over, we jump out: Suvorov, the commander of our gun crew, carries the sight, I, the barrel, Fuat Khudaibergenov, the gun carriage, our Number Four, the base-plate, and our Number Five, the shells. We run directly into the slowly sinking wall of black dust.

We pass the Nazi defence line, but there's nothing there except earth and smoke. Not a single living human being! Well, it seems that it was not in vain that our cadets sacrificed themselves five days ago: learning the position of the enemy guns, our artillery today had a clear knowledge of all the targets, and the counter-attack is a success. We cannot not even see the bodies of enemy soldiers: they were all buried in the course of our bombardment.

I remember some Romanians who surrendered without a fight. 'Antonescu kaputt! Stalin gut! Rus Kamerad gut!' And they kept playing the melody of our *Katiusha* [a very popular Russian song – editor's note] on their mouth organs. Their horses were a pleasure to look at: beautiful and well-groomed. The harnesses were made exclusively of fine, creaking leather, with no shaft-bows or collars, only thick wide straps. The carts were covered in the gypsy manner. Some were very luxurious, with windows, curtains, and running on rubber tyres. Our rifle division instantly turned into cavalry! Everyone got a horse! But next day the horses had to be abandoned.

Our gunners decided to replace their Mongolian ponies with heavy-weight Romanian carthorses. But the next day switched them back again: and they were lucky that the Mongolians, having been rejected, bore no hard feelings, and kept running along like faithful dogs. Hairy and small, mean and fond of biting, Mongolian horses turned out to be very enduring, and served us well till the end of the war. While the Romanian thoroughbreds, one after another, had to be left in the fields. Although well-groomed and beautiful, they were too delicate for wartime.

Have you ever seen a horse wounded in action? I have. It was a horse I rode for several kilometres, until a shell exploded near us. Making a few circles in the air I finally landed. Then I saw the animal: its front legs, set against the ground, made jerky movements as if dancing; its body was covered in sweat, the muscles vibrating with a futile effort. The poor thing didn't understand that it would never rise again. Its nostrils quivered, pink and bloody. It groaned like a human, and looked at me with wide open eyes, tears falling from them. I stood close by but did not have the nerve to shoot it. Some old soldier stopped by and put an end to the suffering of the wounded horse. He stuck a carbine into its ear and fired. I'm crying as I write these lines. What was the dying horse thinking when it looked at me with its wide open eyes? That men are a sick race, a force that disfigures nature? No, this knowledge is accessible only to Man himself. At its final moment, the horse expected from me – a human being – help and salvation.

Kalach-on-Don was first taken by our tank troops. The infantry entered the liberated town only a day later. So we weren't participating in that operation, we just passed through the place. Just before reaching Kalach, when our forces were stretched out on the highroad – some men still on horseback, others walking – we suddenly heard screams . . .

'Air raid!' What, planes? But it's a misty day! Still, I hear the drone of engines. Then I see them: pot-bellied German bombers, no more than 100m [110 yards – editor's note] high. They pass directly over our column, dropping their deadly cargo. Falling close to one another, the bombs pepper the road but do not explode instantly. For several seconds I keep running ahead, jumping over those who, hearing the alarm, have plunged to the ground. I bypass or jump over bombs that have just fallen: there are already about ten of them ahead of me. I can hear explosions behind my back – a continuous roar of thunder – and bits of earth rain down from above. Then it dawns on me that I should change my direction and make a right angle turn away from the road. I do it. But just the same, here in front of me, I see an enormous metal object rolling in a ditch. I don't have time to skirt round it. 'How long ago did it fall?' I ask myself. 'Will I make it?' I feel anger as I fly over it because I'm moving so slowly, as if caught in the clutch of some giant magnet. I have about half a minute, then I must hit the deck. Something flies overhead and flops in front. I jump over it. What was it? A horse's head, a bridle: I recognize our platoon leader's horse. I fall down and press myself close to the ground, seeking sanctuary, the Earth's embrace. The explosion tears the knapsack right off my back and tosses it away. Stupefied, I struggle to my feet and begin coughing and vomiting, as if I'm about to throw up my entrails. Black earth is everywhere around me – the snow disappearing completely – bloody shreds of arms and legs, the smell of burning, excruciating pain in my ears. And in my mind, a scene which my eyes had caught during the wild run: one round bomb crashing into the back of a horse carrying our platoon leader. He was just about to dismount and had one foot on the ground and the other still in the stirrup. The road is now a bloody mess: the remains of those who immediately dropped down upon hearing the alarm.

The bridge over the Don, which was used by our tank men to break into the town, has been destroyed by the Nazi planes: so we cross on the ice, which is so smooth and slippery, that it is almost impossible to make a single step. Laden with our heavy barrels, gun carriages, and base-plates, we will surely break it – especially if someone slips and falls down – and will all end up in the freezing water. We are given an order to fill our helmets and greatcoat tails with sand and keep throwing it in front of us, walking at a distance of about 5m [almost 5 yards 6 inches – editor's note] from one another. In this way, line after line, we begin crossing the thin, glittering ice.

The ice sags beneath our feet, threatening to break any moment. For dozens of metres on either side of me I hear only heavy breathing and muffled grumbling: 'Quiet!' 'You're trampling like an elephant!' 'Careful!' The bridge is close by. Sappers cover it like swarming ants. Automobiles and carts are jamming before it, and more and more keep arriving. Gunners are also waiting for the sappers to repair the damaged span: the ice is too thin for them to cross the river. But we infantrymen are already on the left bank. Where is our armour? All the way from the Don up to the town – in the trenches, ditches, on the road – we see dead Nazis and wrecked machinery. Our tank men really did a great job!

We enter Kalach at dawn. Empty streets bear witness to the hectic flight of the enemy. All kinds of stuff – loot that was left behind – is scattered around. The windows are wide open, broken glass everywhere. It seems the Fritzes leaped through them, into the street below. Over there one can see a dead German in a long shirt leaning on a window-sill . . .

But where is the enemy? Eight kilometres [almost 5 miles – editor's note] away lies Illarionovskaia, a large village. Battalion Commander Ignat Dudko and Commissar Alexander Chetkasov summon me and a certain Mayorov, a cadet from the Orsk Aerial Photography School. We are told that we have four hours to reach the place, find out if the Germans are there and report back. Mayorov is two or three years my senior, a robust, stocky man of middle height. He is put in charge. In order to save time we decide to go as far as we can on captured bicycles. It is 8.00 pm. We pedal down the road, foot-worn by retreating Germans, pass our outposts and dive into darkness.

Soon we find a fork in the road. I don't know about Mayorov, but in the Tashkent Infantry School they taught me the basics of night-time reconnaissance: so when my companion decides that we should split up and take separate roads, I argue that it is too dangerous. What if the village is occupied by Germans and their patrols are somewhere near? I suggest that both roads lead to Illarionovskaia from different directions, and that it would be better to follow one another, so that the man ahead could be covered by the one behind. But Mayorov refuses to listen: 'Are you afraid?' he asks with an air of superiority. Now I have no choice but to comply, for I do not wish to be considered a coward, and because a command is not a thing to discuss. 'We'll meet here!' barks Mayorov, 'if my bicycle is still here wait for me some fifteen or twenty minutes, not more.' And so he takes one road and I take the other . . .

Suddenly the situation seems hopeless. If the Germans are in Illarionovskaia, then they will have posted sentries: well-hidden, camouflaged, lying in wait. And here I am walking towards them, large as life, without anyone covering me: not so much a scout, as a prisoner ready for interrogation – an easy prey for the enemy. In a split second they might appear from nowhere, tie me up, and there'll be nobody to shoot at them from behind my back.

With my left hand I clutch an anti-tank grenade, so that I can pull the pin with my right. I will not let them take me alive. But I am troubled by the senselessness of this 'reconnaissance'. Wait, Mansur! What if your intuition is wrong, and only one of the roads leads to Illarionovskaia? Then Mayorov's decision to split will prove correct! My mind turns over the different possibilities, all the time whispering, 'Be prepared to die, but keep your spirits up, and be ready for anything.'

I lay down on the ground and try to calculate how far can I see in this position – perhaps some 200m [almost 220 yards – editor's note]. The steppe in front of me is covered with snow. I hear no suspicious sounds (I know the ground transmits them well). And so this is how I keep moving on: every 200m I put my ear to the ground, listen for a while, then rise, walk and lie down again . . .

Suddenly I hear the sound of horses' hooves. You're in luck, Mansur! To detect the enemy first is to save one's life! Like a snake I creep aside for a few metres, my sub-machine gun and grenades ready for action.

I see two men on horseback. The horses are not the cavalry type, but carthorses. I am puzzled. Both men are wearing *ushanki* [traditional Russian fur-hats with ear-straps – editor's note], so they are not Nazis. They are riding slowly, speaking softly. Maybe they belong to the *politsai* [police force set up by the Germans and formed by local inhabitants – editor's note]? But I don't see any weapons on them. Now they're right in front of me: 'Stop, hands up!' They instantly halt and raise their hands. 'Who are you? Where from? Where are you heading?' The riders remain silent, looking at me suspiciously. I approach them holding my SMG. Then, seeing my Red Army uniform, they start to jabber all at once: that they come from Illarionovskaia, that the Germans are setting up their defences there. I search them, and convinced that they are telling the truth, I send them back to the regiment, to report. Then I turn back to the place where Mayorov and I left our bicycles. I wait for Mayorov, but he does not return: neither in twenty minutes, nor in forty . . .

We fought over Illarionovskaia for almost five days. After the Germans were finally kicked out, we found Mayorov's maimed body near the Nazi HQ. He was lying facedown. On his head there was a liner without any cap, his overcoat bore the trace of his belt (he had a very wide belt of the Romanian type) and on his feet there were boots with puttees. German prisoners testified that during interrogation Mayorov did not utter a word and was later shot dead. We buried him on a small hill right outside the liberated village. He was born in the Oriol Region.

I realized that I could not be blamed for Mayorov's death but was still tormented by doubts. Maybe I should not have been so ashamed of appearing a coward? Maybe I should have tried to convince him that my plan was better? (In the end, both of those roads did lead to Illarionovskaia.) Or maybe I should have ignored his order and followed him, so as to give him cover? It's too late now to speculate on the possibilities – many of my comrades perished both before and after this incident – but Mayorov's death still bothers me to this day.

One evening, after Illarionovskaia, a certain soldier in our company named Nikolai got wounded. There is a curious story behind our relationship . . .

Happy to leave our train after the bombing I described earlier, my Company was marching from the station at Filonovo towards the River Don. During this hike we did not receive any bread, because our commissaries [logistical troops who organised the transport and distribution of rations – editor's note] lost their way and could not find us. We were so famished, that I began to think it much more likely that we would die from starvation, rather than Nazi bullets. Being so weak, everyone was depressed. We didn't even have the strength to talk or be angry with our commissaries. Soon we would be expected to cross the Don and make our first appearance at the front line. But my head was swirling! If only it had been summer, I might have eaten some grass or roots. I'm sure I would have found something, even though this was the steppe and not the Siberian forest!

After we had reached our destination, the Don River, our commissary, a sergeant major, unexpectedly made his appearance. Although happy to find us, he was, nevertheless, also afraid: for it was his fault that the Company had been left to starve the whole week. At first, I was worried that he had arrived without bread: his face, usually fat and ruddy, was haggard and pale, and obviously weakened by hunger, he could barely move his feet. Yet his horses – pulling a large two-wheeled cart – looked robust, with their withers neatly divided in two, and the cart was heavily laden.

The sergeant major was shuffling between our men – who were lying almost senseless on the ground – inviting them to collect bread, sugar, *makhorka*. We could smell the aroma of rye bread coming from the cart, and so began to move. There was not enough life in us, however, to scold our commissary: so we decided to eat first, and give him a sound beating later!

Each of us got one loaf. The sergeant major hurriedly explained that he had fed his horses with bread. We were not cross: the horses looked so well-groomed, and without that bread they would never have pulled through. Indeed, had they died, our bread would surely have been lost: so the sergeant major was not so bad after all! He cut a small piece from his loaf and advised us to follow his example. He told us not to eat more than 100g [just under 4 ounces – editor's note] at first, or we'd get belly colic: 'Don't you be greedy, boys,' he kept telling us, 'you'll get the gripes! You just suck it a little, like candy, crumb by crumb!' Pavel Suvorov nodded approvingly: 'The sergeant major is right, he knows what he's saying!'

In the damp air of early November hung the sour smell of rye bread. We almost breathed the bread. Our stomachs rejoiced in absorbing it. Life was coming back to us, and we regained our sense of humour, remembering how we had almost died. We laughed at the sergeant major, how he had looked afraid, seeing us lying flat on the ground. We also laughed because now, the once portly commissary was almost as skinny as us: 'I could not look at the bread,' he told us, pleased at having a clear conscience, 'I'd be full but the Company would be starving!' So everything was alright and we had a real feast.

But then something unpleasant happened. I wanted to have another slice but found that my loaf had disappeared from my sack. I could not believe my eyes! Everyone in the Company became excited and agitated. Our shouting attracted the attention of the battalion commander. In those days we were still led by Captain Feodor Gridasov. He was short, had closely-cropped hair and a red face, as if he'd come straight from a *bania* [Russian steam bath – editor's note]. He always wore an Order of the Red Banner on his chest. Gridasov had been wounded, spent some time in a hospital and recently returned to our regiment. He asked what was going on. Reluctantly we told him: 'The scoundrel will be shot on the spot!' and unfastening his holster, Gridasov took out his pistol.

Everyone in the Company grabbed his knapsack, and in an instant, the contents were emptied onto our waterproof capes. Only one kit remained tightly closed, and its owner seemed in no hurry to open it. Realizing that his fate was sealed, he kept lowering his head, unable to meet our penetrating glances. He gave a start when he heard the captain cock his pistol: 'Search it!' the CO pointed at the sack. I dashed towards Nikolai (for that was the name of the thief), pushing aside the man who, following the CO's order, had bent over the sack, and immediately sank my hand into it. There, under my fingers, I felt the two loaves. Everyone waited in silence. I stood up, snapped to attention, and reported: 'The stolen bread is not found!'

For a moment there was an expression of bewilderment on the captain's face, but then it changed, and in his eyes I read, 'Good Man!' He put his pistol back into its holster and without uttering another word, walked away, back to headquarters.

Everyone in the Company breathed a sigh of relief. Without asking any more questions about the missing loaf, each man cut a piece from his own bread, and put it on my waterproof. Nikolai covered his face with his arms, and lay on the ground next to his kit, remaining in that position for some two hours: a man sentenced to a disgraceful death, who had received a pardon . . .

Two or three weeks later that same Nikolai had one of his lungs seriously injured by a shell splinter. We could hear the air hissing as it went in and out of the wound in his chest. This happened one evening, some time after Ilarionovskaia. There were no medical orderlies in our battalion. After a battle, we collected the wounded ourselves and took them to the medical unit, which was situated in the regiment's rear – a bit too far, in my opinion! As luck would have it, the Company – once again – had been left without food for twenty-four hours, and we were impatiently awaiting the arrival of our field kitchen, when I received the order to take the wounded soldier to the rear.

It was rapidly getting dark when I harnessed myself into the wire straps of an improvised litter mounted on skis. I set off immediately, slowly dragging the prostrate man, all the time wondering whether the food had arrived, and when would I make it back. Nikolai was unconscious. I could only tell if he was alive when I stopped, because the skis under the litter made a loud scraping noise, as they passed over the snow. I stopped again and again, each time hearing the hissing sound coming from the wounded soldier's chest: so he was not dead yet. I forced myself on, skirting round shell-holes and trenches.

Night fell, and I was beginning to think that all this effort would be wasted, if the wounded man died before I got him to the medical unit, when suddenly I heard: 'Mansur . . .' I stopped. Was it my imagination? No! Nikolai had regained consciousness. 'Mansur . . .' I struggled to free myself from the straps, and rushed to the injured soldier's side: 'Mansur, shoot me . . . Or leave me, if you can't . . . I've exhausted you . . .'

But his words renewed my strength! I harnessed myself again and rushed ahead, this time without making any stops, as if I were running away from vile and disgraceful thoughts: for I have to admit, that at the beginning of my journey, somewhere in my mind, there had been a hope that Nikolai would die, and I would be free from this burden; that I would be back in time to get my share of the hot food.

Why is good and bad so strangely mixed in a single man – in me?! I must have looked frightening in the dark: wheezing, my teeth bared, my eyes ready to jump out of their sockets. But I was determined to get Nikolai to the medical unit: dead or alive! I can't say that I was saving his life a second time because of a particular liking for him. I rushed on, rather, in pursuit of a clear conscience: filled with a desire to triumph over evil and immorality – things I hate so much – yet which are present in me!

I almost collapsed into the deep ravine crammed with our rear units. The scent of tasty, appetising food, mixed with that of horse manure, gas, and hay, filled my nostrils, making my head swim! As I approached the dugouts, lights could be seen in some of the small windows. I tried one of them and a door swung open: I asked, in a hoarse voice, if I could leave a seriously wounded man there. 'What regiment?' A fat-faced orderly stood in front of me: '1034th' I answered. 'You'll have to move on. Here we have 1026th.' The heavy door slammed shut.

Suddenly I felt totally exhausted, unable to drag Nikolai a step further. He was moaning and talking deliriously. Still, I went on. What could I have done with that bureaucrat? I would've liked to put a bullet through his narrow forehead: but then I would have been court martialled and received a bullet in exchange!

Another dugout (these dugouts were built by the Nazis, a fine piece of work!). I knocked at the door and an orderly appeared, surrounded by a cloud of tasty vapour. I asked: 'What medical unit?' '1036th' he answered. 'Then we're in the right place!' I lied without hesitation: 'here is a seriously wounded soldier!' Without looking back, I strode into the dugout and sat behind a table, as if I owned the place. The nurses brought Nikolai in: he was already lying on a stretcher. 'I want some food,' I said. A plate of wheat porridge – warm, aromatic, and rich – was placed in front of me. I ate some and fell asleep right there at the table.

They woke me up while it was still dark, knowing that I had to return to my company before dawn. I finished the porridge, and they gave me half a loaf of bread for the road. I heard a voice: 'Mansur, come here . . .' I walked to the farthest corner of the dugout: my Nikolai is alive! 'Mansur, as long as I live, I will never forget you . . . May God help you return home safely . . .' Halfway to the medical unit I had been dragging behind me a thief, who had received my pardon; then, after he asked me to shoot or abandon him, I had been running away from my own vile thoughts: now, I said farewell to a real comrade-in-arms, wishing with all my heart that he would recover and live.

Speaking of field kitchens, in our rifle battalion there served as a cook, a lance corporal with a funny surname: 'Tsibulia', which in Ukrainian means 'onion'. His first name was Kuzma. We infantrymen, receiving our share of the porridge, used to laugh at him, making fun of his surname, which seemed to fit his job perfectly: 'Kuzma, tell us the truth! You invented this name for yourself on purpose, so the top brass would give you this cosy place, where you can eat as much as you like?' Skilfully handling his ladle, he would reply, 'Oh, lads! If I had a different name, I would not be toiling like a slave at this business!'

When Tsibulia was giving us porridge, he could perfectly judge – even in the dark of night – what kind of a soldier was standing before him: 'I can see right through you, and I know that you haven't earned your porridge!' The private feels ashamed and doesn't say a word. Now another infantryman comes up with his mess tin: his rifle is shining; his shovel is as sharp as a razor, so it can be used in combat instead of a sword; in his knapsack he has two anti-tank grenades and a full set of cartridges; he is worn-out and thin, like a hard-working peasant. In such cases, Tsibulia is generous with the porridge and gives him a second helping. Then comes a 'dandy': he is wearing an officer's overcoat and a new, wide, officer's belt, which he filched somewhere; on his waist hangs a Parabellum pistol taken from the Germans; and on his head a cap of Astrakhan fur. Instead of a standard soldier's mess tin, the 'dandy' has a metallic case from a German gas mask, which can hold at least four servings of porridge. With a grave air he stands before the cook with this 'bucket' and demands: 'Fill it up!' Tsibulia does not argue with him, but silently slaps in one portion only, all the time looking sternly at the 'dandy'. The latter does not move and insists: 'Why, you dog, you have a full cauldron there!' 'Yeah, for sure, there's more porridge here than brains in your head!' We laugh so heartily, that the Germans, hearing us, send over several rounds. On Tsibulia's greatcoat one can see a medal. He has the right to be proud of it, he really deserved it, for he behaved like a hero . . .

One day our battalion received an order from divisional HQ to attack the enemy, so as to 'straighten out' our sector of the front. At night, under cover of our artillery, we crept up close to the German trenches and rushed them, engaging the enemy in hand-to-hand combat. We lost many men in the encounter – the Fritzes being three times our number – and I was sure that we would be completely destroyed, for our supreme commander-in-chief had issued Order 227, demanding 'No retreat!' [Stalin's Order 227 was as significant as Hitler's 'Stand Fast' order of winter 1941. As a consequence, front line troops were forbidden to retire, and were followed by special units, authorized to shoot any who attempted to do so – editor's note.] At the critical point of this combat, however, a miracle happened! We heard sub-machine gunfire from behind the enemy lines, and suddenly all the Nazis vanished from the trenches! Later, we were amazed to learn that Tsibulia – who had fallen asleep on his two-wheeled cart, carrying the field kitchen – had penetrated the enemy lines! His horses, having been frightened by several shells bursting nearby, had dashed towards the Nazi trenches, carrying the dozing cook along with them. When Tsibulia woke up and realized what had happened, he began shooting at the Fritzes, hoping, at least, to sell his life dearly: this was the heroic deed that brought Tsibulia the medal, 'For Bravery'.

CHAPTER THREE

The Man Killed by a Sewing Machine

Twenty-third November 1942 was the day when the forces of our South-Western Front pushed forward with their advance, whilst receiving a new objective: to link up with the army that was marching to join us from the south. I remember this day as a sequence of unceasing battle scenes.

As usual, heavily laden with gun carriages, barrels and base-plates, we were running ahead to change our position, pressing the enemy, who were putting up a strong resistance. Again I saw our mortarmen falling to the ground. Among those who died was a good and strong fellow from Bodaibo. He was of Siberian origin, a gold-digger, and a man dear to me because I myself grew up at the Miasski Gold Mines.

As the *partorg* of our company, I now had to fulfil my unpleasant duty: for I was expected to collect the dead man's membership card. I turned back and quickly removed the knapsack from his body. But I couldn't understand what weighty object had crushed the back of the Siberian's skull, for it certainly wasn't a mortar component. I unwrapped his waterproof and there – to my horror – I found a portable sewing machine! I felt sick. What a cause of death! The Siberian was an excellent soldier: brave, cool-headed and tough. As a civilian, he was a fine worker and a decent family man. For him a sewing machine was a symbol of prosperity. He wanted to bring it back from the war and present it to his wife.

I remembered my pre-war life: a gramophone, a bicycle, these were scarce enough; as for sewing machines, there were only two for the entire population of our village! Yet one of these machines – such a marvel – had killed the Siberian: for I could not find a single scratch on his body. He just stumbled while running and fell. I didn't tell anyone in the Company about this incident – not wanting the man to be mocked or judged harshly – but maybe I was wrong? Maybe it would have served as a good lesson to the others.

The 69th Tank Brigade was engaged in action in the same sector as our 293rd Rifle Division. Our tank men were having a tough time. The Germans strongly reinforced their anti-tank defences, and our machines suffered much from armour-piercing shells. One of them hit a tank that our Company was following in the course of an attack. It caught fire, burning ferociously, as if it had been made from timber. One tank man jumped out, ablaze from head to foot, crying: 'Save the colonel!' He fell on the snow and started rolling around, trying to extinguish the flames. He kept on screaming: 'Hey, brothers, save the colonel!'

Everyone tries to run around the burning tank. It can blow up any second. I want to slip by, just like the others. I have to hurry up – I'm not being late for tea or anything – I'm in the middle of an attack! My crafty brain invents an excuse: those who passed before me had more time to rescue the trapped man, because a tank usually blows up two or three minutes after it catches fire. But my conscience, on the other hand, is calling: 'There's not a second to lose, climb up that tank!' My brain: 'No use! There's not enough time!' But my conscience gets the upper hand and I feel the hot, hissing armour under my damp gloves. It's slippery. I cannot climb up, and see no cramps or projections to use. But it's too late to stop, and I just keep jumping, till I somehow manage to clamber aboard.

From the hatch on top, hot, stinging smoke rises into my face. Then hands – the live hands of the trapped tank man – seize my greatcoat in a death grip. I sink my arms deeper – the better to pull him out of the narrow hatch – close my eyes, and turn my head away: unable to see a thing because of the thick smoke. Finally (never before has a human body felt so heavy!) I haul him out and we fall on the sweet, snowy ground. Yes, it's sweet, but we can't stay here! The colonel has both legs broken. I lug him as far away from the tank as I can, about 20 or 30m [between 22 and 33 yards – editor's note]. The explosion is a powerful one. The turret shoots some 5m [about 5½ yards – editor's note] into the air, makes a somersault, and tumbles to the ground. Bits of metal keep falling from the sky. The colonel embraces me: 'My dear boy! I won't forget this! What's your surname? Abdulin? I won't forget this! Meanwhile, take this pistol . . .' Some medical orderlies approach us, put him on a ski litter, and drag him away to the rear . . .

Thirty years later, Marshal Oleg Losik, who in those days fought with the 4th Mechanized Corps alongside the 293rd Rifle Division, helped me establish the identity of the colonel: Battalion Commissar G. V. Provanov, of the 69th Tank Brigade.

It's true that we did not fight for decorations. When I climbed the burning tank, I did not think of any reward. My only thought was: 'Will I make it before the explosion!' Nevertheless, my comrades (one of them, Ivan Yevstigneyev, still lives in a village in the Sterlitamak District of Bashkiria: he served in the same regiment and remembers the episode) congratulated me in anticipation of my receiving a medal [the statute included an award for 'saving a commander involving risking one's life' – editor's note]. After the war, I retained some hope of seeing the colonel again; or at least, of finding out what became of him. Then, in 1975, I learned that the men of the 69th Tank Brigade believed that Provanov had died in the burning tank, claiming that his body was never found! Meanwhile, the missing colonel had been posthumously awarded the status of Hero of the Soviet Union. My guess is that the tank men, quickly examining the remains of the tank after the battle, came to the conclusion that their battalion commissar had been burned inside. But what really happened to him after we parted, when the orderlies put him on the ski litter and headed for the medical unit? Was he hit by a shell? Was he killed by a splinter after escaping death in the burning tank? Or did he lose too much blood? In the latter case, surely they would have found some ID on him?

One could say that I was unlucky. Why? Because I didn't receive my decoration. But the colonel – if he really did die just after being miraculously saved – was even more unlucky!

After parting from the colonel, I ran after my comrades . . .

A strange figure on three props – two elbows and one knee – shaking convulsively, is rapidly moving from the enemy lines in my direction. The other leg, in a *valenok* [traditional Russian felt boot – editor's note], seems unnaturally long. Dangling lifelessly, it bounces along the uneven ground, causing the whole body to shudder. I hurry by. The man's leg is half torn off, but he'll be found by the orderlies, sent to the rear, and will stay alive. Suddenly, I hear a terrible howl. But it's not the pitiful sound that makes me stop and stare in horror. Looking back, I see the soldier sit, take a penknife from his pocket, and try the blade with his finger: blunt. Then, with a wild expression, he draws the damaged leg close, and starts cutting the naked sinew from which it is hanging. I always carry a sharp knife with me. Should I help? But my brain is numb, and I just stand and watch how the soldier, with a kind of ferocious grin, cuts his leg off. Finally, the limb drops to the ground right next to him. The soldier takes off his cap, puts it over the stump, and ties it up tightly with his belt. Then he lifts the severed leg, and holds it close to his breast, as if it were a small child. Masha Lutsenko, one of our nurses, rushes up to him, and I force myself to go on running ahead, stumbling.

Artillery barrage! I barely have time to jump into the nearest hole and hide. Another infantryman dives in after me. He screams wildly: 'Give me a smoke!' Shaking off bits of earth that have fallen from above, I take out my pouch and hand it over to him. He answers in a harsh voice with some foul words: '. . . ! . . . ! Roll it!' As I roll the cigarette, trying to understand the reason for this outburst, he yells at me through the roaring explosions: 'My arms are torn off!' I look down and see the dangling sleeves of his overcoat, stained with blood. I stick the cigarette between his lips and give him a light: I notice that they are almost black in colour. The bombardment suddenly ceases, and the soldier leaps up and runs away, shouting to me as if in farewell: 'I'm through with the war, brother . . .'

The lads in the Company assume I've been killed, having seen me climb the burning tank, which blew up moments after. Some, no doubt, looked back and witnessed the explosion, thinking: 'Abdulin is gone.' Now I am reunited with my comrades, and I am as happy as if reaching my father's door: 'He's alive!' they shout, seeing me. It is a wonderful thing to see someone express sincere joy simply because you are alive. I even saw tears in Suvorov's eyes as he gave me a hug: 'Well, Mansur, you're a bit too much!' Was it a reprimand? Or did I sense pride in his words . . . ?

Finally, that afternoon, the troops of the South-Western Front, fighting in our sector, linked up with those moving towards them from the south. In the heat of the battle – ignorant of the fact that there were no more Nazis between us – we kept on shooting: at each other! The heavy fire forced us to lie fixed to the ground. Then we saw a mass of men counter-attacking us. As they came closer, we were puzzled by their appearance: they did not look like Germans . . . Finally, someone realized that we were being assaulted by our own troops and the shooting ceased. In fact, the battle stopped right there.

Then, in complete silence, we ran to meet each other, hearing only the sound of flattened snow beneath our feet: 'Brothers! Friends! How could it happen? We fought with our own men . . . !' We embraced each other. We also cried: for there were dead and wounded on both sides, and each person blamed himself. Later, when clearing the battlefield of bodies, we avoided each other's eyes.

We had now reached the Don Front, closing a net around our enemies. The German army had been encircled, cut off, trapped in a tiny pocket [initially some 25 miles long and 12 miles deep – editor's note]. Our immediate objective, therefore, was to prevent it from breaking out. The hour of the historic Battle of Stalingrad was at hand.

I had been at the front for only three weeks, yet so much had happened. I had given Suvorov many opportunities to worry about me! Nevertheless, my unexpected return – following the news of my 'death' – helped strengthen the bond between us. When things quietened down a bit, we talked about the significance of Order 227 ('No retreat!'). This directive certainly served to simplify things a good deal. When there was a halt, we all halted together. There was no longer any uncertainty. Every soldier knew that when he stopped, his neighbour stopped too. Indeed, everyone stopped, prepared to die right there, knowing that no one would run. The order provided a strong psychological incentive for the men. As did the knowledge that there were special holding detachments in the rear, authorized to shoot anyone who actually did drop back . . .

Our trenches were on the front line. We knew that the Nazis would not sit passively inside their pocket. But how many were in there? No one knew the exact figure. We kept asking our commanders, 'How many soldiers in the pocket?' 'Some 40,000'. Forty thousand! Quite an imposing number. What if half of them were to breakout west-ward, attacking the sector held by our regiment? The truth only dawned on us two months later, when, on 2 February 1943, we discovered that there were actually 330,000 Germans in the pocket! 'Why did you lie to us?' we asked our commanders. They answered us with a sly grin, suggesting that sometimes soldiers are better off left in the dark. They had said '40,000' so as not to scare us. 'Maybe you were right,' we agreed.

In late November 1942, however, our orders were to prepare for any attempt by the enemy to breakout. We worked hard, digging deep trenches. In order to do this, we had to gouge out a 1.5m [almost 5 feet – editor's note] lump of frozen earth, then dig a burrow at the bottom of the trench. Since these burrows were made to fit a particular individual, they differed in size and form. Sometimes, one burrow would shelter two or three people: it was warmer that way. Meanwhile, the frozen ground above protected us almost as well as concrete. One might assume that as soon as we had completed work on a trench, and dug our burrows, we would simply have crawled inside and slept till ordered to fight. But this was not the case. We wanted our dwellings to be comfortable, so we would make a niche for our grenades, another for our cartridges, and a third for our sub-machine guns. Then we would make a niche for our mess tins, and so on. Thus we made our trenches more and more cosy, all the time getting more and more attached to them. In fact, the order, 'Load the mortars! Forward!' was often accompanied by feelings of sadness and regret, at having to part with a piece of ground that had become a kind of home. As for leaving your trench to the enemy, that was totally out of the question!

Our mortarmen saw to it that the enemy did not sleep at night. By day, we would zero in on a ravine, where various Nazi service units were concentrated, and make a detailed plan of their positions. Then, as soon as darkness fell, we would begin firing at regular five-minute intervals. This was called 'wearing out the enemy.' The Germans were shelled all night long, but we managed to get some sleep at least: each crew worked for an hour, firing some 100 bombs, before scurrying back to burrows, kept warm by sleeping comrades.

For some reason the Nazis did not dig any trenches. Maybe they expected to make a successful breakout? Or maybe our frozen ground at Stalingrad proved a bit too much for them? I don't know. Instead, they made their defences from frozen corpses. They would build a wall consisting of two or three layers of dead bodies, cover it with snow, and thus have something to protect themselves from our fire. In this way, the frozen remains of dead Germans defended those still alive from bullets and splinters. But I did not envy the Fritzes when a sudden thaw took place! Besides, such measures were no match for our 76mm guns.

Enemy prisoners, covering their heads with their hands and rocking back and forth, often muttered: 'Oh, mein Gott!' This clearly meant, 'Oh, My God!' But what did 'Gott mit uns' mean? This was inscribed on the belt buckles belonging to Nazi soldiers. The belts were good quality, made of real leather. I often thought of taking one of these belts from a dead man: but this inscription, clearly visible, like lines on a tombstone, made me feel uncomfortable. Not wanting to wear something I didn't understand, I decided to learn what it meant. *'Gott'* obviously meant 'God', but the other two words? I must have passed through a dozen trenches, asking my comrades about the inscription, only to receive replies like: 'Hell knows!' or 'I don't give a damn!' Eventually, I bumped into a private – a former village school teacher – who, with substantial effort, managed to translate the mysterious words. It turned out that they meant: 'God is with us.'

When the Nazi corpse-walls eventually thawed out, these inscriptions looked like bitter mockery.

As it happened, the German rank and file did not even know they were in a pocket. The evidence supplied by prisoners suggested that the Nazi chiefs had done everything to conceal the terrible truth from their soldiers: so they would keep believing in victory and fight us till the very end. I myself saw a captured German, who, being shell-shocked, kept stubbornly repeating, like some broken machine, 'Ich gehe nach Moskau!' – 'I'm going to Moscow.'

It was on the Don Front, in November 1942, that I heard about anti-tank dogs for the first time. As someone who grew up in the Siberian forestland, I really love dogs, and I was appalled to learn about the fate of these poor creatures. What does a meek animal, so dear to children, have to do with this mess? A dog is a faithful friend. Yet we were apparently sending these trusting companions to die under enemy tanks! I decided to go and investigate.

I found the dogs nearby, with the soldiers who looked after them, waiting for their hour to come. They were all shapes and sizes, a big mix of colours and breeds. There was one particular pooch, however, which caught my eye. This curious looking canine had one ear hanging down, and one standing erect. He looked like a real character, a real bad boy! He noticed me, and began twisting his head from side to side, hoping to get some food. Bundles of explosives stood nearby, weighing some 8kg [almost 18lbs – editor's note], and an antenna was visible, connected to a detonator. I learned that one of the dog-breeders – a middle-aged, red-haired man – grew up in the Krasnoyarsk Region, same as me. We talked a little. He told me that the dogs were trained for three months, receiving food only under a moving tank. This was the secret of their heroism. I went back 'home' to my burrow, and described what I had seen to Suvorov.

Soon, some tanks appeared from the direction of the enemy lines and we saw a black, shaggy ball rush towards them. This was followed, a moment later, by a second and a third. The first dog blew up a machine with a powerful blast. Two more explosions were heard soon after. The Nazi tanks made a sharp U-turn and sped away from us. My comrades yelled 'Hurrah!' and I, too, was supposed to be happy – the German attack had been repelled – but instead I wept, cursing the war and the monsters who'd started it.

At night, wave after wave of German transport planes dropped various military supplies into the pocket. Firing captured flare guns, we misled the navigators and got loads of stuff thrown to us: loaves of bread, sausages, tinned meat, woollen socks, straw boots [large, bulky snow shoes, worn over normal boots – editor's note], cigarettes, biscuits, and so on. It was rumoured that the bread, wrapped in plastic, had been baked in 1933! But our soldiers had little enthusiasm for it, considering our crusts to be the tastiest thing in the world.

As it happened, for more than a week, my Company had been unlucky with these 'food parcels', our commissaries, as usual, being lost somewhere. One of my comrades, however, named Victor Marchenko, was fortunate enough to find a knapsack full of sausages, wrapped in gauze. For some reason – contrary to our rules – he decided to keep the spoil to himself and refused to share it with us. He even went so far as to threaten to shoot anyone who might try to take the pack away. Consequently, it was unanimously agreed to leave him alone with his sausages and forget about him. I knew Marchenko before as a perfectly sane person and an honest friend, but something had obviously happened to him: 'Maybe he feels that his death is near?' was my thought. The idea made me feel very uncomfortable . . .

A reasonably quiet day passed. We were impatiently waiting for night – in order to pay a visit to the Fritzes and hopefully bag some rich booty – when suddenly, from the direction of Marchenko's burrow, we heard the dull report of an explosion. When we arrived on the scene, Victor's dugout had collapsed and smoke was rising from it.

I must confess, from my first days at the front, I noticed that those of my comrades who took a watch from a dead Nazi, would soon or a little later die themselves. Just before their demise, such men might turn into complete cowards, losing their self-control, not knowing what to do with themselves; or they might desperately try to look calm. As to myself, I seemed to have a kind of sixth sense, and was always correct in guessing that such a person would die in the next few hours.

One day, in our sector of the front, we saw a German four-barrel automatic anti-aircraft gun. It was a miracle of military engineering: a complicated mechanism with many fly-wheels and handles, standing on a jack. It could revolve on its axis in any direction. The gunner's seat had a back to it, leaving one free to operate the weapon with both hands and feet. Each barrel had a gigantic box containing a set of five shells, to be loaded automatically. The whole machine was excellently balanced: you could aim anywhere you wanted.

Ivan Konski, a mortarmen from our company, is the first to climb inside, immediately turning the handles and fly-wheels. Right next to him stands Gennadi Manuilov, a gunmaker, who explains what's what. But Konski seems to know everything already, and ten minutes later he's talking about the machine as if he'd invented it. In the distance, we hear the engine of an approaching plane. Judging by the sound, the craft is flying low. But it's foggy and as yet, we see nothing. Konski continues playing around with the gun, and points all four barrels in the direction of the growing, growling, noise. Suddenly, a low-flying German transport appears, moving quickly, soon to vanish again in the mist. Konski opens fire: so does the plane. Tracer lines dart between them. Then, just as the craft is about to disappear into dense fog, we hear a wild bellow from its engines. Before our very eyes, the hull breaks off, the fuselage buckles, and a gaping hole appears, from which the contents of the plane start to spill and fall to the ground. Meanwhile, the shattered vessel begins losing height and passes out of sight. We hear a dull noise as it hits the ground, followed by an explosion. Ivan Konski, red-faced, is covered in sweat. He looks at us from the gunner's seat absolutely stupefied. The rest of us scream 'Hurrah!' and run off to see what fell from the interior of the plane.

Our soldiers counted more than thirty bodies of Nazi high-ranking officers. There were hundreds of boxes and suitcases, containing property stolen from the Soviet people. All the documents and valuables were sent to the divisional HQ. And Ivan Konski, as far as I remember, received a grand decoration.

Our mortar company had its own Maxim machine-gun, as well as a German MG-34 machine-gun, which helped us greatly in action. We also had an anti-tank rifle with plenty of ammunition: we sometimes used it to destroy machine-gun nests, but we didn't get a chance to shoot at a tank. It would have been nice to keep the captured anti-aircraft gun for ourselves: with some regret, Ivan Konski had to part with it, handing it over to the gun experts.

The following day proved to be unlucky for Ivan Konski. He found a pistol – maybe it was German, I don't know, but it was definitely foreign made – and put it in his pocket, hoping to take a closer look at the unfamiliar mechanism after the fighting. That evening, when things had quieted down, Konski remembered the new handgun. We all sat down in a circle, and Ivan kept turning the strange thing round and round, trying to understand how it worked. Suddenly there was a report. Konski froze with the fingers of his left hand spread wide apart, the palm bleeding heavily. Very pale, he looked at us one after another. Had anyone been hit? Seeing that the bullet had not hurt anyone else, Ivan stared again at his bleeding palm.

This was when we became frightened. If our superiors found out, Konski would have to face a tribunal. Accident or not, it was a self-inflicted wound, and the Nazi transport plane, shot down only the day before, would not help Ivan. We dressed the wound as fast as we could, and prayed to Heaven that it would heal without any need for a doctor. We then helped Ivan hide his hand inside a large mitten with cuffs, and promised not to say a word to anyone.

Two weeks later Ivan Konski removed the bandage. A small scar was visible on the palm: the bullet had passed through the flesh without damaging the bone. And so you can see that the men of my company were keen students of captured weapons, but that sometimes things went wrong. Here is another example that might have had a tragic end.

Near the railway station at Karpovskaia we captured a train with special carriages. On one of the cars stood an enormous cannon mounted on a platform. It seemed that the Germans had brought it here to fire on Stalingrad.

Its calibre was no less than 400mm [almost 16 inches – editor's note]. The giant fascinated us! We stood around it, expressing our amazement, and of course, we wanted to know how it worked. Nearby, we saw some wicker boxes filled with shells. Each one weighed 100kg! [Over 220lbs – editor's note.] We also noticed a heap of sacks. We opened a few, and discovered what looked like bundles of spaghetti, each strand as thick as a finger and some 70cm [almost 28 inches – editor's note] long. 'Why, it's gunpowder!' Exclaimed a comrade. The others laughed in disbelief. But the soldier – who had guessed correctly – picked up a 'spaghetti' and proceeded to set fire to one end: 'Wow! Look at the way it burns!' Suddenly, the 'spaghetti' leaped from his hand, as if alive, and whirled around the sacks of explosives and boxes of shells.

Some took to their heels, while others attempted to catch the 'spaghetti'. One man tried to step on it, but it rocketed right from under his boot. Then it made a turn, and tried to force its way between two sacks containing more of the strange, volatile substance. Well, if the mountain of ammunition went off, it would – as the saying goes – 'have been too late to begin running yesterday!' So without thinking, I dashed towards the sacks, grabbed the 'spaghetti' – burning my fingers through the gloves – and stepped, not on its blazing end, but on the other one, keeping it securely wedged against the floor till it burned itself out.

Later, this cannon worked on our side day and night. Its shells whizzed high over our heads. Then, somewhere in the distance – inside the pocket – there would be a colossal blast, followed by a bright glow across the horizon . . .

Sitting in the trenches during a time of rest, one thinks about the past. The strongest desire is to get back to a well-heated *izba* [traditional peasant's house – editor's note] to have a good sleep; or a *bania* [steam bathhouse – editor's note], to relax on a bench, enjoying the hot steam. These images would float through my mind like fairytale wishes!

For a whole month, we have not slept in a proper dwelling, but have been reduced to snatching bits of sleep in the open, in between bouts of fighting. Living like this, on the winter steppe, was almost un-bearable, even for my young, strong body. Lice were literally killing me! In the winter there was no getting away from them. I tried to poison them with insect powder: no result. I remember how, sweating after a fight, I would take out a pack of insect powder and empty the contents behind my collar, straight onto my naked body. I powdered myself from head to foot, but the poison had no effect on the lice. Hunger, cold, constant lack of sleep, continuous hard work, took their toll. We drank dirty water from dirty mess tins. We got it by melting sullied snow. How can one endure all that? It's hard to imagine!

Moreover, three or four weeks after my arrival at the front, I began to suffer from incontinence. I had to urinate every five minutes or so, and in order to keep my pants dry, I simply left my fly open all the time. I was sure I'd caught some terrible disease, but I was ashamed to report it. What terrified me most was the fear that this sickness would last forever: I would rather die than be such an invalid! My friend, seeing me urinate so often, reassured me: 'I had the same problem, but when I was sent to hospital, after being wounded, I was back to normal again within a week!'

I used to think: 'Why am I still safe and sound in this hell, when most of my comrades are dead or wounded?' In my sleep, I would see myself as a slain warrior, lying on a field, in a scene from the painting, *Battle of Kulikovskaya* [this is most likely a reference to *After the Battle*, by Vicor Vasnecov – editor's note]. An old Siberian infantryman, hearing of my dreams, told me with envy: 'You will return home from the war, so don't be afraid of such a dream!' Yet I, too, was envious, resenting others, even the seriously wounded. Sometimes I would rush forward into withering German fire, hoping to be wounded. My comrades called me a 'real hero' and a 'fearless man', but I just felt ashamed.

Mud has soaked into our skin. Our faces are so black that they seem covered with soot. We look at each other, and find ourselves so filthy and funny-looking, that we somehow find the strength to laugh. I was glad my beard was not showing yet. The stubble of my older comrades made them look like brigands. Surely our commanders wanted us to look decent? But then, they could not make us to stay clean . . .

In my childhood I was a dreamer. At the mine, at eight years old, kids knew how to sieve for gold. Like ducklings, we would paddle all day long in the Miass river with our scoops and basins. I dreamed of finding a giant nugget, one so big that none of our gold diggers would be able to lift it. At that time, I reasoned that the tiny pieces of gold which we found must have a mother, a massive, maternal nugget, big as a crag!

In those days, we children had to work all the time – around the house, in the vegetable garden, in the fields, and in the forest. Naturally, we wanted to play, but there was no time. Skates and skis were left unattended. During the summer holidays my father arranged for me to work in a gold digging crew, where I was responsible for driving horses. I liked work, but I also wanted time to myself – at least once in ten days – to play in the forest or go fishing. Prospectors, however, work all through the summer without a break. What could I do to invent a holiday? Well, as it happened, I found a way. In the mornings the gold diggers discussed their dreams. If someone had had a real nightmare, the superstitious prospectors would decide to have a day off. So I joined in their conversations, inventing a series of fearsome dreams – children's nightmares were believed to have a special significance – and the foreman would instantly make a decision not to work: I would then run away to the forest or to the river. When I told my father about my ruse, he laughed till the tears streamed down his face!

Being grey-haired I'm still a dreamer, and I was one even in the trenches near Stalingrad in December, 1942 . . .

'How can I stir up my company?' I thought in those days. 'What excuse can I invent to make people achieve the impossible and smarten themselves up?' The solution arrived in a flash. At first I was scared, but when I thought it over, I realized that there was no way I could be exposed, and decided to act. Leaving my company for half an hour or so, I made my reappearance in grand style, breathlessly announcing some stunning 'news': 'Hey, lads, there are rumours that Stalin has arrived at the Don Front!'

The 'news' spread through the trenches like wildfire (the speed of the 'soldiers' telegraph'), and within an hour, there was not a single man in my whole battalion who was not busy improving his appearance. Some scraped the mud from their greatcoats, others sewed up holes in their uniforms, some washed and shaved in the frost: but everybody was frantically trying to look smart.

Then the soldiers started asking their officers about the 'news'. But the commanders were at a loss and could not answer. This made the rank and file trust the rumours even more: 'the officers are supposed to keep such information in secret, for security reasons . . .' So you see, I had been foolish to worry about the consequences of my ruse: even if I had confessed that I was the author of the rumour, no one would have believed me!

One day, as our battalion was advancing further and further, we ran into a row of solidly made dugouts, left by the Germans. I noticed how our soldiers stopped near them, discussed something, and then moved on. Soon I reached the dugouts myself, and saw a big gunner from our regiment writhing on the ground. It looked as if he had accidentally poisoned himself. Such things happened often.

The unfortunate man lifted up his knees, rubbed his belly and groaned like a trumpet. The soldiers took a swift a glance at the gunner and walked on. 'What did he have?' I asked. 'There, you see, he drank something from one of those bottles.' I saw a box containing six large bottles, each filled with some golden, sticky liquid. The 'dying' man was desperately trying to expire with as much suffering as possible. I noticed that this chap had a very crimson face. Just then, he winked his eye at me, and began groaning mournfully in Ukrainian: 'Oh, my God! Oh, my God!'

I learned that inside the dugout there were more boxes, containing even more bottles of the golden liquor. We had our own carts in the mortar company, pulled by a pair of horses. I whispered to one of our men to fetch the cart as fast as possible, and it came right on time, before the artillery transport could come up. Now the Ukrainian really started screaming: 'You bastards, you could leave us at least one box!' 'Nope', laughed our boys, 'there's so little here!' 'Well!' protested the gunner, who had made a miraculous recovery, 'then I'm going with you!'

Some time later, when the gunner (his name was also Marchenko) became a familiar figure in our company, he used to tell the story of how he almost tricked an entire battalion, but a 'sly Tartar' saw right through him: 'Where there's a Tartar, a Ukrainian has nothing to do!' he grudgingly concluded.

CHAPTER FOUR

Born Under a Lucky Star

In order to make our fighting more efficient, Buteiko, the company commander, decided that our crew should become 'nomadic'. From now on, we were to act independently of the battalion, operating in its front, co-ordinating our fire with the rifle company, and selecting our position as the situation demanded.

The result was that the rifle commander, having our crew at his disposal, was able to use mortar shells against targets that were normally beyond his reach. For example, there might be a Nazi sharpshooter hiding behind a knocked out tank: we could take care of him by lobbing over a few shells. Or the Germans might set up a new machine-gun nest: again, mortar-fire would be the best way to get rid of the problem. A messenger would come running to us from the rifle company with news of a target, hiding, let's say, behind the remains of a cannon: like an ambulance crew, we would rush to the scene of the emergency. We already had enough experience to calculate the distances between ourselves and our targets. Working together – Suvorov, Fuat Khudaibergenov and myself – we usually hit the mark with our third shell.

As I mentioned, the main advantage of this 'nomadic' strategy was efficiency. As soon as the enemy presented a new target, we were right there to shell it. At the same time, being on the move helped us dodge Nazi fire. Thanks to our divisional newspaper, *Forward!* this mode of action was adopted by all the mortar companies of our division.

There was, however, one disadvantage: mortar parts are heavy, and it is very hard work lugging them around. For me, the most cumbersome thing was the barrel. Polished with coarse cloth, it glittered as though nickel-plated, and was not only heavy – weighing 20kg [just over 44lbs – editor's note] – but also slippery, sliding from my fingers like a slithering fish. Then I had an idea: I would drag the barrel over the snow and frozen ground on a leash! And so I attached a length of rope and off I went. How nice! Buteiko noticed my invention and said: 'Just be careful that the cover doesn't fall off the barrel, otherwise you'll get soil inside and ruin the mirror.' I was very happy that the CO seemed to approve of my idea. But my joy didn't last long. 'Under these new arrangements,' continued Buteiko, 'the gun-layers will have to carry the shell box too.' 'Yes, sir!'

Now I had 20kg on a leash and a further 22kg on my back! 'Well, Mansur,' grinned my comrades, 'no time to loaf about!' Despite the humour, things were very difficult indeed. It was rare that our detachment consisted of the five crew members stipulated by the regulations. Our losses were heavy, and the company had already been fully remanned twice. We might, on occasion, have a 'Number Four' in the crew, but as for a 'Number Five', this was just a pipe dream. Usually, there were only three of us to carry the shells, the gun carriage, and the base-plate. If necessary, we could manage with two: as long as each and every mortar was firing at the enemy!

Still, our losses were not as heavy as in the rifle companies. There, life expectancy was one or two weeks. Yet each night brought more reinforcements, and I knew that our military production line would keep churning out soldiers till we reached our final destination – Berlin.

It was touching to see how the rifle companies cared for us mortarmen. They would get shells for us, and even find good firing positions for our mortars. Their morale rose when we were near. And because of the tubular mortar barrels, which looked like chimneys, they called us 'Samovar men'. One day, the riflemen warned me that a Nazi sharpshooter had appeared in front of the enemy lines, and had already killed seven of our soldiers. I sat down beside their bodies, thinking to myself, 'We must finish off this sharpshooter!'

I returned to my company and told Suvorov about the sniper, and how good it would be if we could discover him: 'There's no harm in dreaming!' Smiled Pavel, adding, 'it's a difficult job, Mansur!'

The only way of finding the sniper's position was by using a scout's periscope. I took one, returned to the rifle company, and began a long and laborious survey of No Man's Land: shell holes, corpses, debris ... To catch a sniper in that chaos would be like finding a needle in a haystack! For the hundredth time I swept the endless plain with my periscope, trying to remember the outlines of suspicious-looking hillocks: 'He can't stay in the cold forever,' said someone behind my back, 'he'll have to leave sooner or later!'

I was jumping up and down in the trench, trying to keep warm, when a young company commander, following my example, also took the periscope. But he soon tired of squinting, and assuming the air of a man with more important things on his mind, walked away, sternly snapping out orders: 'Be careful! Stay low! Understand?'

Meanwhile, I got excited by the game, and took the periscope once more. Soon I knew all the minute details of the terrain, as if it was my own palm. Restlessly scrutinising the ground from left to right, I began systematically eliminating the possible number of hiding places, all the time narrowing the circle. By noon I was concentrating my attention on one particular 'hillock', when suddenly it moved! I couldn't believe my eyes – it was him! Now I was terrified that after all my efforts I might lose him. What if he crawled away to safety before we had chance to do something?

Suvorov appeared in the nick of time. Without looking away from the periscope, I reported the situation. We decided to use a rifle belonging to an old soldier from Siberia: 'My gun always gets the bullet home,' said the private, handing me his weapon, 'I wish they'd give it to me after the war, to take back to the forestland! I don't want no orders or medals, just my rifle!' I carefully laid the gun on the parapet, while Suvorov thought how best to provoke the sniper into firing, so that I might take advantage of the ten 'dead' seconds it would take him to reload.

With no time to lose, Pavel wrapped an entrenching shovel in a piece of cloth, marked two eyes and a mouth with mud, stuck his cap on top, and cautiously lifted it above the breastwork. The 'hillock' gave a start, and the shovel clinked. I instantly put the rifle butt against my shoulder and fired. The 'hillock' sank down. Then, there was a burst of automatic fire from the enemy lines, and our machine-guns snapped back.

Soon afterwards, when everything was quiet again, we spotted two figures crawling like lizards from the enemy lines towards the 'hillock'. These Nazis also got their due, and when night came, some of our more daring men approached the dead sniper and brought back some booty. This included a notebook, which contained a chilling piece of accounting: the figure '87'.

That same night I committed a serious offence. Our chiefs expected the encircled Germans to attempt a breakout in the west – our sector of the front. But days had passed without a peep from the Fritzes, and in the euphoria following our sniper 'kill', the last thing we expected was trouble. Our orders were to sleep in shifts, and I suggested to Suvorov that he might take his turn first, while I stood watch. Well, Suvorov was soon sound asleep. But then I, too, completely dozed off, and it is still a mystery to me how I lost consciousness so quickly and so completely. Did I just faint after a hard day? I don't know, but it would never happen again . . .

The Germans came at us like an avalanche with all their armour, cars and tow-trucks, moving in columns over our heads, in an attempt to break out of the pocket. Our gunners opened fire and hit several tanks and other vehicles, but the Fritzes kept on coming. Our rifle companies fell back. In fact, all our front line units, unable to withstand the massive German onslaught, slowly and methodically retreated on the second echelon of our lines, thus allowing the artillery to fire unhindered.

But we keep on sleeping! I see the battle in my dream. Yes, my mind perceives it as a phantasm, and at first, does not order me to wake up. But then, from somewhere deep in my brain, comes a vigilant voice: 'Wake up! This is no dream!' What should I do? What should I believe? 'Oh, I'll just open my eyes,' I decide at last. But lying there awake, I see the same pictures as in my dream! What the hell is going on? Suvorov wakes up: 'Well, Mansur, what's up?' 'The Nazis broke through our defence,' I murmur. 'And we're sleeping?!'

Suvorov carefully listened to the sounds above our heads. The Germans were trying to avoid a tank that was burning before our trench, so our position in this 'dead zone' saved us from being discovered. Suvorov ordered me to sit still, while he rose and cautiously poked his head above the parapet of the trench. Then he came crawling back down and we discussed what we should do.

In my dream, I correctly guessed what was going on. Judging by what Suvorov managed to see, the Nazis had stopped at the second echelon of our defences. The roar of guns was not moving away from us, but seemed fixed about 2 or 3km [approximately 1½ miles – editor's note] to the west, just where our second line was located. We had little choice but to sit tight and wait for a couple of hours: but if the regiment failed to return, then we'd have to try and reach our comrades under cover of night.

Suvorov returned to his observation post and I hid myself at the bottom of the trench. How could I have switched off like that and fallen asleep when I was supposed to be keeping watch? I hated myself for this! If I had been left alone it would not have been so bad, but poor Suvorov! He didn't blame me, but that just made things worse. I tried to imagine what Suvorov was thinking: 'Mansur is just a feather-brained boy with no sense of responsibility. A sucker. If I get out of this OK, I won't be on friendly terms with him anymore. I don't need such a disorganized loafer. One can't trust him at all, he's busy sleeping when he's needed . . .' And so on.

There I sat, trying to analyse myself as best as I could, and my conclusion was: 'Yes, Suvorov has no need for such a friend. I have no need for myself either! Why am I such a good-for-nothing? If we do get out of this trap and return to our battalion, the commander will have nothing to thank me for! They'll take away my medal "For Bravery" and expel me from the Communist Party.' I would have shot myself but I didn't want to let Suvorov down again. I couldn't kill myself and leave him alone at this dangerous moment.

Meanwhile, above my head, I heard the din of battle, as the Nazis continued moving west. Our gunners, in an effort to halt them, fired high explosive shells and mortar bombs: these blasts, which doubtless killed many enemy soldiers, could just as easily have destroyed us as well.

At last, the Germans began to fall back, bringing with them a cacophony of sounds, caught by my ears while the chaos raged above my head: desperate shouts, deafening explosions, growling engines, the moans of those in agony. The great, grey wave, it seemed, was rolling back faster and faster into the pocket. We were getting the upper hand. Half an hour later I could hear the music of Russian swearing, which sent a shiver down my spine! Our dear *muzhik* soldiers! [the word *muzhik* is a term for a peasant, or old man – editor's note]. Hey boys, swear at me too, because I'm sitting here, while you're risking your asses! Our soldiers are really furious – they won't forgive me for falling asleep!

Suvorov came down, grabbed several hand grenades, a few cartridge-drums, and said with a solemn air: 'Let's try to get a pardon from our men. Come on!' I was greedy and took with me a huge arsenal of grenades and cartridge-drums. Standing beside Suvorov, I was ready to open fire. The Fritzes were retreating, following their own tracks, and coming within firing range: 'Keep running, you scoundrels!' We waited just a little more, and at the most critical moment, opened fire into the faces of our fleeing enemies. They had no time to take care of us. They simply tried to skirt round our trench from both sides. We continued firing: all the time anxious about hitting our own men – who were now in hot pursuit of the Germans – and of being rushed from behind by those Fritzes who had escaped our bullets. Finally, we turned to shoot the Nazis in the back, our rear having been recaptured by our comrades. And so the battalion, having lost half its men, regained its positions.

Thus it happened that in a single night, Suvorov and myself, without moving anywhere, had found ourselves behind enemy lines! Exhausted by life in the trenches, we had slept through a full scale attack: these days we are bothered by a tram rattling under our windows!

The company commander was happy to see us alive: 'At least you did not run: on the contrary!' he laughed. But the battalion commander said: 'Now you will not receive your decoration for the destroyed sharpshooter.' I was happy to get off so lightly. For such an offence, they could have done something much worse to me. Our men, of course, made fun of us in whatever way they could. For several days we became the object of endless ridicule. When everything was over, Suvorov just shook his head and said: 'One of us, Mansur, was born under a lucky star.'

It's cold. Morning. The Nazis sit quietly in the pocket. We are all silent. The snow falls slowly to the ground.

In front of us, in the pocket, there are five hills occupied by the Germans. We cannot see them, but on the map, to the North of Karpov, they are marked as 'Height 126' and so on.

Our regiment was ordered to occupy the five heights and entrench there. When the time of the attack came, our artillery opened fire and rifle battalions began moving ahead to the front. This was in early December. The snow that winter was deep, no less than 40cm [almost 16 inches – editor's note], and in low-lying places even more.

The end of the artillery barrage was a signal to advance. Our battalions arose, and screaming, 'Hurrah for the Motherland!' rushed ahead. The assault began without a hitch, and encountering no enemy resistance, we approached the five hills. The Germans retreated in a cowardly manner: 'The Fritzes are worn out, they don't want to fight,' I remember thinking to myself.

Well, since there was no resistance, the companies and battalions had little desire to plough through the deep snow. One after the other, the soldiers regrouped, forming a single lengthy column, which endeavoured to march only where the snow was well-trodden and compact. In this way, our regiment neared its objective. One more kilometre and the hills would be in our hands. This was probably the first time on the Don Front that we pressed the Fritzes so easily; the first time they retreated without a fight: 'If this is the way they are acting now,' I thought, 'the Stalingrad battle will be over in a week.'

At that moment, from everywhere around us, German machine-guns and artillery opened up on us. Now, a soldier cannot see the general picture of a battle on the scale of, let's say, a division. His mind is only able to grasp what is before his eyes. And so I will not try to outline the overall course of this battle, for it would be easy for me to make a mistake. Instead, I will describe only what has been left imprinted on my memory.

Our regiment, like a giant living creature, began twisting round and round, without moving anywhere. From all directions a hail of bullets and shells was hitting us. We heard the howls of enemy six-barrel mortars, their bombs killing with splinters anyone within their reach, and I quickly came up with an idea: 'I must find my way out of the crowd and dash towards one of the hills; or even better, run back, in the hope that the Nazis won't not bother with solitary targets!' Suvorov and I pushed aside from the main mass of people, so as to escape the zone of fire. Soon, along with some fifty other men, we were tramping through virgin snow. Our feet sank deep into the snow, but here, some 100m [almost 110 yards – editor's note] away, at least the enemy was no longer shooting at us. In order to move faster, we took off our greatcoats and even our *vatniks* [padded jackets – editor's note]. The Germans did not fire at us. We escaped from the trap alive, though soaked with sweat, as if we had just jumped out of water.

In the distance, we could clearly see the panorama of our catas-trophe. The Germans had skilfully ambushed us, and continued to meticulously gun down our men, while their tanks – hidden in pits with only their turrets visible – poured in a storm of shells. Our regiment was out of control, and it was terrible to witness its slaughter: we felt ashamed but there was nothing we could do.

Suddenly we heard the growl of approaching Diesel engines. Then we saw our tanks – some twenty or thirty – and behind them, in white winter camouflage cloaks, came our skiing soldiers, armed with sub-machine guns, and holding ropes attached to the armour. What a scene! Our soldiers, led by a captain, seemed to appear out of nowhere. They were curiously clean – spick and span – and were wearing flashy white fur coats. They even had brand new SMGs. Then it dawned on me: it was a holding detachment! [Reserve troops, detailed to enforce Stalin's policy of 'No retreat', by shooting front line soldiers who attempted to fall back – editor's note.]

I was ready to say goodbye to this world, when the captain shook my hand warmly, and in an Estonian accent, calmly said: 'No one is going to shoot you! You are not cowards. You managed to break out of the trap!' We could hardly believe our eyes and ears, and our relief must have been obvious. The captain could see the steam rising from us, as if we had just come out of a *bania,* and our blouses were so soaked that you could literally wring them out. 'Now take some *vatniks* and greatcoats from the dead,' he continued kindly, 'and go to our dugout. There is a stove there.'

Later, the soldiers told us about their captain. His name was Yan Tukhru, and as I'd guessed, he was an Estonian. He is now a retired major general. He read my book, and having found his name there, invited me to visit him in the city of Tallinn. After we had relived our past defeats and victories – including this episode – I asked him a question which had bothered me all these years: 'Please tell me why you never shot retreating soldiers – including myself and my comrades – unlike the other "holders"?'

'Mansur, did you notice anything special about the men commanding those "holders"?'

'No, I didn't.'

'I'll answer your question: because I'm Estonian.' I thought of all the commanders who had enthusiastically implemented Order 227 ('No retreat!'): it was true that there was not a single Estonian among them. 'At the time, my superiors were suspicious about my reluctance to carry out the order, considering me to be too self-willed.'

The battle ended an hour later. The hills were finally taken, but we couldn't look each other in the face. What a disgrace! Commanding officers kept visiting us all through the night.

Some soldiers told us that the neighbouring regiment had been in a similar tight spot; but at the critical moment, Chief-of-Staff Captain Pavel Bilaonov appeared among the men. His thunderous voice and iron will made the soldiers hold firm and lie low. First he halted the battalion, then he organized a counter-attack. His personal example and bravery became a model for the rank and file. Two retreating battalions, seeing Bilaonov's actions, returned to their advance positions.

Our battalion commander was replaced by someone else. Thirteen Nazi tanks, six guns and eight mortars were destroyed. Some 100 German soldiers were taken prisoner. Possession of those five hills cost us dearly.

The following morning we lost a soldier by the name of Akhmet Garipov. Our men had seen him the night before with a pot of hot coals, over which he had proceeded to fix his waterproof cape, making a sort of tent. They found his body beneath the cape: the poor fellow had been poisoned by the gas.

Latyp-aka, an old Uzbek, shook his head sadly, speaking in broken Russian: 'Oh, Garib, Garib! He wanted to make a small Tashkent! He wanted to make our Uzbek *sandal*. A *sandal* is a pit. A lot of hot coals. Then all the family and the guests lie around the *sandal*, cover themselves with lots of blankets. *Sandal* will be good, will be warm, but one should put only one's legs and belly under the *sandal*, and the head must be outside, to breath fresh air. If you put your head under the *sandal*, you'll die. Garib hid his head. Bad death. One should die when one is old, after you raised your fifteenth child. Garib, Garib, what a foolish head Allah gave you. It's better to die of a bullet in a fight . . .'

I listened to the aged Uzbek and remembered how, in the military school, I fainted in the Tashkent summer heat. What a vast country we have! Some are more used to a cold climate, others to a hot one. In December 1942, the temperature in the Stalingrad area sometimes fell to minus 40 °C [minus 40 °F – editor's note]. Of course, a man might survive minus 50 or even minus 70 °C if there is no wind. But at Stalingrad there was this terrible steppe wind, and only one place to hide: the trench. I was born in Siberia, but these conditions were too much even for me. As for the Uzbeks, they were used to living in the south, and it would have been better to spare them the freezing weather: but when the enemy was pushing from all directions, and the country was under threat, there was no place for such prudence.

In the neighbouring rifle company there was also an unexpected tragedy. Some soldiers found in a field near the trenches a round hole, the size of a tank hatch. A warm smell rose from beneath, as from a freshly made stove, used for the first time. The men found that the hole led into a chamber, resembling a pot some 5 or 6m in diameter [no more than 20 feet – editor's note], and created by the blast of a high explosive bomb. The sticky clay soil and been compressed like brick, and the walls of the 'pot' appeared roasted, with narrow fissures in them. Some of the more resolute soldiers decided to have a nice nap in this cosy place. Eighteen men got inside and went to sleep forever. It turned out that from the small but deep fissures, nitric oxide – created by the explosion – continued to seep inside. Who could have known about this danger? A miner, perhaps. Well, I'm a miner: but if I'd found this wonderful bedroom, I would have forgotten myself, and been the first to go down and grab a place. When will we stop being so foolish?

Several nights ago, Nazi transport planes dropped some very valuable items near our battalion: a load of warm boots made of felt with leather soles, very well made, snug and waterproof. In fact, we found them better than our traditional *valenki*, and everyone was happy to put them on. The Fritzes were furious with us for taking their boots, shouting: 'Russ, give our *valenki*, take our guns!' (We had many German sub-machine guns and lots of ammunition for them).

So now our feet are fine. But in the meantime, we have lost our waterproof capes, and the rest of our bodies are soaking wet with rain and melting snow! What can we do?

Well, yesterday, in No Man's Land – not more than 200m [almost 220 yards – editor's note] away from our trenches – I saw some parcels that the Germans had dropped for their men. The packages were ripped, and I could see that they contained clothing, including some waterproof stuff. Brand new waterproofs! If only one could get to them . . .

I keep looking out into No Man's Land, hoping that someone will run towards the stranded parcels: if everything is OK, then I'll try myself. I point out the waterproofs to Suvorov. He doesn't say a word. Now I am in an embarrassing situation, because it looks like I'm hinting that he should go. Better to have kept my mouth shut! Now I have to go or be labelled a coward. And so I find myself walking across the neutral zone. I come up to the ripped parcels and looked around: where are the German trenches? I must be a good mark for a sharpshooter! Still, if he misses with the first bullet, I'll be able to slip away. But it is quiet and I don't see anything suspicious.

I grab the corner of a waterproof and begin pulling it from under some other stuff. Then, out of nowhere, several Nazi soldiers appear. I am so afraid that I cannot breathe, and think that there must be at least seventeen of them. But wait, I don't have any weapons on me! Even my pistol, presented to me by the tank colonel, is not here! The Germans stand in a semicircle, smiling and laughing: they have decided to have some fun. A hundred thoughts flash through my mind in a split second. But I am fortunate that fear has not made me blind: for a few steps ahead, I notice a pit containing an open box filled with anti-personnel hand grenades.

The Germans keep laughing: 'Russ Ivan! Russ Ivan!' Twisting their fingers against their temples, as if to say, 'what a fool you are, bringing your ass here for a waterproof!' Maybe they are bored, and want to cheer up their men, who are doubtless watching this comedy. But our boys can also see me, and I wish I had time to grab one of those grenades. Still, what have I got to lose? So I put my hands on my belly, as if fear was killing my stomach, and jump into the pit. Grabbing hold of a grenade, I realize that the Germans either have not noticed the box, or are too tipsy to be afraid of one Ivan in the open. 'If only I could make it before they open fire!' I think, as my hands automatically go to work, and while the Fritzes are laughing: 'Ha-ha-ha' and 'Ho-ho-ho' and 'Ivan *Kaputt*! Ivan, *valenki* off!' I prepare more than ten grenades. Two sub-machine guns, covered by a thin layer of snow, are lying right next to me. Are they loaded? I stoop, and my hands feel the magazine. I remove it. The cartridges are tightly packed: it's full. 'Let's go!'

The grenades come with such speed that the first one explodes, as I'm throwing the third. I keep flinging them like red-hot coals. Then I jump out of the pit with the gun, and without even looking at what is happening on the spot where, some seconds ago, the Fritzes were roaring with laughter, I loose off a few rounds. Now they are roaring with something else! Out of spite, I grab the corner of the waterproof and take to my heels, hearing bullets whistling past me . . .

I fell into the trench next to Suvorov. My dear commander howled with delight and began pounding me with his fists and kicking me. And since that day, even while digging frozen ground for a trench, I always kept my sub-machine gun hanging on my back. It's a nuisance when you're at work, but never again did I part with my weapon, not for a minute!

CHAPTER FIVE

Holiday Presents for the Fritzes

At night some envoys came to our lines. I think they were from a Romanian brigade. Our battalion commander summoned me to HQ, so that the envoys could take a closer look at me: it turned out that they had seen me snatch the waterproof from under the Germans' noses. There were eight of them, and they all wore thick black sweaters. I thought that they looked like our Georgians or Armenians. Though it was pretty dark at HQ – with light coming only from bullet cases filled with gas – the Romanians had a look at me. Then they talked amongst themselves something, and our commander sent me back.

It turned out that they had come to discuss the terms of their surrender, and the following night, several hundred men from the enemy brigade operating in our sector of the front, laid down their arms.

The envoys provided our chiefs with a lot of valuable information, and gave away the plan of German positions facing our division. We saw the results of our artillery attack against enemy lines several days later, when our troops advanced. They also showed our battalion commander a place where, every night at 11.00 pm, a German field kitchen served out hot food.

We mortarmen were ordered to take care of that kitchen. We checked its location on our fire scheme, and realized that if we adjusted our angle a few degrees to the right of target No. 3, we'd have a direct hit.

We brought some captured bombs to our firing-point: thirty for each mortar. Lieutenant Stukach and I carefully made it to the observation post, which was right up against the German front line. Then, keeping our eyes peeled, and our mouths shut, we waited. The night was bright, even though there was a thin crescent moon in the sky. Then, at 11.00 pm sharp, just as we'd been told, a field kitchen appeared. The Germans, each carrying two or three mess tins, began arriving from everywhere around. No less than 100 people crowded round the kitchen. The cook took his time. So did we. Then, we opened up a volley with all of our nine mortars. We did not spare the Nazis an ample serving of their own shells.

There's no pleasure in killing. But why did the Germans come to our home? Why did they bring death and suffering to our land? Did they expect us to give up without a fight? I saw them later, when they were leaving Stalingrad, sinuous columns of frostbitten half-corpses. It occurred to me that each one of them had a mother who was waiting. Suddenly, I felt a lump of compassion in my throat. But it soon disappeared. With what thoughts, what hopes, did these mothers send off their sons to this war? And what did they expect from us?

Once more we're worn out by hunger. Our kitchen was blown apart by the Germans. Furthermore, Hitler had ceased to provide Paulus's army with food by air, so we no longer got any captured provisions. I went to see a comrade of mine, Sergeant Major Smirnov, commander of a service platoon. We had been friends since Malaya Yelshanka, where our regiment had stayed for several days on its way to the front.

There, in Malaya Yelshanka, along with our uniforms, they gave us puttees. It was the first time I had seen them, as army cadets wore socks. I kept asking myself: 'how are these slippery, knitted bands supposed to stay my feet, when the legs become narrower towards the end?' If they had become wider at the end, then things might have been simpler. We had not been taught to deal with puttees at the military school, but I didn't want to look like a fool, so I wrapped my feet as tight as I could, with all the strength of a coal miner, so the puttees wouldn't slip down. My feet instantly became numb but I decided to put up with it. Then came an order to assume formation: tactical exercises with gas masks, which had been distributed earlier. I marched, but I couldn't feel my feet! Well, we'd covered 1km [just over 100 yards – editor's note], when I fell to the ground, roaring because of the terrible pain in my knees. Sergeant Major Smirnov ran up to me and instantly realized what had happened. In a second, he untied the puttees and the bindings loosened like a steel spring. My legs were blue and looked like the crimped hose of a gas mask. For ten minutes, Smirnov massaged my legs and feet, until I felt a million needles pricking me, and my skin resumed its normal colour. The sergeant major rubbed and swore like hell: 'What a fool! And where did you get the strength to wrap it up so tight, eh?' For half an hour the whole company waited while I squatted and jumped, following the sergeant major's directions. I could see that he was happy everything had ended fine: but he now realized the problems he faced with cadets who had swallowed a three-year training program in six months. He personally wrapped my feet very gently, and sticking my spoon behind the bindings, ordered: 'Don't touch it!'

Now I find him in a deep ravine, where he has safely hidden himself, along with his whole platoon, plus their horses and two-wheel carts. Sergeant Major Nikolai Smirnov is sitting in a concrete dugout like a sultan or a khan, full-fed, clean-shaven, and with a double chin. He threw a scared glance at me, then recognized who I was: 'Oh, Mansur, come in, sit down. Still alive?'

'Listen, Smirnov, give me something to eat.'

'I have nothing, we're starving ourselves.'

'Knock off the jokes. At least give me a crust for Suvorov.'

'I have nothing, I'm serious. You know yourself, Mansur, I would never in my life refuse you.'

I sat there thinking: is he lying or not? But then I remembered his anxious advice on the other bank of the Don before our first fight, when he found us completely exhausted and lying flat on the ground: 'Don't you be greedy, boys! You'll have the gripes! Belly colic, God forbid. You just suck it a little, crumb by crumb!' I remembered how he had fed his horses with bread, while starving himself, just to bring us our rations. I felt ashamed that I did not trust him. Maybe he's not lying after all. And then Smirnov came up with an idea: 'I can give you mixed fodder. For horses.'

'OK.'

Five minutes later his soldiers brought a sack. Inside were some briquettes of oatmeal chaff with flour, thorny like a hedgehog. 'Well,' I thought, 'there was a time when horses ate our bread, now it's our turn to try their food.'

'Put it into a kettle with water,' instructed Smirnov, 'boil it, then squeeze out the chaff and drink the liquid. It will ease your hunger.' I shouldered the fodder sack and rushed home. The men of our company got together and boiled several briquettes. We were so hungry that we ate the chaff as well: it seemed to soften, and we hoped that we would be OK.

Next day something totally unexpected happened: I wanted to defecate but it hurt. I tried to stop but it was no use, I simply had to carry on. But the agony! Sharp, like claws! Everything went dark before my eyes, and I was roaring like a hog in a slaughterhouse – they could hear me miles away! Then, stooping, groaning, clutching my gut, I crawled back to the trench, as if to a hospital ward after a difficult operation. 'Well,' I thought, 'if the Fritzes don't kill me, my own stupidity will. Why did I eat the chaff? Smirnov warned me!' Then I heard another soldier screaming somewhere at the other end of the trench: my comrades were, of course, sentenced to suffer the same fate . . .

In late December 1942 our regiment lost many men and reinforcements arrived from the Central Asian republics. Barely understanding Russian, Uzbeks, Tadzhiks and our other friends from the south, finding themselves without their green tea, in a frost of minus thirty, died in silence, like flies. The day after they joined us, the Germans began joking through their loudspeakers: 'Ivan! Let's trade the Uzbeks for the Romanians!'

Next morning, at daybreak, a tidal wave of incessant mortar and artillery fire crashed into our trenches and enemy planes showered us with bombs. The wild roar of flying shells was enough to completely stupefy us! The ground, like raw rubber or jelly, rocked back and forth. There was no air to breath, as if the oxygen had been burned away by exploding bombs and shells. Deafened, like all my comrades, I crawled into my burrow at the bottom of the trench, keeping my legs outside, so that I might be pulled out if I got buried by crumbling earth. It was a good thing that the soil here was hard and solid and our burrows could still hold. When we hacked them from the frozen ground – getting bloody callouses on our palms – Mother Earth heard a lot of strong language: but in the middle of that barrage, hiding in my burrow, I asked Her forgiveness.

Above my head, the blasts followed in quick succession, and it seemed to me that all of them were directly over my hole. We used to console ourselves with the fantasy that 'a shell hole cannot be hit a second time.' Often, under heavy gun and mortar fire, I told myself: 'Well, boy! This time you've surely had it!' I would feel frightened:

'Maybe I'm the only one left here?' Then I would pop out of my burrow, like some gopher, and quickly look around to see what was going on. My comrades – plagued by fears of their own – would also poke their heads out in the same manner. When I could see that my neighbours were alive, and had not run away, I would feel ashamed, and dive back into my burrow once more!

The artillery barrage ceased as suddenly as it had begun. Those of us who were still alive crawled out. But many men were left to lie in their holes forever. They had no need for a burial. But we had no time to express our regret – or our joy – for the Fritzes and their allies had begun their assault. The enemy waves came closer: the first row was made up of Romanians, the second of Germans, the third of Hungarians, and the fourth of Germans again. We witnessed a horrifying sight in No Man's Land: some Romanians and Hungarians raised their hands, in a gesture of surrender, and the Germans shot them down. After a slight pause, the enemy regrouped and continued the attack. We met them with the full force of our machine-guns and mortars and the assault was repelled. Then once again, we were showered with shells and forced to dive into our burrows. In this way we clung onto our trenches for ten days without water, bread, *makhorka* or our kitchen!

The snow was so mixed with earth, that we couldn't boil it for water anymore. Our rear had been smashed to pieces. Our telephones were dead and we had no connection with the outside world. The Germans in the pocket were much better off because they had villages with wells. One of our more resourceful soldiers ran to a ravine, and there, at the very bottom he found thawed soil. He waited for the dirty, smelly water to concentrate into a puddle, scooped some into his mess tin, and drank as much as he could. Then he scooped some more and brought it back to us. I lifted the mess tin to my lips and almost fainted: it smelled of rotten eggs! But we drank it all up, and used every opportunity to rush back to the ravine to get more of that bitter, smelly water. Then, after the first hole froze, we dug another one, and kept doing this till we unearthed the bodies of some dead Germans. For many of us, this discovery was nothing special: 'It's all the same, to die of poison, or to be shot!' I felt sick but did not throw up, because for three days I did not even have a single bread crumb.

One friend of mine, a real joker, reassured us: 'Man is 80 per cent water! Each of us has three or four buckets more than a camel! Without water we'll last three or even four weeks! Without food just as long! Because each of us has some 50kg [just over 110lbs – editor's note] of meat!' In those ten days we turned into walking skeletons. Through our skin, as through parchment, one could see our skulls with large, black, holes instead of eyes. Our lips were dried, our teeth exposed all the time. One of our soldiers remarked: 'We should take scythes in our hands and hang on our chests a sign: "Death to the German Occupants!"'

Finally, one night a field kitchen belonging to some other battalion bumped into us. The cook was ready to turn back to find his men, but he was grabbed by our boys, who emptied the pot containing someone else's porridge. That same night, before daybreak, some news-papermen with notebooks and a camera came to see us. We were too weak to describe how we defended our lines. They took a photo of us. A day later we read about our heroism in a paper but for some reason there were no pictures. Our commissar explained: 'The snap-shots didn't turn out that well . . .' Of course, it was not possible to show live skeletons in a newspaper!

It was a great joy for us to receive a letter, a note, or a parcel from home. Also, in each box containing shells, bombs or cartridges, we found pleasant surprises: a piece of paper bearing the address of an unknown girl, so that one could write her, or tobacco pouches filled with makhorka. These were embroidered and you could instantly tell if it was the work of a young girl or a child. The old soldiers – the muzhiks – preferred the latter, while the boys instantly grabbed the pouches embroidered by young girls. And they never confused them!

In these pouches one might find a photo and a letter. You were the hero of the day if you were lucky enough to get one! Certain 'heroes', however, passed their letter or photo to some comrade: these were the boys who were engaged, and who had given promises to their fiancées. On the pouches one might read: 'Death to the German occupants!' 'Come back with victory!' 'Greetings from the Komsomol girls of the Collective Farm, Dawn of Communism!' 'Avenge my deceased father!' or 'Soldier, avenge my deceased little brother!' And we, who took such a pouch, would faithfully do what was asked of us: the next Nazi one destroyed was regarded as fulfilling a special request. We fastened these pouches to our webbing, on top of our uniforms, where they could be easily seen.

That winter, when we were near Stalingrad, we often received parcels from my native Siberia containing warm clothes: woollen socks, scarves, mittens or handmade sweaters. These parcels cheered us up. We felt that our whole country was with us in the trenches.

On 28 December 1942, we learned from a German prisoner (captured by our regimental scouts, led by Andrei Bogdanov) that the Nazis were planning to send us 'season's greetings' at midnight, New Year's Eve. Consequently, our chiefs ordered us to move into new firing positions, so we could make a pre-emptive strike against the enemy batteries. This order came after a hard but successful fight, in which we seized a comfortable ravine from the Germans. We had just dug ourselves in, and were preparing, finally, to get some rest for the night, when our company commander, gave the order: 'Company! Load the mortars!' We were exhausted, worn out, broken-hearted. But a command is a command. Cursing the whole world, we obeyed him and began packing. Our firing line sounded like a troubled beehive. From every direction I heard foul language and malicious cries: 'Boys! This is treason or at the very least downright humiliation!' Someone else screamed: 'Shut up! Things are bad enough without you yelling!' I was on the verge of tears when a vile thought crossed my mind: 'It's better to die than to suffer this way!' And if I, a nineteen-year-old miner used to hard labour since childhood, couldn't take it any longer, what about those who had just finished ninth or tenth grade? [Boys of seventeen and eighteen years of age – editor's note.] Or those who were unused to manual labour?

At last our company, headed by the CO, began climbing the steep slope of the ravine, up onto the steppe, and into the teeth of a ferocious hurricane. If we had not been so heavily laden with equipment, we would have been swept away like leaves of grass to God knows where! Sand, dust, and grains of ice blinded us, filled our noses and mouths, and even penetrated our clothes. It was minus thirty, and the frost bored deep into our bones. I felt like I was totally naked. Facing the wind, bent double, my nose almost touching the ground, I struggled after the CO with my last scrap of strength. Then, I suddenly fell face down on the frozen ground, as if someone had stabbed me in the back with a ramrod, right under my left shoulder blade, and pierced my heart. A thought flashed through my brain: 'Well, Mansur, that's it!' The shooting pain was so bad I could hardly breathe, let alone move. And so I lay paralysed with pain – a kind of neuralgia – until at length, the sensation began to ebb away, as if the 'ramrod' were being slowly withdrawn. I drew in a deep breath, got up, and prepared to push on. But first, I looked up at the sky: there was a cold, round moon, and black, ragged clouds, rushing southwards like herds of wild Mongolian horses without riders.

After an agonising half-hour march, our CO made a gesture with his hand, bidding us lie flat, like walruses on a block of ice. Then he, together with his liaison man, disappeared into the darkness, bound for the rifle company in order to check our position. Fifteen minutes later they returned, and the CO ordered us to dig in. I glanced at my pocket watch: it was 1.00 am, no less than eight hours before daybreak . . .

The first to begin is my comrade, Pavel Suvorov. He has a captured artillery pick in his hands. The shaft is made of oak, nearly 1m long [almost 40 inches – editor's note], and the ends are curved, with longitudinal ribs to make them stronger. One end is like a pike, the other like a chisel. Thanks to this pick, our gun crew is always the first to dig in. But Suvorov looks gloomy and depressed. He just stands there, his head sunk on his chest, leaning with both hands on the shaft. Then he raises the pick, and with a roar, smashes the ground with all his strength. But when I hear the clunk of the Swedish steel, and see the red sparks fly from the spot where his blow fell, I realize that we're finished. Everyone else thinks the same. Fuat, who rarely speaks, yells in my ear: 'It's the end for our company!' He walks away and freezes into a stone statue with a sad Mongolian face. If Suvorov, a professional miner, has failed, it seems useless for anyone else to try.

But our platoon commanders, Stukach and Isayev, encourage us to go on: 'Come on, boys! Come on! Dig in!' I should give a hand – after all, I am the *partorg* – but I just bob up and down like some machine, trying to keep warm. A blow! Another blow! Buteiko himself makes a series of them: but the hole he creates is only as big as a sparrow's nest. One cannot even stick a pair of ammonite cartridges into it. The other mortarmen crowd together, stamping their feet in a bid to keep warm. They have small entrenching shovels, which are useless against frozen earth. Meanwhile, barely able to move my numb feet, I circle round the group, like some shaman performing a sacred dance to ward off evil spirits. I am frozen through to my bones; my brain is deadened with cold; my mind refuses to work. Only two cells remain active: one tries to convince me to lie on the ground and have a nice nap; while the other screams, 'Don't do that! If you go to sleep now, you'll die!' I keep walking. It takes an enormous effort to make a single stride. Maybe this will be the final step of my life? My little brain cell continues to scream: 'Hold on! Hold on! Keep going!' I take one more tread. Suddenly, beneath my feet, I feel something like a cotton wool mattress. My legs fail me and I fall on my knees. A miracle. I have stumbled into a cesspit!

I automatically grab my entrenching shovel and furiously slice through the upper layer of the 'mattress' to the moist, warm, muck below. Almost instantly, I smell the bitter scent of ammonium chloride. I inhale it. I drink it in. My brain revives with each breath and eventually warmth enters my body. Blood returns to my fingers. Suddenly they began to ache! I call out to my comrades but cannot produce words, only some hissing sounds. I call them mentally, my eyes wet with tears: 'Boys! Fuat! Come over here now!' It seems Fuat and the others hear my thoughts: 'What's wrong, Mansur? Did you call us?' Fuat, seeing the vapour rising from the ground, guesses what I have found, and falling face down on the rotting dung, sticks his freezing arms right in up to the elbows. Suvorov and Latyp-aka also run up and embrace the warm manure. Suvorov jokes: 'Mansur is lucky with shit! He was born under a lucky star!' Other mortarmen hurry to join us, but Suvorov proposes they disperse to look for more heaps of musty old manure. Within the hour, all our mortarmen are snugly embedded in the warm Mother Earth, as if into a grandmother's armpit.

Long before sunrise, we were ready for battle. Suddenly, we heard the boom of engines coming from the sky: German transports bringing holiday presents for the Fritzes. Immediately, we began shooting our captured flare pistols. Then, our anti-aircraft guns opened up, and minutes later, enormous parachutes carrying huge packages descended on our lines. We ripped them open. Soon our trenches were full of Christmas presents. It would be impossible to name all the goods: sausage, butter, raisins, dried apricots, honey, chocolate, biscuits, brandy, Champagne, schnapps and many other things. There was also warm underwear, woollen socks, sleeping bags and thousands of sets of photos, showing naked beauties and boys, coupled together like the figures in a number 69. At first, we could not work out what they were doing, but when we finally realized, we couldn't believe our eyes! My Uzbek friend was so appalled, I had to calm him down by convincing him that the Germans did not use humans for these photos, but painted rubber dolls, just for fun. This is how I came to know about pornography [obscene or indecent images and literature were forbidden in the Soviet Union – editor's note].

By daybreak, on 29 December, we had divided up the Christmas presents that fell from the sky. The front was quiet and we rested for two days. Then, on 31 December, at 11.00 pm sharp, we opened up a volley fire against the Nazi artillery batteries, together with our divisional guns. Without sparing our shells, we continued our bombardment for half an hour. The German guns did not get the opportunity to reply. Some minutes later, however, we heard the dreary howl of a forlorn six-barrel mortar coming from enemy lines. Six shells flew over our heads and exploded somewhere in the ravine that we had left behind.

I remember, on our way to the front, at the village Malaya Yelshanka, where we received our new field uniforms, mess tins, chemical kits, and so on, we were also given a plastic capsule with a screw top. Inside was a small piece of tape, on which each soldier had to write his personal details. Then, the capsule had to be tightly closed, to keep away moisture, and placed in a small pocket. We called these things 'passports of death' and I don't know about others, but I quietly threw the mine away. In its place I carried a mascot, hoping to save it till the end of the war. All my comrades had something that served them as a lucky charm, but we were not in the habit of talking about such things: a mascot could only preserve its power if kept secret.

I made my mascot with my own hands. When we were marching to the Stalingrad Front, our columns, after detraining, moved only at night. In the daytime we camouflaged ourselves, tried to keep quiet, and slept. During these stops we also visited our field kitchen, dried our puttees, and so on. I decided to make a wooden cigarette holder. When I finished it I said to myself: 'If I do not lose it, then I'll return home alive from the war.' But before I had time to hide it in my trouser pocket, our sergeant major, passing by, snatched it out of my hand and went on his way. I immediately went numb with fear: 'I made a bet with fate that I wouldn't lose it! This means I won't get home alive!' I sat there thinking: 'I can't fight with an officer, and he will not give me back this holder.' I felt sick and depressed. I don't want to die! But at that moment a thought crossed my mind: 'I must immediately make another cigarette holder, a more beautiful one.' In half an hour the new one was ready, and as luck would have it, I passed the sergeant major holding it in my mouth. He saw it and proposed an exchange, promising to give me a pack of *makhorka* in addition. I gladly agreed, and quickly returned to my place, where I secretly sewed up the mascot in my small trouser pocket. I was overjoyed! This means I'll return home safely!

Once, before an attack, our soldiers found themselves among some T-34 and KV tanks. Their crews were walking around in order to have some fresh air. We were curious to talk to them.

Tank men respected the infantry and were likewise happy to see us. Lots of jokes were made. Some discovered that they came from the same part of the country. Everyone was having a good time. But one tank driver looked gloomy: 'You know, my infantry friend, I'll be burned today,' he suddenly told me. We were standing some distance from the others. I said to him: 'Each one of us has an equal chance of staying alive. You should keep your spirit up, especially now.' The tank man remarked with some irony: 'And you, you think you speak like a commissar? I've been driving a tank since the first days of the war. This is my fifth machine. I'm finished today and that's it. You're just a kid, you don't understand. I've lost my mascot . . .' I had a sick feeling in the pit of my stomach, but I didn't show it.

Just before the beginning of the attack, I told this story to Suvorov, as if laughing at the tank man's fear. But quite unexpectedly, Suvorov took the whole thing seriously. So we decided to follow that tank during the attack, just in case something did happen and we could help out the crew. I kept running with my eyes fixed on our machine, watching it speed ahead, manoeuvre, and evade thermite shells [in the Red Army, this was the name for hollow charge shells – editor's note]. The thermites were flying about with a roar, raising fountains of sparks. Several machines to the left and to the right caught fire, but our tank kept on shooting! I finally became convinced that nothing could go wrong. That man knows how to fight! But suddenly, in full motion, the tank blew up. Because of the momentum, its wrecked form rolled ahead for another 10m [almost 11 yards – editor's note] then caught fire. Suvorov and I rushed to help, but all we could hear was the dry cracking of exploding cartridges coming from inside the tank.

Here is another interesting story. Several of us were standing on a two-wheel cart, watching the action on our left flank, where a neighbouring regiment was fending off an enemy attack. The Nazis were trying to recapture a height they had just lost. There were five or six of us on the cart. I was the first, and Lieutenant Stukach, the last to climb up. Suddenly, we heard the whizz of a spent bullet, coming from somewhere afar. I stooped, and losing my balance, jumped down, dragging the rest – we were holding each other by the straps – with me. Stukach, however, managed to hold on, but did not have time to stoop. The bullet hit him in the temple, and even though it had lost much of its speed, the blow was enough to knock him down. But we could see he was still alive! He found the bullet in his bloodstained hair, looked at it, and sat there with a broad smile, unable to understand how he had survived. After a moment of total amazement, we began throwing him up in the air, shouting: 'Hurrah! Bullets can't kill the lieutenant!' A crowd instantly surrounded us. Everyone was interested: 'How come bullets can't kill him?' I remember thinking at that moment: 'probably Lieutenant Stukach has a mascot . . .'

I desperately want to get through this war and stay alive: to see life as it's going to be lived afterwards. I'll agree to any conditions. As long as there's a place where I can have a good sleep. As to the rest, there's enough to make everyone happy: sunshine, clear spring water, our Siberian mother-forest. But what if I lose an arm, both legs, an eye? What would be the worst scenario that I would accept, in order to save my life? I could agree to anything, but not death, not the end. If I ended up an invalid, perhaps I could start drawing? I love drawing! And I don't need any decorations: well, perhaps the medal 'For Bravery', that would be enough, just so that people would know I had fought in the war. Thus I was secretly dreaming and sometimes touching my mascot. It's here. I can take it out, have a look, and then put it back again.

Yes, it was a superstition, but it was not the only one I had. There some things I simply would not do. For example, I would never take a watch from a dead man, for I noticed that if someone broke this rule, he died soon after. There was some strange connection. I don't believe in Allah or in God. But the night I was dragging Nikolai – the soldier who had stolen my bread – to the medical unit, and he asked me to leave him, somehow I was absolutely certain, that if I did, my own faith in a higher justice would severely punish me. And because I didn't desert him, my faith rewarded me, for I am still alive.

Another thing I noticed: if a man tried to hide like a coward, he would inevitably be killed. This was a rule. And so I would often guess, 'He'll die,' and I rarely made a mistake. Sometimes a man would lose his nerve after being wounded, and returning to the front from hospital. I can tell a story about one of my comrades, a machine-gunner called Nikolai Belozerov (he is the only man in this book, whose surname I changed). Nikolai used up more bullets than any other machine-gunner. He had two No. 2s, who took care of his cartridges. He was a brave soldier and never abandoned his post without an order. One day he was lightly wounded and sent to the rear. Some time after that I met him at our regimental HQ, where I was attending a meeting of our Communist Party Bureau. Belozerov looked spick and span, had gained some weight, and had an Order of the Red Banner on his blouse. He wore the uniform of a junior lieutenant. I was glad to see him: 'Tell me, how was it at the hospital?' I asked him with envy (yes, I must confess that I was jealous of people with light wounds – they got to sleep in a clean bed), 'did you have enough sleep?' Belozerov told me about his girls, even though I knew nothing about women at the time. Well, I gave him an account of what happened while he was away. We each had a sip of alcohol, grabbed a bite, and walked out of the ravine to take a path leading to our battalion. We were running across a field when German mortars suddenly roared into life.

We jump into the nearest trench. Several of our men are already in there. Nikolai puts on his helmet. But like everyone else, I'm not wearing one. I think to myself: 'Now he is commanding a machine-gun company, he wants to give an example to his soldiers by wearing a helmet, even though they're good for nothing.' I look at his eyes, they are staring at the ground: 'Nikolai is now afraid,' I tell myself, 'he was different before.' The incoming shells strike nearby, bursting with hot, screeching splinters. We leap out and dash forward. I run to the next trench with the others, but Nikolai suddenly turns back and jumps into our previous hiding place. Again the deafening explosions follow one another. Once more I leap out, ready to dart forward. I scream: 'Nikolai, let's go!' Where is he? Is he still in that trench? No, there must be something wrong. I run back to the place. Nikolai's helmet is pierced by splinters and spattered with grey-red brain, his face is black, his arms mutilated. The bomb hit the rear wall of his trench.

Everything belonging to Belozerov – his documents, a new pistol, and the Order of the Red Banner – I handed over to the battalion commissar.

Suvorov once said to me: 'You seem to be born under a lucky star, Mansur. How many times you have escaped death?' I listened to him and felt for my mascot – it's here . . .

During the last couple of weeks my friend Suvorov was in an especially sombre mood. I asked him: 'What happened to our humorist Suvorov?'

But he's silent. Just answers 'yes' or 'no' and that's all. Once he took out all his documents, placed before himself, and read them aloud so I could hear. He has a small daughter, a wife, a mother. Slowly, deliberately, he read out his home address. Then he collected the papers, wrapped them in a piece of cloth, and placed them in his blouse pocket: 'You'll send all this to Kuchkar, to my family.' My heart sank. 'I can sense, Mansur, that my end is near.'

I tried to cheer him up as best as I could, but it felt like he was building a wall around himself and was completely withdrawn. He became indifferent to everything. Maybe he had lost something? But I was afraid to ask. You see, if Suvorov really had got a mascot, I shouldn't know about it.

On 10 January 1943, after the battle for the village of Dmitriyevka, when it was quiet again, Pavel Suvorov was hit in the head with an explosive bullet. The single, stray projectile came from afar, with a prolonged hissing sound. Not a single enemy shot followed after this had happened.

I cried, like women cry beside the dead body of their beloved. I howled, like little children howl, when they are greatly and unfairly offended by someone.

He once told me how he got his Order of the Red Star. At the very beginning of the war his regiment was retreating eastwards from the town of Brest. On one railway station they found a boxcar with explosives, parked on a dead end sidetrack. It was to be used in some mining works. There were no sappers in the regiment, so Suvorov explained that he was a mining engineer, and volunteered to take a closer look at the cargo. There was ammonite in some sacks and a metal safe containing detonators. The safety fuses, wires, and electric brazing equipment were stored separately. The village had three decent buildings: a school, a hospital, and a hotel. It was decided to mine them. There was little time but Suvorov managed. He even had enough wire to make a reserve detonating system. After the population was evacuated, the regiment left the village. When the Nazis finally occupied the place and settled in these buildings, several huge explosions shook the ground.

We buried Suvorov near the village Dmitriyevka. All battalion officers were present. Pavel was the instructor of our entire mortar company, and our mortar was the principal one in the unit, our detachment referred to as 'Suvorovski'.

Fuat and I now felt like we lost a father, and I thought that I would never recover. While Suvorov was with us, I tried in every way to please him, as if I lived and acted with just one motive: to get his approval. I'm grateful to all my comrades. They took care of me and behaved like true friends.

We wrote letters to Suvorov's family, to Kuchkar in the Urals. But whatever expressions you choose to console someone, the words 'died a valiant death' cannot be substituted for anything else.

CHAPTER SIX

Pitomnik Airfield

We broke into the small village of Pitomnik. As long as I live I will never forget that airfield in Pitomnik. The Nazis had brought their wounded here, but did not have time to evacuate them. The wounded Germans were dying, freezing on the snowy concrete. Thousands of people freezing to death. Some were crawling across the airfield, leaning on their hands, from which the fingers had already fallen off.

A German is looking at me, his eyes growing dim. His nose is practically gone, his face frostbitten. He is emaciated and unshaven, unable to move his jaw. His brain is almost frozen and his heart is barely beating. It is unbearable to see the man suffer so much, begging with his eyes for a bullet, but I don't have the strength to finish him off. Another one falls to the ground and will sink into the desired peace in ten or fifteen minutes. It is impossible to save them: an irreversible process of dying, all their limbs frostbitten.

I'm ashamed to think the way I do; I'm ashamed to feel this unwanted pity. I hope our boys don't notice. Remember, I've lost a friend and must avenge him! And then I see one of our soldiers, with the same fear as mine, looking into the eyes of a German crouching on all fours. Both are glancing in turn into each other's eyes and at a pistol in the hand of the soldier. The German is so numb that he cannot even nod his head. He blinks: 'Yes . . .' The soldier shoots him in the temple. The man is dead but he doesn't fall, he's too frozen. He remains on all fours, like a bench, with no blood flowing from the wound in his head.

On the airfield in Pitomnik we found huge piles of parcels, ready to be flown to Germany, with valuable loot inside. Pitomnik itself consisted of a handful of houses, yet it was very important: it was a base for German motor transport. The vehicles were in excellent condition and neatly assembled in rows, in accordance with their unit numbers, and totalling some 17,000. It looked like a little town with streets and blocks.

Together with Fuat Khadaibergenov I entered a dugout. What a comfortable dwelling: a kitchen, a bedroom, and a lavatory! The smell of perfume. Different drinks in bottles, flasks and thermoses. The coffee was still warm. Yes, well, not bad at all (and until very recently) was the life of the commanders of those soldiers freezing on the airfield. On one of the double beds lay a small dog with shaggy, snow-white hair. For some reason it was trembling. We had some sausages in our knapsacks. We gave a piece to the dog and went away, closing the door, and writing on it with a piece of coal: 'Mined'. It would have been a pity if, in the heat of the moment, one of our men had shot the trembling animal. It had nothing to do with all of this.

I was never particularly interested in trophies, but in that dugout I noticed a box trimmed with velvet. I opened it. Inside was an impressive collection of decorations and I decided to take it back to our regimental HQ [in the Red Army, the possession of German decorations and other items of 'propaganda' was strictly forbidden – editor's note]. The following day, I was summoned by our battalion commander. There I saw an unknown senior officer, middle-aged with a double chin. I reported to my CO. 'At ease. Sit down. Tell the Representative of the Special Department what booty you found yesterday.' He nodded towards the stranger.

'German decorations.'

'Why didn't you hand them over to your chief?'

'I didn't have time.'

'Well, give them to Comrade Colonel, while you're still alright.' [A euphemism for 'not yet punished' – editor's note.]

'Permit me to bring them now.'

'Go ahead.'

As I left the dugout, the Fritzes began bombarding our trenches. After several mortar volleys they rushed to the attack but our fire stopped them. When things quieted down I went back to collect the German decorations but amidst the devastation could find neither the trench nor my pack: 'this is very, "while you're still alright,"' I thought, and returned to my battalion commander empty-handed.

We entered another dugout. This must have been a place for the maintenance staff. At first glance, it seemed to contain nothing of interest. But in a corner, under a thick layer of blankets, a man was lying curled up. I pointed him out to Fuat, who nodded. I lifted one corner of a blanket and saw a German officer in a new uniform: 'Halt! Hände hoch!' I ordered. The officer sat up. 'Halt, halt,' I pointed my sub-machine gun at his hands, suggesting that he should surrender. The officer was about to rise, leaning on his left hand, when his right suddenly dashed for his holster. Well, it's your choice. A short round prevented him from taking out his Parabellum. We left the dugout, promising to be more careful in future. This could have ended much worse.

In Pitomnik we found a car full of chocolate. Who was it intended for? Definitely not for those German soldiers who gnawed on horses' hooves, so as not to die of starvation.

After Pitomnik there was Gumrak. The Nazis retreated from the station after a short struggle. We entered a concentration camp for Soviet prisoners. Some of the men were on the verge of death: they were speedily evacuated to hospital. Several thousand corpses were stacked in an open field. One horror followed another. How can I survive this nightmare? If a bullet doesn't find me, surely I'll lose my mind . . .

Gumrak is only 15km [just over 9 miles – editor's note] from Stalingrad. The Nazis offer no resistance, they simply flee.

We were proud that our division had its share in the decisive victory at Stalingrad. Beginning with the breakthrough of the German defences near Kletskaia on 19 November 1942, followed by the taking of Kalach, of Illarionovskaia, the fight near Raspopinskaia station – where an entire Nazi regiment was destroyed and 3,000 Romanians taken prisoner – the bloody battle for the five hills north of Karpovka, and the attack near Marinovka, we had stubbornly pushed on towards Stalingrad. We knew that people there were fighting over every bit of land. Pavlov, an ordinary sergeant, had been defending a house in the city centre since September, and was still holding on . . .

Meanwhile, our company of 82mm mortars had completely run out of bombs. We had even used all the captured ammunition. But our resourceful CO, Senior Lieutenant Buteiko, paid a visit to some neighbouring gunners. There he found the driver of a 3-ton truck, who, having just delivered a load of artillery shells, was about to return to a dump in the rear for some more. Buteiko promised the driver a reward – a captured watch – if he would bring us back some shells. The CO summoned me to his dugout and explained: 'As the *partorg* of the company you are ordered to go along with the driver and return in three hours with some bombs!' 'Yes, sir.'

The driver, a lively and merry fellow of about forty, was impatiently hurrying me. 'Come on, *paria!*' Hearing the Siberian word *'paria'* ['fella' or 'chap' – editor's note], I gladly got into the beat up wooden cab (it had a box instead of a seat), made myself comfortable, and asked the driver: 'Where are you from, *paria?*' Happy to see a fellow Siberian, he answered: 'I'm from Krasnoyarsk. And you?' 'I'm from the Kemerovo Region.' 'Then we're neighbours!' 'You bet!' The engine roared and we rushed ahead, into the dark night.

The rumble of the wooden cab and the roar of the old engine were so loud that in order to be heard, the driver had to bring his unshaven face close to my ear and yell: 'Neighbour! My name is Ivan Sobolevski. And yours?' 'Mansur Abdulin!' I shouted, and Ivan twice repeated my name, in order to remember it better, and once more screamed into my ear: 'Alright, I'll do everything to try and help my neighbour out! And I don't want your captured watch!'

We were driving at top speed. Ivan concentrated on the road. His powerful hands seemed glued to the steering wheel, which he turned with such force that I was scared he'd tear it off. On both sides of the road were wrecked tanks, automobiles, armoured troop carriers, planes, and so on. Our lorry kept making sharp turns, barely avoiding the frozen metallic monsters. A hundred times, dashing to the right or to the left, we managed to miss crashing into some iron debris. At maximum speed, with blacked-out headlamps and motor roaring, we sped on. With all the noise, Ivan could hardly hear me even when I screamed right into his ear. Meanwhile, the thin, jumping rays of the headlights, like two spectral swords, snatched from the darkness only fleeting glimpses of the road, as we zigzagged between the battered machines. I was thrown to and fro in the cab with such force that after fifteen minutes, I felt as if I had been beaten within an inch of my life. Fear and pain almost made me jump out at full speed. But where could I go in this dark and freezing night in the desolate steppe?

Our lorry, without slowing down, rushed ahead, dodging all the deadly obstacles. I found myself wondering about the frequent flaps coming from the wheels. It seemed as though we were riding over some boards or slabs. Bump, bump, under the front wheels, and then bump, bump, under the back. I was curious so I yelled into the driver's ear: 'Ivan! What's that flapping under our wheels? As if someone scattered boards or slabs in the steppe?' He replied: 'These, Mansur, are not slabs, but dead bodies! They were flattened by cars and are now making this flapping sound, like boards!' I was totally taken aback and cried out: 'Impossible!' Ivan stopped the lorry and we jumped out. 'Well, Mansur, see for yourself!' I switched on my pocket flashlight and saw the 'slabs' and 'boards': there was one of our soldiers in a grey greatcoat, there was a Fritz in a green one. I felt my feet slipping on the 'slabs' and 'boards', while Ivan explained: 'This is because they're greasy. Look at our wheels, it's like they're covered with grease. And if you want to replace a flat tyre, the wheel should be cleaned with gas first. You see? Let's go!'

After skidding along for a time, we finally began driving properly once more. Eventually we carried out the CO's order – Ivan refused to take the watch – and we exchanged home and field addresses.

After the war, when I happened to be in Krasnoyarsk, I found the house of my comrade Ivan. In the yard I met a woman, who one day must have been beautiful, but now looked much older than her age, worn out by hard labour and starvation. 'Does Ivan Sobolevski live here?'

She did not answer, but with a nod of her head invited me to come in. The house looked poor and sad. I sat down on a broad wooden bench, which had not been cleaned for a long time. The floor was dirty, the large oven was covered with soot and needed whitewashing. The woman went out of the room and soon returned with a piece of grey paper, which she handed to me in silence. It was an official letter announcing his death. It happened on 18 January 1943. She said quietly: 'I seem to know you. He wrote to me about your meeting. You're Mansur Abdulin?' She didn't cry. Somehow I felt ashamed that I had survived and Ivan had died. Then I remembered the terrifying sight of the 'slabs' on the road.

Twenty-first of January 1943 was a significant day in the history of our division: 'Fighting for our Soviet Motherland against the German invaders, the 293rd Rifle Division proved to be a model of bravery, courage, discipline and order. Engaged in continuous combat . . . the division inflicted heavy casualties on the Fascist forces and with its shattering blows destroyed enemy manpower and equipment, mercilessly crushing the German invaders . . .' This is an extract from order No. 34, dated 21 January 1943 and signed by Joseph Stalin, People's Defence Commissar of the USSR.

'For the courage demonstrated in fighting for the Fatherland,' continues the order, 'the 293rd Rifle Division is to be reorganized into the 66th Guards Rifle Division . . .' So we were now guardsmen, and our regiment renamed the 193rd Guards. This was a great honour. Not many of my old comrades had lived to witness it. After the Battle of Stalingrad, our new regimental commander, Guards Captain Pavel Bilaonov, would take 1,613 men to the Kursk Salient, most of whom were recent reinforcements. How many wonderful lads had been left lying in the ground between the Don and the Volga? By sacrificing their lives, they had brought about a decisive turn in the war.

I received a letter from the office of the Tashkent radio. A certain Rashidova informed me that owing to weather conditions, the post could not be delivered to the Sargardon Mine in the Tien Shan Mountains: that was why letters from the front (including mine) were being read over the radio. I felt ashamed that my letters had become known to complete strangers, as well as my family, but also grateful to the staff of the radio station, for showing so much kind consideration. 'All of us,' I thought, 'both at the front and at the rear, live with only one idea: to free our country from the invaders as soon as possible.'

One dark night in late January 1943, our mortar company received fresh reinforcements. Among the twenty-five newcomers there was one soldier who was notable for his athletic figure, fiery red hair, and large red beard. His frank expression, big blue eyes, and pug nose, made him look like a typical merchant from the Russian heartland: a good model for some nineteenth century painting.

When we received reinforcements, the veterans of our company tried hard to recruit such strong men as this red-haired lad for their gun crews. An 82mm mortar is not a carbine or a sub-machine gun! During a fight we often had to lug it around. It was taken apart to make up three 20kg loads [just over 44lbs – editor's note], plus boxes with bombs, each weighing 25kg. All our mortarmen envied my detachment, because it already had two mighty soldiers: the Uzbek Fuat Khudoibergenov, a heavyweight weightlifting champion of Uzbekistan and Azhura Tuichiyev (whom we nicknamed Palvan), and the freestyle wrestling champion of Tadzhikistan, who had arrived only a week before. Even though I myself was not exceptionally strong, I was a young miner used to hard labour and physical strain.

I fixed my eyes on the red-haired boy and kept thinking: 'How good it would be to have this giant in the crew.' But the chances seemed slim. There was a universal agreement in the army that if people came from the same area, they were allowed to serve together in the same gun crew or squad. In this sense I was lucky because I am a Tartar, a Siberian, a man who lived in the Urals and in Central Asia, and a Moslem, all rolled into one! But this red-haired Russian fellow surely had nothing in common with me.

I started looking at the other boys and was ready to pick one robust fellow of medium height, who was peacefully dozing in a cosy corner of the dugout, when our old sergeant major started listing the men. He was responsible for recording the newcomers' personal details for our unit's roll. And we veterans always pricked up our ears in order to find out where the new recruits came from.

Five of my fellow-soldiers had already found new comrades-in-arms, and everyone was happy! People greeted each other! The sergeant major grew angry: 'Calm down!' Finally it was the turn of the red-haired boy. A moment of silence. The dim light, coming from a bullet case filled with gas, into which a piece of cloth was stuck, seemed motionless, as if expecting an answer. The red-haired soldier replied cheerfully: 'Private Rashid Sadykovich Sadykov.' Hearing the Central Asian name I almost jumped in amazement: 'Why, he's from the same area as me!' Everyone started laughing. The sergeant major again ordered us to be quiet. The red-haired boy continued: '. . . born 1918, Uzbek, home address, 15 Lenin Street, Gazyl-Kent Village, Bostandykski District, South Kazakhstan Region.' I could no longer restrain myself: 'We're both from the same district, I'm from Brichmulla!' And Rashid answered: 'I have many relatives there!' I don't remember how he began embracing me, but everyone in the dugout could hear my bones crunch. When the introduction was over, I, accompanied by friendly laughter, grabbed Rashid by the hand and led him back to our trench, where my comrades were impatiently awaiting my arrival with a 'new boy'. Fuat and Dzhura were as happy to see a new crew member as I was. We celebrated our meeting with some alcohol and talked till morning. I told the story of how I first met Dzhura. This was how it happened . . .

I entered a dugout, where gun crew commanders had assembled to take a look at some newcomers, and instantly noticed a coal-black Asian, almost 2m tall [over 6½ feet – editor's note]. I ran up to him and addressed him with a traditional Central Asian greeting. Pleased at hearing the familiar words, he answered with enthusiasm. We began talking: 'Where are you from?' 'And you?' 'I'm from Brichmulla' 'And I'm from Natkal!' Then I approached the sergeant major and our company commander: 'Well, I'm taking this man with me. We come from the same parts. And he has agreed.' But the sergeant major answered me sternly: 'Wait a minute. Do you know any Tadzhik language? If you do, say something, and Dzhura will translate it for us. In this way you'll prove that you come from the same parts.' Everyone in the dugout became quiet, expecting an interesting show. Then, in my best Tadzhik, I cursed the sergeant major, using the foulest language I knew. If only he could have understood my monologue, he would have probably died of apoplexy. At first, Dzhura was frightened, but when he realized that the sergeant major did not understand a word of Tadzhik, he burst into laughter. All the other mortarmen began laughing and demanded an exact translation from Dzhura. But the soldier was quick-witted: 'I don't understand Russian!' he replied in a strong accent.

The red-haired recruit, Rashid, told us about his life. We learned that he was not actually Uzbek but Russian. He didn't know his parents because they left him in a market in Tashkent when he was just six months old. Or maybe they died. At any rate, the baby was taken and adopted by a certain honest man, a smith, whose son was born shortly before that. This child could not suck up all his mother's milk, and the woman suffered a lot, her breasts becoming inflamed. However, with the appearance of a 'second son' this problem was solved. This was how Rashid found his Uzbek parents and his brother Usman. The smith and his wife died at an early age, and the boys moved from Tashkent to the village Gazyl-Kent. Working there at a collective farm, they each built a house and planted a garden around it. In 1938 both got married and had sons. In 1941, when the war began, they went to the front together. Usman perished near Moscow.

Losing many comrades in the bloody fighting, we kept pressing the Fritzes deeper into the pocket. With our nine mortars my company bombarded the Germans almost twenty-four hours a day, inflicting heavy casualties. Rashid did everything to avenge his deceased brother. I also fought desperately: to avenge my comrades, my fellow-countrymen – whose lives had been blighted by the war – and my Motherland. We were not afraid to die, but we wanted to survive, in order to see life in our great country after the war. On 30 January 1943, the forces of the Don Front managed to split the encircled German troops into two pockets, north and south. During this battle our gun crew bombarded the enemy with such intensity that smoke would rise from the paint on the mortar! Dzhura was killed by a German bullet. We buried him in an old trench, in a yard near a four-storey building.

Changing our firing position once more, we cross an open field, running after our tanks so as to stay in the 'dead zone', where enemy bullets can't reach us. You should never fall behind, even if you're loaded like a camel; even if you're choking with thick, poisonous exhaust. Suddenly, Fuat screams: 'Rashid is wounded!' Throwing down the heavy equipment, I rush back to the place where Rashid is lying. A group of infantrymen, headed by a young lieutenant, are running in the opposite direction. The boy, shaking his pistol, yells in a squeaky voice as loud as he can: 'For our Motherland! For Sta-a-a-a-lin! No retreat! I'll sho-o-o-ot you!' I am frightened because this nut could easily mistake me for a deserter and open fire. The lieutenant has already made a warning shot upwards, but then he suddenly collapses, his head falling back. Strange are the ways of war. Maybe this German bullet, by cutting down the young lieutenant, saved my life . . .

When I reach Rashid, I see that he is bleeding heavily, holding his leg above the knee with both hands. I slit the quilted cloth of his trousers, and place a gauze bandage over the bullet wound, so as to stop the blood. Rashid is trying to get up. The bone is not damaged, and he even makes several steps. Then I place him on a waterproof and drag him to the rear. On both sides, left and right, I can see other wounded men being carried along, so I must be going in the correct direction. I must hurry to get Rashid to a medical unit. Behind my back the roar of battle has suddenly ceased, and I realize that the Germans must have stopped resisting. In this area of the front the war is over. Finally, I bring my comrade to the so-called trans-shipment point, where the wounded are being loaded into lorries, for trans-portation to the rear. With the aid of an orderly, I help Rashid descend into a gigantic pit, where about 200 men are awaiting their turn to be evacuated. The orderly promises that in half an hour all the boys will be taken away. Saying goodbye to my friend, I run off to find Fuat and my gun crew . . .

'So how's Rashid?' they asked me. 'OK'. But my heart was heavy. I was worried about my comrade. The Fritzes were quiet. So were we: waiting for what happens next. It was not yet dark, and I, obtaining permission from my company commander, rushed back to see how Rashid was doing. When I reached the place, there was not a soul in sight. I felt relieved: it seemed that everyone had been evacuated. But glancing into the pit, I was struck with horror: 200 wounded men were lying silent and motionless, seemingly asleep, their heads covered with fresh snow. I jumped into the pit and hit the nearest soldier hard on the shoulder. But his frozen body had petrified. I yelled at the top of my voice: 'Lads! Answer me! Is anyone alive?' Silence. The boys, it seemed, had sunk into a sub-zero slumber, never to wake again. Where was Rashid? There! I took off his cap. The fiery red hair was already covered with hoarfrost. I jumped out of this communal grave, and in a frenzy began looking for the orderly and his CO. But what could I do? There was no trace of them. I went back to my company. I told the boys that everything was fine: I did not want to hurt their feelings. As for myself, I simply had to find the strength to go on, after seeing such a terrible scene; after seeing our soldiers die in such a senseless way.

In November 1943 I was seriously wounded, and after being treated for half a year in various hospitals, returned home to Brichmulla, partly disabled. Passing Gazyl-Kent, I did not stop to see Rashid's family, because I did not have the strength to conceal from his wife and child the terrible tragedy of my comrade's death, which would certainly have made their grief even worse. I decided to visit Gazyl-Kent later, in civilian clothes, if only to have a look at them. After resting for about two weeks in Brichmulla, I went to the Bostandykski Military Registration Bureau, to report my arrival. On my way back I made a stop in Gazyl-Kent. I went down Lenin Street, along the side with odd numbers. There was a yard, and on the gate I read the number 15 painted in tar. I knocked. A dog barked somewhere behind the fence. I heard a barefooted boy running to the gate. It opened and before me I seemed to see Rashid himself, but only five or six years old! I almost cried out: 'Rashid!' His son, Ruslan – a sturdy boy with blue eyes and a pleasant smile – decided to greet me first: 'Hello! You want to see my mother? She'll be with you in a minute, I'll call her.'

Barely recovering after such a surprise, I told him: 'No, thanks, brother. Sorry, I seem to have come to the wrong place.' The boy looked distressed. I quickly turned away and went down the street. When I was about to turn around the corner I glanced back and saw Ruslan together with his mother. They were standing there looking at me.

CHAPTER SEVEN

A Captured Gold Watch

Thirty-first of January 1943. We reach the outskirts of Stalingrad. A demolished city. No words can describe the scene that opened before us. There was not a single house left intact! No roofs, no floors. Bare walls with empty windows, through which one can see only huge mounds of bricks. Our men tell each other that the Germans are split into two separate pockets. But where are they?

Armed with grenades and knives, we are ready for street fighting. Our knapsacks are packed with cartridge-drums. Everything superfluous should be left behind. We move on towards the centre of the city. For the first time our artillery has nothing to do: the pocket has become so small that to shell it now would be too dangerous. Even we mortarmen are ordered not to fire beyond a neighbouring house or street for fear of hitting our own men.

We hear a shot! So, the Nazis are here after all! Over there in that house, which can be described better as a heap of ruins. We quickly put our mortar in place and our 'presents' fall on the heads of the Fritzes. We're afraid to fire farther, because we might hit our troops in the next building. There's no clear battle-line. I have a feeling that we are mingled with the enemy like figures on a chessboard. Be careful with every shot you make!

First of February 1943. An exclamation of amazement wakes me up. It is already daylight. Several of our boys, leaning on each other, are staring at the opposite side of the street. What's happening? I scramble up some backs to see what's going on. No one protests. They're too preoccupied with some scene. I look at the empty windows of the house facing us and still can't understand what it is. White cloths are hanging from the window sills, and on a mound of broken bricks, white rags have been neatly arranged. It is quiet. Not a sound.

'Capitulation.' I don't remember who uttered the word, but it was mouthed softly, delicately, as if the speaker were afraid to scare it away.

Should we quit our cover? And what if this is a trap? Just the evening before, the Germans were putting up a desperate fight. But our curiosity is too strong. What if this really is a capitulation? I suddenly see embarrassment on the boys' faces. They are looking at each other with meek smiles. We're as black as devils: dirty, covered with soot. Should we accept the capitulation? But we need someone impressive for such an occasion: 'And where are they, those who have an imposing look?' I thought. But we must accept now, or else the enemy will think that we're afraid and change his mind!

I crawl over the heads of the boys, jump down, and walk into the centre of the street. My legs feel like they're made of wood. I move slowly. The white rags and cloths can be seen on many houses, some of which we never suspected of containing Nazis. But where are they? Some distance away, I see other 'representatives' apprehensively looking around, standing in the middle of the street. We cast sheepish glances at each other: look at us! Naïve fools, making targets of ourselves! If, at this moment, we heard a shot, we would feel nothing but shame. I emphatically hang my sub-machine gun behind my shoulder: if they open fire, I won't have enough time to use it anyway.

Then, all at once, they begin appearing out of the ruins. Creeping out of their holes in slow motion, they throw their SMGs on the snow and raise their hands. They seem indifferent to my scruffy, un-imposing appearance! A pistol falls at my feet. This status symbol is the only clue that the man who threw it – a scarecrow wrapped in blankets – is an officer. The swine barely missed me: 'You can be as mad as you like,' I thought, 'but just surrender!'

Our boys, seeing the Germans dressed in such a way, assume a dignified air and begin crowding the street. Compared to us, the enemy troops look like ragamuffins. They throw down their guns and silently form up in columns. Suddenly there comes a dull and solitary report: an officer, it seems, has shot himself in the heart . . .

A company from our Special Department arrives in Willys jeeps. They ride up to the Fritzes, surround them, and begin confiscating all their valuables for the Defence Fund [a voluntary pool of money and valuables given for the war effort, which eventually totalled some 20 million roubles – editor's note]. A young captain permits me to take something for myself from a pile of watches, cigarette cases, lighters and jewellery. My comrades watch enviously as I quickly stuff my pockets with loot. But I am thinking of them too – there are some seventeen men in my company – and everyone gets a captured watch.

All, that is, except for one soldier, Victor Kozlov, who decided to leave me without a watch as well. He reported to our CO that I had kept the best and most expensive watch for myself. The company commander proposed that I should voluntarily hand it over to the Defence Fund. I immediately gave it to him. Later, I found out that my watch ended up in the pocket of our sergeant major.

Soon after this incident, our divisional commander organized a meeting for the active participants of the Stalingrad battle. He made a speech and outlined our future objectives concerning the further destruction of Hitler's war machine. At the end of this meeting I was the first to report to the general that our sergeant major, who was present, had kept for himself a captured gold watch, which I had voluntarily handed over to the Defence Fund. The general was outraged and ordered the sergeant major to surrender the watch immediately. He obeyed and gave it to the general. In 1975 I met our general in Poltava, at the first post-war meeting of our regiment, and saw that same captured gold watch . . .

On the evening of 2 February, we were suddenly ordered to 'move during the night to the "north" German group, which continued staunch resistance . . .' It seemed a particularly sad prospect to be killed in this last fight, when the war was almost over. Well, at least here in Stalingrad. We were on the spot before daybreak, and one might imagine our joy when here too we saw white flags! We were almost on the verge of embracing those damned Fritzes!

During the day we went to have a look at the supermarket where Paulus's HQ had been situated. White rags everywhere in the city. We had barely managed to relax, when in the evening we received a report that isolated groups of Nazis were still resisting. For a whole week more we searched the streets, smoking the surviving fanatics out of the sewers. Then, slowly passing before us on their way out of the battered but triumphant city, came the columns of prisoners. The sick and wounded trailed along at the back of each column, wrapped in blankets from head to foot. I asked the soldiers who guarded them: 'Where to?' 'To Gumrak,' they unwillingly answered.

Those of us who survived received medals, 'For the Defence of

Stalingrad.' But we were few. By the end of the battle, only a handful of infantrymen who finished the Tashkent Military School with me remained on active service. It was decided that we should be distributed between freshly formed companies. Fuat was transferred to another battalion and so we had to part. I never saw him again.

I already wrote that after arriving on the Stalingrad Front, I and all the other soldiers were attacked by masses of lice, which to us seemed more like scorpions. They covered you from head to foot: your cap, blouse, vatnik, greatcoat, and mittens were swarming with them. For us, lice were the bloodthirsty Enemy Number 1, and the Germans Enemy Number 2. For the Fritzes gave us a little rest, but the lice attacked us twenty-four hours a day! And they were not at all afraid of the poisonous insecticide, with which I daily powdered my tormented body. This treatment made me sick and clouded my mind. Tortured by lice, I was on the verge of jumping into the flames of a burning tank more than once!

Because of the lice I couldn't sleep, and even if I fell dead tired, my hands would instinctively reach for the most inaccessible areas of my body, and my nails would scratch until I felt blood. I used every opportunity to place my cap on the mortar base-plate and crush the lice with my gun. Not just the cap, but the plate itself would be spattered with blood.

In the Village Karpovskaia, where our newly-formed 66th Guards Division was quartered, we finally declared a merciless war on the lice and had our sweet revenge! We quickly designed and built hothouses and saunas or banias. Every day we washed ourselves and sweated in hot steam, while in the hothouses, our uniforms were warmed over a fire until smoke began rising from them. But the lice still survived. What a plague! What could we do? I secretly decided to leave a lighter in my trouser pocket, and put thrice the usual amount of firewood into the oven. Our hothouse completely burned down. The Special Department launched an investigation, but could not find any proof of arson, and so we were given brand new uniforms. From that day the lice completely vanished: 'They capitulated!' we joked. Then one after another, the hothouses belonging to other companies caught fire. This time the Special Department didn't even bother looking into the business. At last I got a good night's sleep!

At the station Karpovskaia, where there was a lot of captured equipment, I had a chance to see German prisoners at work. That was something! Here is an engine, it is repaired and put on a special testing platform. Someone starts it and it seems to run beautifully. The senior German technician, like a doctor, carefully listens to it from different sides. His face, like some device, accurately reflects the quality of the work. Our mechanics think that the engine is ready to be installed in place. But the German prisoner cuts them short in an angry voice: 'Nein!' It seems he hears something that our mechanics do not. Some alien sound. In German, he gives instructions to his aides: they once more disassemble the engine and tighten some unimportant looking nut or screw on the con-rod. 'Hitler Kaputt? Stalin gut!' They nod their heads: 'Russ Kamerad gut!' Are these the same men who, two weeks ago, fought so ferociously against us? Our soldiers are totally baffled: 'How can it be!' We had a feeling that the war was about to end. But the real end was so far away! How many people would die between that spring of 1943 and the spring of 1945?

As a unit of the 32nd Guards Rifle Corps, our 66th Guards Rifle Division was put on troop trains and transported through the Tambov, Lipetsk, and Voronezh Regions in the direction of Kursk.

I still remember a nice railroad station in the Lipetsk Region, where our train stopped for several days. The station and the adjacent village were called Dobrinka [in Russian, *dobry* means 'good' or 'kind' – editor's note]. The name attracted our attention, and we wanted to have a closer look at the inhabitants. We were especially popular among the children, with whom we shared our food.

Even though in those days life was very hard, there was a festive mood in the streets, and everyone was sure that the war would soon be over. The old people and the women tried to give us as much as they could, but the main thing was that we felt their love for us and for our army. It was spring, a time when rations were especially low, and so we shared our meagre supplies with the people of Dobrinka. Even a piece of bread or a crust was accepted with gratitude. The children did not gobble the bread, but sucked it, like candy, in order to prolong their pleasure.

I am sorry, dear reader, if the description of those several days in Dobrinka created an impression of excessive sweetness! But just as my dirty, lousy, body demanded hot water and clean clothes after the Stalingrad battle, so did my mind, in order to maintain its balance, seek purification in kindness and humanity. It was a necessary process of restoring one's soul. Because it is my deep conviction that only good people should fight against evil. Dear inhabitants of the village Dobrinka! I want to thank you for those spring days of 1943 when, after the horrors of Stalingrad, we spent some time with you!

Was it at that station where I received news from home? My father did not read my letter of 6 November 1942, when I wrote about the first Nazi I destroyed. On 12 November he died in an accident in the mine. He was forty-five years old.

I loved my father more than anyone else. I was proud to be his son. In 1934 he had an opportunity to keep 4kg [almost 9lbs – editor's note] of gold for himself, without any danger of being caught, but he did not do it. Even the inspector called him a fool for handing it over. My father was strict, but just. He was a Communist. I faintly remember that in those days Party members working in the mines established a limit for their pay – not more than forty *roubles* a month. My mother was somewhat displeased with my father, because non-Party miners earned twice as much and led a better life. But my father could always convince my mother that he was doing the correct thing. Did my father love me? I think so. But he tried to hide his love from us kids: 'If I hear or learn from someone that you used foul language, I'll give you a beating you won't forget!'

Then one day my father found me a job in the mine, driving the horse that moved the drum next to the shaft. My duty was to keep the horse going. There was a number of commands that the men working in the shaft used. I easily learned them and began earning my bread.

I'm ten years old. It's a hot day. The wayward animal is dilly-dallying, bitten by gadflies. Horses are smart creatures: 'Oh, he's just a boy. I'll show him!' But what kind of a driver am I, if I order the animal in a boy's voice? I am not more stupid than my horse: so I begin to show my character. I try to speak in a low voice, imitating the bass of some *muzhik*, and using the foulest language I know. It works! The horse begins reacting to my commands. I am glad to be doing as well as any grown-up. I feel ashamed pronouncing the obscene words, but I have to do it, because horses are used to it. Besides, I had often seen peasant women, who, before climbing into a cart, cursed with the most foul language both their own fate and that of the horse!

I have been working as a driver for several hours. Everything is OK. I go on saying the obscene words, shouting myself hoarse. That's the way it's done! And then I feel a glance piercing my back. I turn.

There's my father standing and hiding a grin in his big black moustache. I am so terrified that my first thought was to run away. Then my heart sinks and I lower my eyes, afraid to lift them. My father comes up to me, hands me half a litre of milk [a little less than a pint – editor's note] and some bread, and as if nothing has happened, suggests I go sit in the shade and have my lunch – he will take over while I am busy eating.

I admired the way he worked. His mere presence was enough to make the horse move. The animal fixed its sly eye on my father, as if it understood that the new driver was the lord of all horses. It turned out that the beast didn't need any special words to keep it going. During the brief stops, father gently tapped it on the withers with his large palm.

I always wanted to help my father the best I could. I wasn't afraid of any kind of work. If my father praised me and was happy, it was the best reward I could have. And now I'm deprived of this greatest of rewards. My father never learned that I received the medal, 'For Bravery'. He is no more. Suvorov also is dead. Who will approve of me now? Who is interested in me? Who needs me to be good? My soul was suffering from a desire to love.

On 9 April 1943, at the station of Davydovka we detrained and began our march towards Stary Oskol.

We are now in the Voronezh Region. 'Everything for the Front! Everything for the Victory!' and 'Death to the Fascist Invaders!' These are the slogans we see everywhere. The farmers look emaciated, dressed in threadbare clothes with tattered boots on their feet. We cross the border of the Voronezh Region and enter the Lipetsk Region, heading in the direction of Belgorod and Kursk.

Not far from the town of Stary Oskol, in a wood near the village Tioply Kolodets, our 193rd Guards Rifle Regiment stopped to rest. Here, in early June, we were officially presented with the new Guards banner, the whole ceremony being well-camouflaged. General Alexander Rodimtsev, commander of the 32nd Guards Corps, personally handed over the new banner. I remember how interesting it was for us to have a look at the renowned general, Hero of the Soviet Union since Spain, and to see the Gold Star on his chest [Colonel-General Aleksandr Rodimtsev was first made a Hero of the soviet Union in 1937 for his actions in the Spanish Civil War, and then again in 1945 for his service in the Great Patriotic War – editor's note].

The devastation of war brings grief and tears to Russian soil.

Mansur Abdulin, 1944.

The first days of the war: volunteers wait to be recruited into the Red Army.

Major Nikolai Kartoshenko, battalion commander, is sitting on the right, 1944.

Lieutenant General Aleksandr Rodimts commander of the 32nd Guards Rifle Corps. Distinguished himself as the commander of the 13th Guards Rifle Division in the Battle of Stalingrad.

A typical group portrait showing the ordinary men and women of the Red Army during th last days of the war. Matriona Shepilova, from Novosibirsk, is on the left of the front row.

Aleksei Yanson's letter from the front. Very often letters from the front were not put into envelopes. A sheet of paper with the text was folded into a triangle. An address was written on one side, and the post office and the field censor made their marks on the other side.

·ksei Yanson. This photo was taken in end of 1943 for an identity card.

xim heavy machine-gun crew changing positions.

An 82mm mortar aiming at the enemy.

An 82mm mortar crew moves through forest.

An 82mm mortar crew changing positions.

A mortar crew practise firing.

Mortar crew in winter conditions.

The crew of an 82mm mortar on well-prepared positions. It was possible to organize such positions only when the front line stabilized.

Anti-tank riflemen with a PTRD rifle.

Soldiers on rest break. The photo was taken early in the war. Note an early model PPSh SMG and a 'Budenov' cap on the head of the soldier to the right.

Soldiers wrestling.

A field kitchen arrives. Hot meals like this 'kasha' helped soldiers to survive the harsh conditions of a Russian winter.

At rest. Soviet soldiers, presumably medics from a rear area medical battalion (the woman on the right is a captain, so she can only be from regimental medical service or higher), take their time to dry foot bindings and boil some tea.

Let's have a smoke! Soldiers were issued with tobacco and had to make cigarettes themselves. Note the shape of the hand-rolled cigarette of the soldier on the left. It is called 'Koz'ia nozhka', or 'goat's leg'.

A minute of calm. A barber arrives at the front, 1944.

Soldiers going to the front. The usual means of transportation for the troops were 'teplushka' rail cars, originally designed for carrying goods.

Red Army troops mounting a GAZ-AA truck.

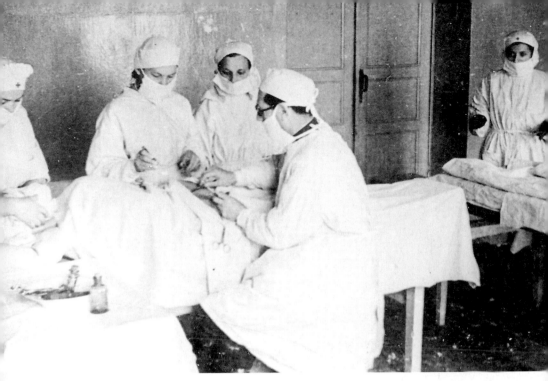

Surgery at a hospital.

Political information: a commissar armed with a PPD submachine-gun reading *Pravda* to soldiers. The soldier on the right is a sniper armed with a Mosin bolt rifle with a PE optical sight.

An infantry lieutenant urges troops to attack waving his TT pistol. This photo became a symbol of the Great Patriotic War in post-war Soviet Union.

Infantry attack supported by T-34 tank.

The thin cartridge belt in the Maxim machine-gun indicates that these dead Russian soldiers did their duty to the last.

German soldier killed near his APC vehicle.

Feodor Gridasov, battalion commander, 1970s.

Nikolai Kobylin, 1976.

Major General I. Tukhru, 1983.

Mansur Abdulin, 1998.

Guards Captain Ivan Tukhru, deputy commander of the regiment, bent down on one knee and kissed the fringe of the banner. We also kneeled in reverence. Next to the celebrated general, and much taller than him, stood Guards Captain Pavel Bilaonov, commander of our regiment, leaning on crutches.

We had learned that our 293rd Rifle Division was to become the 66th Guards while still near Stalingrad: now we were impatient to receive the Guards badge. It closely resembled the Order of the Red Banner, and we wanted to get it as soon as possible, so we could go around looking smart. If one of our comrades met a Guardsmen from another unit wearing this badge, then the news would spread fast and we would come running to see the beautiful thing with our own eyes. In June, after we received the banner, the Guards badges were at last sent to our regiment. Finally, each of us had one! In those days soldiers rarely had medals, let alone orders. For many Guardsmen the badge was the only decoration on their blouse, and it often seemed to a soldier that he did not need anything else.

After the Guards badge, we were awarded the medal, 'For the Defence of Stalingrad.' That was the time when, having those two decorations, everyone became especially enthusiastic about winning the war and returning home! Men started painting Guards signs on tanks, guns, cars, towing trucks and even on two-wheel carts. We made the same signs out of brass and cut them into the stocks of our sub-machine guns and rifles. It was a mystery where the soldiers found the time or the materials to make them. In winter we wore our Guards badges on our greatcoats, so that everyone could see that we were Guardsmen! Members of the Komsomol would also wear their Komsomol badge: so eventually there was an impression that each of us had several decorations, which made us feel more confident.

If there was some scouting to be done, a soldier carefully removed his medals and badges from his blouse or greatcoat, and together with his documents, handed them over to the political instructor until his return. People had the following idea: the war has been going on for two years and it is embarrassing not to have at least one medal, especially after Stalingrad. What were you doing there after all, if you haven't deserved a single decoration? Well, all of us who survived received the medal, 'For the Defence of Stalingrad.' I was also presented with the medal, 'For Bravery', after I shot my first Nazi soldier. But how many other Fritzes were destroyed between my receiving the two decorations?

While still near Stalingrad we were all given half-litre bottles with some potion: a smelly liquid containing spirit, which was supposed to be used in case of mustard gas poisoning. You could not drink it but it was handy for starting fires. Yet we were specifically ordered not to use it in this way. One political instructor – I don't remember his surname, but he replaced Fatkulla Khismatullin who was killed in our first engagement – was especially strict with those who disobeyed the order. If he found out that someone had misused the potion, the man was in danger of facing a tribunal. But cold, like hunger, gives its own commands, and we continued to burn this liquid anyway. Once, the Political Instructor could not stand the frost anymore, so he hid himself in a dugout and decided to warm up. He sprinkled some of the liquid into an oven, but he was so awkward that the hand holding the bottle caught fire. He instinctively jerked his arm, spilling yet more liquid, and could easily have burned to death. Later, when we were bandaging the unfortunate man, I could not help making a sarcastic remark: 'Don't break your own rules.' He never forgave me my irony. But I still think I was right. It's wrong and unwise to prohibit others from doing something, only to go and do it yourself. It was my duty to tell him: after all, I was the *partorg* of the company.

During the war I met many political instructors. On the whole, they were good commanders and able teachers. They kept the soldiers' spirits up and educated them by personal example. I must note that the rank and file, especially the more simple men, respected the political instructors, who could plainly describe the object of the war, and the situation at the front and in the world. What are the most important things for a soldier? He should be well-fed, know why he is fighting, and have respect for his commander. As to myself, I was brought up on the principle that Communists should be a model for non-members. This is why it was hard for me to accept the fact that a political instructor could be inadequate for the post that he occupied. But I was unlucky with one other political instructor in our company. His surname was either Snesar or Snesal, I don't exactly remember.

One day he saw a captured wristwatch I had. 'Give it to me!' I'm not greedy, but there was something about his tone that I didn't like: 'Get one from a Nazi in a fight, like I did.' 'Give it to me and I'll reward you.' I was surprised: 'In what way?' 'I'll recommend you for a decoration.' I thought: 'Should I punch him or not?' Then I imagined a tribunal, the judge, and the sentence: 'Capital punishment'. No, better not punch him, I would pay dearly for it! So I said aloud: 'You petty businessman! You're full of shit! What are you trying to sell? The Motherland will give me a decoration, if I'm worth it, not you!' To my surprise he calmly listened to these insults and with a sarcastic smile called me 'Sucker boy'. It was a nice chat we had. The Motherland awards one with decorations, but specific people recommend you.

I can't say that I reflected a lot on the issue of decorations when we stayed in that wood near Stary Oskol, gathering strength for future battles. I realized that almost all my old comrades had perished, and that for me the best reward was to be alive.

At the Tashkent Military School I was a leading singer: 'commander's voice', our instructors used to say. I did not become a commander, but was quite successful with my singing. We loved to sing 'Katiusha', 'Tachanka-Rostovchanka', 'Three Tank men', 'Gunners, Stalin Gave an Order,' 'Holy War'. There was also another song, which we called 'Kalinka'. The tune came from the well-known song, but the words we wrote ourselves. It was about a water-carrier from Vologda. The text was at the same time satirical, lyrical, witty and humorous. It was a real hit. We accompanied it with whistling and whooping.

First, we would make our audience (mainly women, young girls, old people and children) cry by singing something like, 'There is a darling girl near every house, there is a darling wife' or 'In the window the girl has put up a light.' Then, after our listeners had wept for a while, we would suddenly strike up our 'Kalinka' and everyone would smile from ear to ear. Soon, the audience would be waving their hands at us, covering their faces with their shawls, blushing. The bravest would start dancing. And we would sing so much that our voices became hoarse! But still the people would beg us for one more 'Kalinka'. 'Mansur,' they would ask, 'are you an actor?' 'No, a miner!' Our regimental commander, Pavel Bilaonov remembered me among the thousands of soldiers only because of my prankish singing. He liked our 'Kalinka' a lot and often asked us to perform it for him.

As to myself, I remembered Bilaonov from Buzuluk. He was a senior lieutenant then. He was very tall, and had an athletic figure, thick hair, a high forehead, and eyebrows resembling the outline of an eagle's wings. All this, along with his self-confident and authoritative look, his strong commanding voice, and an Order of the Red Banner on his blouse, made a magical impression on us recruits. We spotted him instantly among the rest of the officers from the divisional HQ, who greeted us as we detrained. 'Who is he?' whispered the men, elbowing each other in order to have a look. Soon the 'soldiers' telegraph' reported: 'Pavel Bilaonov, Head of the Operations Department of the Divisional Staff, born in the Caucasus, in Osetia . . .' That explained the imposing bearing of this dashing horseman. So now Guards Captain Pavel Bilaonov was heading our 193rd Guards Rifle Regiment.

I must confess that every soldier wanted to fight under the command of Chapayev, Budionny, Kotovski or Blukher [famous Red Army commanders and heroes of the Civil War – editor's note]. Men are not interested in fighting when there's no Chapayev! Of course, strictly speaking, it doesn't matter who your commander is: a soldier is simply expected to observe army regulations, full stop! But regulations aside, the rank and file want to love their commander. This love is rarely expressed or mentioned, but it helps the soldier endure the hard front line existence.

And so, whether we like it or not, a commander's looks, bearing, voice, charm, are all important. And if your CO is not only handsome, but fearless and resolute during a fight, soldiers will follow him into the worst of hells. Our Stalingrad veterans told the new men how, during the storming of the five hills, Bilaonov had suddenly appeared at the critical moment and stopped our battalions from retreating. Full of pride, we referred to our regiment as that of Bilaonov, and called ourselves 'Bilaonov's Men'. Bilaonov's deputies were Guards Captain Vladimir Yegorov, the Regimental commissar and Guards Captain Ivan Tukhru, who was Estonian by nationality. So now our regiment was headed by three Guards captains!

Late June, 1943. Seventy kilometres [about 43½ miles – editor's note] to the north-east of us lies the village Prokhorovka. It is very hot. Not a cloud in the sky, not a drop of rain. The air is motionless and dry. All day long our regiment is involved in tactical exercises. I am now commander of the first and main mortar gun crew and assistant platoon commander. We train our new recruits, sharing our Stalingrad experiences, and also learn some of the things which we didn't have time for at the Tashkent Military School.

We knew all the technical characteristics of Tigers, Panthers, Ferdinands and other enemy tanks and self-propelled guns. Our gunners received new anti-tank weapons. We also became acquainted with new self-propelled 152mm guns [SU-152 – editor's note]. The infantry had enough reliable anti-tank weapons: all the soldiers carried anti-tank grenades and there was an ample supply of Molotov cocktails.

We lost no time. Every day our T-34 Tanks helped us practice. We learned how to throw cocktail bottles, and the heavy percussion grenades. Such a grenade can explode in your hand if you accidentally strike it against the side of the trench when throwing it. But if it hits a tank, the powerful blast could stop it dead. We veterans explained to the greenhorns the particular weaknesses of Tigers, Ferdinands, Panthers, and so on. You should always act in pairs. The enemy tank must ride over you, over your trench, then one soldier fires at the accompanying infantrymen, while the other throws the bottle or grenade. Because of the intensive exercises involving tanks, we realized that very soon we'd be taking part in some heavy fighting between large armoured forces.

One day, after picking out our firing position, we began digging trenches. At last, we had some heavy rain, but we kept on working until it got dark. We were taking our exercises very seriously! We also made a dugout with a thick layer of earth over the roof. It was a dry and pretty comfortable dwelling. Then our field kitchen arrived and we had a hearty meal. It was still raining heavily. The boys began preparing for sleep. Our sentry went to his post. As usual, before lying down, I checked my lucky mascot: but my trouser pocket was empty!

At first I sat there absolutely stunned. Then I began thinking. Should I look for it? But where? In the wet earth, churned up by dozens of soldiers' boots? In the tall grass, under heavy rain, in the dark? In the open field, where piles of earth lie around the trenches? The situation seemed hopeless. I had lost my lucky charm! This means I'll be killed. How mysterious the human mind is! I sat there in the dugout and kept repeating to myself that to die now was not as bad as at the very beginning, before I shot my first Nazi. Since then I've finished off a lot of them! But I want to live very much. Especially having survived Stalingrad. And it looks like the war is nearly over . . .

I tried to convince myself that my superstitious fears were nonsense. After all, my mascot was simply a symbol which I had invented for myself. What possible connection could there be between this little thing and my life or death? Why did I ever decide to put my faith in it? But some unknown force ordered me: 'Go look for it!' The rain suddenly stopped. I crawled out of the dugout. But I had not the faintest hope of finding my mascot.

Wet clay everywhere with many deep traces of boots, filled with water. I see a gigantic footprint. This must be Ivan Konski's boot or Sergei Lopunov's. Their feet are the size of an elephant's. Then I suddenly noticed some kind of a thin stick, like a match, in the imprint of the heel. I bent down, plucked it out with my finger and saw that it was a small stick with a cavity. I brought my flashlight closer and then sniffed it. I could smell the odour of nicotine. My hands began to tremble! Afraid to give way to the wild joy about to flood me, I carefully examined the footprint further, and found three more sticks with cavities. Yes, it was my cigarette holder, crushed and broken into four parts. My mascot!

Returning back to the dugout I took a piece of string out of my knapsack, put the four parts together and tied them up tightly. Then I hid my mascot in my trouser pocket and sewed it up. After the enormous strain and dread brought about by my mascot's temporary loss, I became drowsy and fell into sleep. In my dream, I saw myself once more lying dead with outstretched arms and legs. I awoke with a start. Everyone in the dugout was sleeping. No one saw a thing. 'I will probably be seriously wounded,' I thought.

CHAPTER EIGHT

Kostia's Tiger

Before the Battle of Kursk began, our 66th Guards Rifle Division (being a unit of the 32nd Guards Rifle Corps, attached to the 5th Guards Army of the Steppe Front) was stationed in the second echelon of our lines, 70km [almost 44 miles – editor's note] north of Prokhorovka. But when the Germans pierced our defences, throwing our advance troops back, we marched straight into action at daybreak on 12 July 1943.

Neither before nor since had I seen so much artillery. The commanders of artillery units, with their guns of different calibre, had a hard time finding positions from which they could fire without disturbing their neighbours. There was not enough space for the gunners on the battlefield!

The roar of guns continued all day without pause. We infantrymen – surrounded by thick black smoke and covered in soot – looked like stokers, endlessly throwing coal into a furnace. Only the whites of our eyes and teeth were shining. We moved at a furious pace, among burning tanks, exploding shells, and fire from every conceivable sort of weapon. Every soldier, covered in sweat, was systematically doing his job, as if toiling in a giant workshop; forgetting about his fear and pinning his hopes on chance: 'Will I be killed or not?' There's nothing one can do to save oneself in this carnage, and the hands did what was necessary automatically.

Having been thrown back, the Germans began another onslaught, again without success. How many times a day did both sides crash against one another? Who would win? It was a case of might versus might, power versus power.

The heat of the fighting can be illustrated by the fact that along the battlefront clouds formed from which rain fell. These leaden clouds marked the curved outline of the front, while in our rear (and that of the Germans) the sky was absolutely clear. I have never again seen anything like it! It was a blazing hell and the hot air rose upwards night and day.

All day long planes fired at each other in the sky. There was a hail of splinters and bullets. That was familiar enough: but watch out, you might get killed by falling aircraft! Pilots parachuted here and there. One had to be careful not to confuse our men with the Germans. We could often see how the parachuting pilots continued their fight by firing pistols at each other. We wanted to help them, but how? If only our parachutes had had stars on them or the fabric was of a specific colour.

At the front I rarely had an opportunity to draw: it is a difficult thing to do when you're in action! Nevertheless, when we were fighting near Prokhorovka, I managed to create a sort of a poster: our sluggish artillery grinding German tanks, preventing them from slipping through our lines. On 12 July, in just one encounter, Leonid Nochovny's platoon destroyed five Tigers. One should not have the erroneous notion that gunners fire only from some cover and from behind the firing line. No. In the majority of cases, if a cannon was not more than 152mm, it was used alongside the infantry, even though we often had to change our position, leaving our gunners to face the Nazis alone. Seeing my poster, one of our soldiers was seized with a fit of hysterics: 'How can he draw here?!' he kept crowing, sniggering like some maniac. He simply refused to understand how a man could draw in such a place, amidst corpses, knocked out tanks and guns.

In order to be more efficient against enemy tanks, our soldiers made special bundles consisting of two grenades and a Molotov cocktail (what our men called 'a bottle of Champagne for a hangover!'). These bundles had to be thrown from a distance of no less than 50m [over 54½ yards – editor's note], because the blast was so powerful that it could injure you! Not many men in our company were strong enough to do it: Sergei Lapunov, Vasili Shamrai, Matvei Yershov, Aleksei Yanson and a couple more. Skinny soldiers, like Kostia Martynov or Piotr Shkolnikov, had to be content with making the bundles, using strips of strong captured telephone wire. But our comrade Kostia desperately wanted to destroy a Tiger with his own hands. Several times he dug a reserve trench some 30m or 40m away [between 33 and 44 yards – editor's note] in No Man's Land, from which he planned to throw his heavy bundle under the caterpillar track of a German tank. One day he got his chance . . .

The Germans have decided to try and dislodge us from a so-called 'domineering height' (though it doesn't look that important to us). They launch a tank attack supported by 100 infantrymen with sub-machine guns. One of the tanks is rapidly rolling in the direction of Kostia's reserve trench, so he grabs his bundle of grenades, and keeping as low as possible, makes a dash for his dugout. Vasili Shamrai separates the enemy infantrymen from their tanks by firing several long bursts from his machine-gun, which makes them jump for cover. Meanwhile, Kostia's Tiger comes up close and stops, preparing to destroy our position with its gun. Seeing this, Shamrai dives deep into his hiding place. Simultaneously, we see Kostia jump out of his trench and throw the bundle of explosives underneath the caterpillar of the tank. It seems to us that Kostia has plenty of time to take cover before the blast. Then comes the powerful, deafening explosion. The Tiger loses its track and twitches, trying to resume its forward movement. But having only one caterpillar, it turns and collapses on its side. Our boys bring up some fresh 'Champagne' bottles and soon the Tiger is in flames.

We finally repelled the German counter-attack. The Nazis lost two of their Tigers and some fifty soldiers. We had ten men killed, including Kostia and twelve wounded. We found him with blood flowing from his ears and his eyes almost falling out of their sockets. Kostia was born in 1925, in the Miasski District of the Cheliabinsk Region. He was posthumously awarded the Order of the Red Star.

One morning I joined the battalion *partorg* in order to inspect our new reinforcements. What I saw was a line of pale spectres, shocked by the sight of burning tanks and decomposing bodies (with their unbearable stench). Our greenhorns, like deaf-mutes, did not answer our questions, but remained silent with a rueful look.

How can such a battalion attack? And if we do get them moving, what can we expect from such soldiers in close combat, if they're already destroyed morally?

Unable to think of a way of bringing them out of this state of shock, we reported the situation to Guards Captain Feodor Gridasov, our battalion commander. Something had to be done instantly because the Fritzes could attack at any minute. Our CO ordered: 'Bring my horse!' He always kept his horse nearby. It was brought to the command point. What happened next none of us could have guessed! Within fifteen minutes, our captain was in the saddle and boldly urging his horse into No Man's Land! There, with a dashing air, he began galloping back and forth right under the nose of the enemy. We expected machine-guns to open up from the German trenches, but instead, to our surprise, we heard the cry 'Br-r-r-a-v-o!' I glanced at our recruits. Suddenly, forgetting all their fears, they screamed in support of their CO like football fans at a cup final. Meanwhile, our captain instinctively felt that this circus should come to an end and suddenly disappeared from the arena. The Germans finally opened fire but it was too late.

Unreasonable? But what other method was there to instantly pull 100 people out of a fatal state of shock, just before an engagement? Make a pathetic speech? That wouldn't have helped!

And so the soldiers regained their spirit. They now felt embarrassed to look at their CO, who had demonstrated to them how fearless he was. Within the hour, our battalion – pressing the counter-attacking enemy – successfully moved ahead, and we finally reached the lines, which our advancing forces had occupied prior to 6 July.

Just as we began to secure our new positions, the Nazis opened heavy artillery fire, signalling yet another counter-attack. Not having time to entrench myself, I rushed towards a burned out German tank. As I crawled beneath it, I saw a Russian soldier lying motionless on his back. He had boots on his feet and his legs appeared to be unharmed. I moved forward, thinking that if he were dead, the body would have swelled in this hot weather. I touched his legs and even pulled a little harder. Nothing happened. Finally, I crawled up to his head and was taken aback by a sickening sight: all I could see was a swarm of maggots, resembling ant's eggs or rice! Forgetting the bursts of gunfire all around the tank, I noticed how the soldier's chest slowly rose and fell. I put my ear against his blouse and heard his heart beating. I carefully remembered the position of the tank.

In the evening the fight quieted down. We repelled the counter-attack and successfully defended our lines. I later found that tank again. Some orderlies brought a stretcher, pulled the soldier from under it, and took him to a medical unit. His name was Feodor Ignatov. I read it with my own eyes on his Red Army ID. Is he still alive? Where does he live? I saved him. Accidentally, of course. I simply noticed that a fresh 'corpse' was lying on ground that had been in German hands for five days. I don't know how many more hours this mighty man could have survived. What strange force helped him last for five whole days without water, without help?

The following day our men learned that Feodor Ignatov had recovered consciousness. He told his doctors that he had been wounded in the head on 6 July, when his battalion was retreating. Coming to his senses for a short time, he realized that he was surrounded by the enemy. He saw the tank – which he had previously set ablaze – and noticed that the flames had almost gone: so he decided to creep under it. After that he couldn't remember a thing. I was happy to hear that the man was alive, and I wanted to pay a visit to the medical point to congratulate him on his miraculous rescue, but that was impossible.

Mid-July, 1943. Early in the morning we saw in a field, on the German side, something strange and mysterious. The whole meadow was covered with enormous sheaves of wheat! We were just trying to imagine why the Nazis would want to mow wheat during the night and assemble it in such order, when their artillery began shelling No Man's Land. The shells exploded upon hitting the ground, producing thick white smoke. We became frightened, thinking it was a gas attack. The wind carried the smoke along our lines, but its direction might have changed any moment! It was a long time since we had discarded our gas masks (many soldiers had kept only the bags, now stuffed with cartridges and grenades). What could we do? Where could I find a gas mask? I was such a fool to part with it!

We sat there, staring straight ahead. More and more shells – bang! bang! – and more smoke rising. Eventually, we couldn't see a thing. What are the Fritzes up to? Only the growl of engines tells us that German tanks were approaching, hidden by the smoke screen. Well, Allah be praised, tanks are better than poisonous gas! When the smoke lifted a little, we could see that the mysterious sheaves of wheat had been transformed into tanks! One machine fired its gun, just as it rolled over our trench, and totally deafened us. The pain in our ears was terrible. Stunned by the sound waves, we fell over each other. The tank rushed on and was followed by several others, their tracks crumbling the sides of our trenches. When we managed to free ourselves from the fallen earth, we grabbed our grenades and Molotov cocktails, and ran to do our duty. Destroy the machines! Some time later I felt my ears partly unclog and I was happy to hear once more the terrible roar and thundering of engines.

Suffering from the stench of burning tanks (and their crews trapped inside), some of our men were on the verge of collapsing. In this hell of blasts and crashing armour, we could not tell who was winning. One of our soldiers was rushing about the trench. He had lost his sight and was screaming in panic: 'Don't leave me here! Or else shoot me!' In order to calm him down I shouted loudly into his ear: 'Take it easy!' He grabbed the sleeve of my blouse and said: 'I recognized your voice! You're our *partorg!* Am I right?' 'Calm down, we never leave our comrades behind and we'll surely take you with us! Just calm down and let us do our business!' He became quiet and I helped him to one of the rifle-pits, where he sat down and took a sip of water from my flask: 'Who's winning?' he asked. 'At present we are!' I answered with confidence. He let go of me and remained sitting: silent, anxious. As soon as I moved away from him a little, a tank suddenly fell with one caterpillar into our trench, its bottom leaning against the edge of the wall. The engine let out a mighty roar but the tank was stuck for good. Then, Boris Polyga appeared from nowhere, and threw a Molotov cocktail on its back platform. The flames rose and then disappeared, diving inside.

In the afternoon, it suddenly became quiet on the battlefield. Our boys began climbing out of the trench – even though it was dangerous – to have a look at the results of the fight. As evening approached, several officers appeared in our trench. They had cameras, were clean-shaven, smelled of perfume, and wore brand new blouses with wide belts, from which hung holsters with glittering pistols. On their heads were new helmets. They walked in the trench, stooping timidly. Addressing all of us with an air of authority, one of them asked: 'Who is the man in charge?' The boys threw a glance at me: should they answer? I gently shook my head: 'No.' Then Boris Polyga replied: 'It's a military secret!' And accompanied by our roaring laughter, the guests left.

Thirty years after the war, during the first meeting of our veterans in Poltava (our division was named after this town), my friend Nikolai Korsunov – who had been the adjutant of our regimental commander – told me that after the Battle of the Kursk Salient, our divisional commander had been given a list of those worthy of being awarded the honour, 'Hero of the Soviet Union'. My name was on the list, but he didn't sign the papers because his name was not mentioned.

*   *   *

Reinforcements keep coming to us from the hinterland. I look for people from my area of the country. We ask about the home front. And we answer questions about the Nazis. Of course, the Germans are no longer the same. They had occupied half of Europe with one blow – in a year and ten months – without much difficulty. Now it's a different story: for the last two years they have been forced to fight one bloody battle after another.

A native of Krasnoyarsk, in Siberia, named Aleksei Yanson, joined our mortar company. He looked like a weightlifter or a wrestler. Or was he a miner? In any case, he was as mighty as a fairytale giant! But it also seemed that he had some decent education. God knows how! We'll find out later. Meanwhile, I have to get him for my detachment! He looks so strong: I'm sure he'd be able to carry a whole mortar by himself, in place of three men!

I want to say a few words about Boris Polyga. He joined our company in July. I suspected that something was wrong: he looked too young, even though his date of birth was listed as 1925. I didn't believe it. He must be hiding something. Could he be so small if he's really eighteen? We couldn't use him as a mortarmen. What else could he do? I proposed that we should accept him as a runner, to communicate with our observation post. Lieutenant Stukach, our company commander, agreed and Boris was happy.

I am a very curious person, and a great lover of sincere eye-to-eye conversation with people, even if it's just a small child. I often managed to establish intimate contact with the most reserved men. It's easy for me to win a total stranger's trust. People tell me things they wouldn't dream of revealing to their own families! Why? Because I value their confidence and can keep a secret. Boris Polyga told me that his father was a general, the head of a military school. I don't remember to what place this school was evacuated, but before the war it was in Leningrad. Since his childhood, Boris was used to spending time among his father's cadets. When he grew up and decided to become a soldier himself, he entered a different military school in another place. But he became known as 'general's boy', and people hinted that his father would find him a cosy place on the general staff or something like it. So, pretending that he planned to visit his parents, Boris took a week's leave, jumped on a troop train, and rode to the front. Now he was worried that he might be tried for deserting or leaving his unit without permission. He was in a difficult situation, and there was nothing I could do for him. But he could not be called a deserter! As for leaving his unit without permission? It seemed to me that there was no crime here: so I advised him to write a letter to the head of his school. But Boris didn't do it and I never reminded him.

There were other fights, and Komsomol member Polyga delivered messages and followed orders with great diligence. I promised not to tell anyone about his father being a general, or that he had run away from military school. There was a liking for Boris in our company. He seemed to become more mature. He also confessed to me that he had added two years to his age: he was really born in 1927. This explained why he was so short – he was only sixteen.

After a series of fierce battles, the Germans retreated but began burning everything in their path. Villages and fields were set ablaze. They destroyed anything they could, strictly following their 'scorched earth' orders. We marched through endless smoke. We seized two large villages, Tamarovka and Borisovka, where storehouses of tobacco were set on fire: everyone had his share of tobacco smoke, whether he was a smoker or not!

Driving the Germans out of Tamarovka, we prepared our defences and decided to dig in just in case. Our squad was ordered to entrench in a certain yard. The woman who owned it suddenly began running back and forth, weeping hysterically, and begging: 'Don't dig here! There's a bomb here! Really!' She kept crossing herself incessantly: 'No! No! Not here!' It all looked a bit suspicious and we couldn't understand. Even our company commander became curious: 'What's going on?' Then he turned to me, snapping: 'Settle this business!' The woman looked me straight in the eyes, and as I met her gaze, I saw three small emaciated children in the window behind. Suddenly, I understood why she was worried. I moved back about three paces and began digging: the woman calmed down and went into the house. The children continued to stare but seemed relieved. In the evening, I went to the woman and asked: 'So what are you hiding there in the yard?' 'Lard. We hid it from the Germans last autumn. I want to thank you, I know that you are hungry yourself. Now I will save my children from starving.'

I don't remember exactly, but I think the village was called Dragunsk. The Germans made a stronghold out of it, building up a defensive line of several echelons. Attacking them, we only managed to cut into it, rather than through it, and found ourselves entangled in an intricate web of trenches. We were so close to the Nazis that sometimes we could hear their subdued conversation. Now our big guns were of no use, so we resorted to our so-called 'pocket artillery'. This was grenade warfare. But throwing a grenade requires considerable skill. One should do it only after a two second pause: if you throw it immediately, the enemy has time to fling it back at you! This is how it should be done: first you pull the pin, then lower the safety switch and hold the hissing grenade for two seconds, then you throw it. Grenades explode like shrapnel over the heads of enemy troops. But it is nerve-racking to lower the safety switch and wait those two seconds. I sometimes wondered if the worker who assembled the fuse might have made a mistake, and that the thing would go off in my face! But the mechanism was always reliable. With a feeling of deep gratitude, I remembered our people in the rear, who day and night produced these F-1 'pineapples'. They realized that even the smallest mistake in making the fuse could cost a soldier his life. During the first day of our action against Dragunsk, when there was a shortage of grenades, we squeezed the Nazis out from their labyrinthine lines with our entrenching shovels, shooting at them point-blank with machine-guns, pistols, and even with flare guns. But later we had enough grenades.

Starting from Prokhorovka, our 32nd Guards Corps was constantly engaged in action with the German SS Divisions, Totenkopf, Gross Deutschland and Das Reich. We also had encounters with the Russian Liberation Army of the traitor, General Vlasov. Vlasov's men knew they were doomed but fought desperately. We did not take them prisoner.

Dragunsk was still holding out against us. Our battalion was now facing a machine-gun pillbox. Situated in No Man's Land, which was as flat as a table, it made any advance by our infantry impossible. The Germans thoroughly protected it on both flanks. At night, they constantly lighted flares so no one could quietly crawl up to the concrete hood and fling a couple of grenades into it. Our gunners could not help because they were afraid of hitting their own men. As to mortar bombs, their explosions were not powerful enough to destroy the pillbox. Guards Captain Ignat Dudko, our battalion commander, tried desperately to find a way of getting rid of that machine-gun. But it kept on firing . . .

One day I was on duty at our observation post with Boris Polyga. Since there was nothing to do, Boris began studying No Man's Land through our periscope. The pillbox was well positioned: there was not a single fold of earth around the hood. Even the surrounding grass had been cut short by our bombs. We tried firing an anti-tank gun at it. No use. The machine-gun was still a deadly threat to us.

Then I noticed that Boris had disappeared from the observation post. At the same time, Lieutenant Nikolai Korsunov, the adjutant of our Regimental Commander Bilaonov, was ordered to come to the battalion's HQ. Nikolai, who was a likeable character, reported to the battalion commander, and they began discussing a way of destroying the pillbox. Suddenly, someone from the rifle company brought news that private Polyga had taken six 'pineapples' and crawled away in the direction of the Nazi trenches. As soon as I heard that, I immediately phoned our mortarmen, telling them that Boris was trying to blow up the pillbox, and that they must refrain from firing in that direction.

I searched for Boris through the periscope but could not see where he was. Our battalion commander disapproved of the brave boy's initiative: to go alone on such a mission meant a senseless, inevitable death. But Boris had a plan of his own. Realizing that the hood of the pillbox should be approached from the German side, our tiny Boris crept way out to the enemy flank, and slipped unnoticed into the rear of the German infantrymen.

At last I caught him in my binoculars! Yes, he was crawling towards the pillbox from the side of the enemy lines! The CO ordered our rifle companies to be ready for an attack, and when Boris, rising, began throwing one 'pineapple' after another into the pillbox, they surged forward into No Man's Land. The Germans reacted in a few seconds, but these moments saved Boris's life: the men from the rifle companies, crying 'Hurrah-ah-ah!' attracted the fire of the Nazis. Our battalion finally forced its way ahead.

When I ran up to him, Boris was looking at once guilty and proud. He was happy but his eyes were full of tears. He had been sure that immediately after destroying the pillbox, he would be killed. Nikolai Korsunov and some other staff officers surrounded him, so I didn't have a chance to say anything. Later, we heard that Regimental Commander Belaonov decided to recommend the brave boy for the Order of the Red Banner.

What force made a hero out of this young soldier? He didn't have a single chance of surviving after he threw his first grenade and this was perfectly clear to him. Boris later showed me a letter, which he wrote to his father. I remembered the first two lines. 'Hi, dad! I'm writing from the front. Today I destroyed a machine-gun fire-point, a Hitlerite pillbox . . .' And I can recall one other sentence further on: 'Now I won't be ashamed if someone calls me "general's boy"'

Several days later Boris Polyga was wounded in the head by a shell splinter and evacuated to the rear.

We entered Dragunsk early in the morning. The Germans retreated during the night. The streets were empty, various bits of rubbish and pieces of paper lying around. There was no sense of danger. We happily marched down the street towards the centre of the village.

Here come our planes. They'll catch up with the retreating Fritzes and tear them to pieces! Our 'flying tanks' make a circle over the horizon, as if picking the best target, then return and begin diving. Are they crazy? Now I can see only the wings and the noses of the aircraft, pointing straight at me. Unwilling to believe that our planes are about to attack us, I – just in case – plunge through the basement floor window of the nearest house. Immediately, I hear the sound of explosions in the street above my head. Earth, broken glass, plaster, and bitter lime dust fall on my head . . .

I thought that the thunder smoke would never cease. And the planes, having fired all their missiles, started shooting at us with their guns. They tore our regiment to pieces and then safely returned to their airfield.

With some difficulty I managed to crawl out of my cover. My eyes met with a scene of total destruction. Then, out of nowhere – as if from another world – the survivors appeared. I didn't recognize them, even though I knew their voices well. Gripped by fear, we cautiously looked around and at each other. One recruit, a young lad, yelled at the top of his voice: 'Mummy, where are you?!' A nurse I knew came up with crazed, unblinking eyes, and leaning on me, whispered: 'Mansur? Are you really alive? Answer me!' I nodded my head. She took some bandages from her bag, and tearing them into strips, began handing them out, so we could wipe our faces.

The street was like a trench turned into a communal grave, into which someone had dropped a mass of dead men and horses, mixed with automobiles, guns, and other flotsam. I felt guilty that some miracle saved my life: I couldn't explain how it had happened! Among our officers, the first to appear was Major Bilaonov, our regimental commander. Seeing him so deathly pale, I wished the earth would swallow me up: I somehow felt that I was to blame for this catastrophe. Bilaonov was so distraught that I was scared he might shoot himself in the heart. He saw me and turned away. Some high-ranking army representatives soon appeared. They examined the place in silence. One of them barked at our major, like a teacher reprimanding a pupil: 'And why didn't you hang your identification flags for the pilots?!' 'There they are, on the cleft poplars . . .' Unable to look each other in the eye, the representatives quickly left to report what they had seen to Zhadov, the army commander.

It seemed that the infantrymen of our regiment were doomed to be targets for a variety of our own powerful weapons. We were often hit from behind by long-range artillery and even by our favourite *Katiushas* [common name for the 132mm truck-mounted multiple rocket launcher – editor's note]. I remember how once, in the Stalingrad area, our battalion was under *Katiusha* fire. When it ended there was nothing left of our men or of our equipment. An avalanche of fire and thunder came on our heads with those rockets, and after just a minute of this volcanic eruption, there were only fuming shell holes everywhere. My friend and fellow-Siberian, Ivan Borodin, who had arrived with some other men the night before, lost his leg in this incident. He cried like a cruelly wronged child: not just because of the pain, but because of bitter resentment that he had lost his leg thanks to our own *Katiushas*. But at the same time, he could not conceal a kind of wild joy: 'You see, Mansur, my war is over! Goodbye, neighbour! It seems I really was born under a lucky star! They always told me at home that I was lucky! Well, now I get home alright! I'll be OK there! The forest will feed a man even if he is without legs.' Listening to Ivan, I felt glad that so far (fingers crossed!), I had come through this hell unharmed. But at the same time I envied him. Ivan felt sorry for me because I was destined to go on with this trench life, with its constant danger, hard work, hunger and lice. He tried to console me by saying that, beginning with this day, he would be praying to all gods to keep me alive! Some time after I had to experience another shock.

We finally got together, we veterans of the Battle of Stalingrad, and embraced each other like brothers. There was a pause in the fighting, but we decided to make some solid trenches, just in case. We agreed that as soon as we had finished them, we'd get together and celebrate our meeting. We selected a spot for our picnic under an enormous solitary tree, and left our knapsacks there with all the necessary stuff. One of the 'Stalingrad men' was picked out to prepare a dinner from our modest supplies. Then we unfastened our flasks (containing *Narkom*'s vodka) and began digging in.

Soon, my comrades – seven men in all – finished their trenches, and gathered together under the tree to await my arrival. I was hurrying, slicing the clay with my bayonet, impatient to have my meal with the others. I heard the boys yelling: 'Mansur! Come on! We're waiting!' I threw down my spade and was about to jump out of the trench, when I heard a whizzing shell, fired from a German gun in advance of our position. I expected it to fly over our lines and explode somewhere in the rear but it went off in mid-air, close to the tree where my comrades were waiting. Several squealing splinters sank into the opposite side of my trench. When I climbed out, I saw that the tree had been sliced in two. Beneath it lay the motionless bodies of my comrades. A single shell had killed seven veterans of our regiment, survivors of the Battle of Stalingrad.

In our battalion, gun crews were undermanned, each lacking two or three people. Nevertheless, it was necessary to keep our nine mortars in action constantly. I decided to help out one mortar detachment, replacing their absent gun-layer. At one point, the commander of the crew ordered me to bring more boxes of bombs, which were stored under cover, while he himself acted as gun-layer. Right after I had brought the first set of bombs, and rushed back for more, I heard a tremendous explosion behind my back. Pausing for a moment, I returned to the mortar and saw its barrel in shreds, spread out like the petals of a camomile flower. Kozhevnikov, the charger, had been too hasty, and sunk a second bomb into the barrel before the first one had fired. The mortar was completely destroyed by the blast of the two shells. We buried the dead in the trench and put the mutilated mortar barrel on the ground over them, like they do with pilots, when they put a propeller from their shot down plane over the grave.

Five young nurses arrived with some new reinforcements. After graduating from school, they finished short-term medical courses and were sent to the front. Being the *partorg* of the company, it was my duty to meet them in order to get them registered. I learned their names and where they came from. Galia was from Penza, Tonia from Riazan, Zina from Tiumen and Shura from Novosibirsk. But Shura, on her Komsomol membership card, was referred to as Matriona. I demanded an explanation. 'None of your business!' she replied impudently. Some of those present began laughing, but I was curious, so I asked her once more: 'Neighbour, I'm from the Kemerovo Region myself, please tell me!' She went on in the same manner: 'What is it to you? My papers say that I'm Matriona, but I want people to call me Shura, that's my pseudonym. Understand, neighbour?' After our first meeting, I would greet this nurse as 'Shura', but then in a low voice, or whispering in her ear, call her 'Matriona', and she didn't seem to mind. Even though she was short, she easily carried her big medical bag with the red cross on it. She also had – unlike other nurses – a unique gift: in broad daylight, she could crawl up to a wounded man lying in No Man's Land, and save his life under the very nose of the Germans! We could only help by covering her with our machine-guns and mortars. Before creeping out, she would meticulously examine the lie of the land, selecting the safest route, via slight folds in the ground. Then she would tie the medical bag to her leg, and without raising her head to check her position, crawl up to her man unobserved by the enemy. She moved blindly! How can one remember a winding route of some 100m? [Almost 110 yards – editor's note] Even experienced soldiers could not understand it! And Matriona herself could not explain: 'How? I have no idea! But I never got lost in a large forest,' she told them. Sometimes we tried to talk her out of it: 'Don't do it! The ground is very open! The Fritzes might see you and kill you!' But she always stubbornly refused: 'I can't make the wounded men wait until night!'

One day, after a brief fight, when once again we were pressing the enemy westwards, Matriona, who was running next to me, was hit by a German bullet. She fell down, holding with both hands a bad wound, which was situated well below the stomach. I realized where she was wounded and asked timidly: 'Shall I dress the wound for you?' Feeling severe pain, she flatly refused, even though she understood that with her help I could bandage the wound and stop the blood. 'You'd better run and find one of our girls.' I realized that she felt shy in front of me, and rushed to find one of the other nurses, but with no success. Seeing our signallers, who were installing a telephone line, I ran up to them and explained what had happened. They immediately contacted the regimental HQ. I talked to Captain Yegorov, deputy-commander for political affairs. He promised that Sviatnenko, the head of the medical company, would help the wounded nurse right away and take her to the sanitary battalion. With a sense of relief, I joined my advancing comrades. When the battle was over, I phoned the regimental HQ and learned that Matriona had been evacuated from the battlefield, that she was alright, and sent me her best regards. In 1980 I visited Tashkent and stayed there with some of my wartime friends. I asked if Matriona was in touch with any of our veterans. I learned that some people were exchanging letters with Matriona, that she lived in Novosibirsk, was married, and had three children and two grandchildren. I found out her address and wrote to her. She replied, telling me that her wound was dressed by a man after all, Vladimir Sviatnenko, commander of the medical unit.

One of our mortarmen, Aleksei Yanson wanted to join the Communist Party. I took care of the paperwork and learned the following: 'born in 1906, Aleksei Ivanovich Yanson is the son of a *Kulak* [rich peasants persecuted by the Soviet authorities – editor's note]. In 1932 he graduated from the Forestry Engineering Academy in Leningrad with a Ph.D. degree. He then became Head of a department in the Krasnoyarsk Forestry Engineering Institute, and is married with two children. He volunteered to go to the front, even though he was exempt from service.' As the *partorg* of the company, I had to consult with Guards Captain Yegorov, our Regimental commissar, regarding the point, 'son of a Kulak'. He told me that it didn't matter at all. In due course, Aleksei Yanson was unanimously elected as a new Party member.

I was so young and naïve at that time, I thought that if a person had graduated from an academy, he must be an academician. So everyone in our company began referring to Yanson in this way. Soon our 'Academician' really proved that he was worthy of the nickname.

One day, the Germans unexpectedly began a tank attack. Our battalion was stormed by two dozen tanks and some infantry. Our rifle companies and machine-gunners checked the enemy foot soldiers, but the tanks continued their advance. As ill-luck had it, our anti-tank gunners were still toiling up to the new position from the rear with their heavy equipment: so Yanson proposed that we fire our mortars at the approaching tanks. In fact, fragmentation bombs could do little against tank armour, but there was nothing else to do!

We opened volley fire and a miracle happened: the tanks broke up their assault formation and actually began to retreat! Some of our shells had fallen directly on the German armour and the bomb blasts had confused the tank men. The effect of our fire, then, had been psychological, and this was what our 'Academician' had hoped for. The Nazis lost their nerve and turned back, while we gained time.

The Fritzes soon realized their mistake, but now our gunners had appeared, and set up their cannon ready for action. They didn't have long to wait. Yes! Those same tanks were attacking our battalion again, moving even faster than before. We used our mortars once more, in order to fool the enemy into thinking that the Russians here do not have anti-tank guns. The Nazi armour approached at speed, confident that nothing could be done to repel their attack. Who's afraid of mortar bombs?! But suddenly one tank went up in flames. Then a second, and a third. In the end, only five or six of them managed to escape, while around eighteen were destroyed, thanks to our ingenious 'Academician'.

We pressed the Germans hard, but they retreated in an organized way, ambushing us as best they could. For this purpose, they mostly used tanks placed in caponiers. You only saw a turret above ground level, which fired at you with its cannon and machine-gun. It was very hard to destroy such a pillbox!

One day, our regimental scouts returned and reported to Battalion Commander Kartoshenko that there were no Germans ahead of us for more than 2km [approximately 1¼ miles – editor's note]. They also informed regimental HQ about the situation. Soon our units were ordered to move forward. Since we were moving through heavy terrain, we had to march in columns. As dusk was falling, we suddenly found ourselves under close-range enemy fire, apparently coming from every direction. Those were well-camouflaged tanks! We lay low, and like moles, began digging in. But the fire was so intense that many infantrymen did not have time to dig a foxhole and were killed. Those who did shelter themselves could not peep out, in order to see what was happening: if you raised a finger, you'd lose it! I was stunned by the thought: 'What if I'm left alone here?' The Germans had done their job well: they had lured us into a well-prepared trap. When darkness fell they dropped their fire. But we distrusted this silence, and did not dare stick our noses out. Indeed, the Germans might have moved a long time ago to prepare a similar mousetrap somewhere in front of us . . .

But as usual, we stubbornly pushed on, forcing our way ahead at any cost, constantly receiving new marching companies from the rear. Our units were remanned every three or four days. Frontline infantrymen like myself, the 'veterans', were never indignant at our failures and unjustified losses. We never blamed anyone for them. I had nothing to say about this state of affairs. War is war.

Sometimes I think that we might not have won that dreadful war, if we had stuck to the rules. There were occasions when a seemingly senseless act helped the soldiers achieve miracles: things which would have been impossible under normal circumstances.

I remember one day, when the German fire was particularly heavy, some news spread along the trench that was impossible to believe. Choosing my moment carefully, I poked my head out of the trench to see for myself. What a sight! Our regimental staff, headed by Bilaonov, Yegorov and Tukhru, as if attending a demonstration, were marching forward under fire! Next to Bilaonov – who was still using his crutches with his head still bandaged – hurried on Nikolai Korsunov, trying to keep pace with his commander. Next to Yegorov I could see sergeant major Nosov! Were they under some spell? Now I felt ashamed to be hiding, lacking the nerve to rise up for an attack. This feeling became stronger and stronger, and there was nothing I could do about it! Our battalion commander, Nikolai Dolinny, was unable to remain under cover any longer, and signalling 'attack!' with flares, rushed out of his HQ, jumped into his Willys jeep, and darted ahead. The whole battalion instantly rose, crying: 'Hurrah! For the Motherland!' and plunged forward. Our units were running after our CO, who was rapidly approaching the German lines. Then we saw the jeep blow up. Later, we found the Order of the Red Star, which had been given to our battalion commander not long before.

Our attack was repelled, but during the night some soldiers from our battalion, headed by Senior Lieutenant Yundendorzh (a Mongolian who died several days later in another onslaught), managed to reach the German lines, destroying a Tiger tank by throwing several Molotov cocktails at it. Afterwards, a company of sub-machine gunners fought their way through the gap and destroyed yet another tank. The Nazis panicked and retreated from their positions. And so, by personal example, our officers showed the rank and file that the desire to survive at all costs was not the only path to follow. Self-preservation is, of course, a basic instinct. It is natural to want to stay alive. But if it becomes your dominant motive, you'll never get out of a trench!

CHAPTER NINE

The Drunkards' Cemetery

Our regiment crossed the border between the Belgorod Region and Ukraine. Vladimir Yegorov, our commissar, explained that from now on we were liberating Ukraine from the German invaders.

After the death of Nikolai Dolinny, Guards Captain Nikolai Kartoshenko became our new battalion commander. I was appointed *komsorg* of the battalion, and Aleksei Yanson took over my post as the company *partorg*. Guards Captain Vladimir Yegorov, our battalion commissar, recommended me for this new appointment. He told me frankly that on average, a battalion *komsorg* survived no more than two or three attacks, because his duty demanded that he be the first to rise upon hearing the order to advance. 'If you think you can, Mansur, take the post. If not, I won't blame you.'

I was puzzled by the commissar's words, and at first I did not know what to do. Yegorov watched me keenly, waiting for my answer. There has always been a *komsorg* in our battalion, and I was aware that others had willingly accepted the post before me. I did not want to be taken for a coward, so what should I do? A man can die but once! I felt for my lucky mascot – it was there. 'All right!' Yegorov gave me a grateful look. He knew he could count on me.

The average number of Komsomol members in our battalion ranged from 240–280. There was a high turnover. I had lots of work to do with all the fierce fighting and heavy casualties, there was never enough time. Every three or four days we received reinforcements. Each Komsomol member had to be registered. As to political instructions, they were the same for everyone: to do as much as possible, since at war one's life may end any minute. To kill one Nazi, at least! Perhaps two if you're lucky: one for yourself and one for a friend who did not have the opportunity to finish off a single bastard! As the *komsorg* I spread my philosophy 'to kill at least one Nazi' among all the Komsomol members of our battalion. This combat philosophy was universally accepted and no one thought otherwise. How else will we get our victory? There was no other way.

By nature I am a tender and sensitive person. I was never a hooligan or a brawler. But when I went to war I wanted to destroy the Fritzes: 'Kill or be killed.' This was my message to the newcomers. I was consumed by the idea that while alive, I would have my revenge on the Germans in advance: for I never expected to survive that slaughter. Once, on my initiative, we shot no less than 200 wounded Nazis in some vegetable store. I must note with some regret, however, that the majority of our soldiers were passive, and either perished or were wounded without trying to destroy even a single German (sometimes without even seeing the enemy). I felt great despair and anguish when I witnessed the death of our soldiers, who had just arrived from the rear. I wept. I could not contain my emotions.

There were exceptions however. I would like to mention a machine-gunner by the name of Nikolai Kobylin. A couple of years younger than me, his two elder brothers had both been killed in action, and he had volunteered to go to the front.

Nikolai desperately wanted to become a machine-gunner. A Maxim is a good weapon but heavy. It weighs 65kg [the Maxim consisted of two parts, which were separated on the march: the body, which weighed 24.8kg/almost 4 stone, and the mount, which weighed 29.4kg/over 4½ stone. The ammunition box, containing 250 rounds, weighed 7.5kg/16½lbs – editor's note]. If you're defending your lines, there is no better machine-gun. But during offensive action it's hard to carry it around. Our machine-gunners were usually hit when they were changing their position: they made good targets for the enemy. But Nikolai invented an interesting and simple strategy. When moving to a new position, he left his Maxim behind and first of all, ran there himself as fast as he could. Then he hauled his gun to the new spot using a thin, multiple wire: thus his Maxim, as if self-propelled, followed its owner!

Nikolai Kobylin would fire both day and night. During the day, he studied his field of fire, setting his gun accordingly. At night, when the Nazis appeared inside his sector, Nikolai would open fire. For him it was no show. Kobylin coolly avenged his brothers and finished off a couple of hundred Germans.

I can recall another Komsomol member, Vasili Shamrai, who was also a machine-gunner. Like myself, he had been born in 1923, had been a miner, exempt from military service, but had volunteered to go to the front. There were times when Nazi counter-attacks were repelled only because of the bravery of these two Komsomol members. Both of them are alive. Kobylin lives in Izhevsk, and Shamrai in the Kremenchug District of the Poltava Region. Kim Dobkin, our poet, also survived. As a scout he was very lucky. He now resides in Rostov-on-Don. And Andrei Bogdanov lives on the Island of Sakhalin.

Everyone wanted to join the Komsomol and often fresh members did not even get the chance to receive their cards. There was severe fighting, and in one month practically the whole list of the organisation would consist of new names. The *komsorg* never gathered others for a meeting, neither did he keep the minutes, make speeches or listen to debates. Engaged in action, the Komsomol organisation of the battalion was in a state of one, continuous 'meeting'. Komsomol life was intensive and did not require any minutes. As the *komsorg* I constantly heard dozens of requests and questions: 'We're running out of cartridges!' 'We have a shortage of shells!' 'Where are the grenades?' 'Why is there still no mail?' 'We have nothing to smoke!' 'Why didn't our field kitchen arrive at night?'

I also served as an interpreter, translating from Tartar, Kazakh, Uzbek, Bashkir and Kyrghiz languages into Russian. All my comrades envied me, that I, being a Tartar, knew so many languages!

I can still remember my emotions during an attack. It was my duty to rise first, and my whole battalion waited for the moment. If the *komsorg* or the *partorg* began the onslaught, no one had the right to stay back. Everyone must follow. Overcoming my fear I would stand up and scream at the top of my voice: 'Forward! For the Motherland! For Stalin!' I would roar and yell so that everyone would hear and follow me: in order to take a nameless height, or dislodge the Germans from a peasant house, or win back a street.

I often wanted to glance back: was anyone following me? But I could not allow myself to turn, because I would reveal my fear and lack of trust in my fellow-Komsomol members. So I ran forward, pressing on, as if I were pushing an overloaded miner's tub uphill. And whenever I felt unable to go on, or that I was doomed to die at any second, a deafening 'Hurrah-ah-ah!' would sweep me along, and soon I would hear the heavy, intense breathing of those running after me, which was music to my ears.

At that instant my fear would vanish with the last of my energy, and exhausted, I would fall to the ground, as if shot dead. Then I would hear a wild cry: 'Our *komsorg* is killed!' And I would force myself to rise and rush headlong into the attack, so none of our boys would have any doubts about their *komsorg*. After the fight I often heard people talk about me: 'He was born under a lucky star.' When I heard this, it was like getting a decoration. At the same time, nothing could be worse than hearing the soldiers speak bad about you: 'Our *komsorg*, he's a sissy, a coward . . .' One's reputation had to be rebuilt everyday, with each new round of fighting.

Once I found myself in a tight spot. I was passing a group of men sitting in a trench and quietly enjoying a meal: schnapps and captured sausage. 'Hey, Mansur! Join us, komsorg!' They poured me 100gm [around 3½ fluid ounces – editor's note] of schnapps and handed me a piece of sausage. I should have refused, saying something like, 'I don't like this German swill'; but all the boys were older than me, and had two or three medals each, while I had just the one, 'For Bravery'. We drank and talked a little. Then someone said: 'Mansur, another 100?' 'Why not?' But then they stopped drinking, making a show of having no more liquor, and rifling through their knapsacks. 'Wasn't there one more bottle?' I should have kept my mouth shut, but instead I asked: 'Where did you get it?' One of the lads pointed, 'Over there. There's more, but the Fritzes are watching. Two of our men have been killed already.' I sat there thinking: 'Now I have swallowed the bait. I have to return the favour and treat them to a drink. If I don't go, they'll tell everyone that I'm a coward.' They tried to dissuaded me: 'Don't go, *komsorg*.' But I see in their eyes: 'You know you have to.' Those boys were counted among the leaders of the brave soldiers. It was not just a bottle of schnapps which was at stake . . .

Between me and the armoured carrier, which got stuck in the No Man's Land, lies a glade about 100m wide. I jump out of the trench, and darting and dodging like a rabbit, run at top speed to the APC. When the Germans open machine-gun fire, I am already in the 'dead zone'. I take two bottles from a box I find inside, pause for breath, and carefully look around. I must choose a different route for the return sprint back to our lines. The Germans are waiting for me. But which way do they expect me to go? And where are the bodies of the other two men? Over there, close to the trench. That means they'll want to cut me down on the same spot. Think, Mansur! 'Right, it's time!' I dash directly towards the bodies of those two soldiers: they are my finishing line. I reach the fatal point – the bullets are hitting the ground before me – and plunge down next to the bodies, as if I'm shot dead. I lie there, relaxed and motionless, even my eyelids are half open. Close to my nose, on the boot of one of the dead soldiers, I see a small insect. It is creeping around on its own business, and does not know that there is a war, and that the man it is looking at, but not seeing, might end his life right now. Well, have I convinced Fritz that I'm a corpse? Is his finger still on the trigger? Has he turned away? I fly up like a steel spring and in three leaps, dive into our trench safe and sound. The machine-gun clattered, but it was too late.

But where are my boys? Gone! Only the sausage remains. It turned out that my comrades also thought I'd been killed. They felt bad that they were to blame for the senseless death of the young *komsorg* and were now in no mood to continue their treat! Shaking off the dust and grabbing my bag, I ran down the trench to find my comrades in order to return the favour. Here they are: 'Why it's our *komsorg!* What a resurrection! You're something! You must be a real actor! You collapsed with such skill that we thought you were finished!'

The following day, the boys laughed at me: how I dodged and jumped like a rabbit running to the troop carrier (one can laugh at a live man). But they also praised me for the ruse on my way back. Everyone in the battalion instantly learned that 'our *komsorg* is not a coward.' I fully enjoyed the results.

On the whole, I must say that I'm not only indifferent towards schnapps, but towards any alcohol. It all goes back to my childhood. Being a kid, I often visited the yard of the mine, where our 'drunkards' cemetery' was situated. Graves with real crosses, empty bottles, and pegs with boards, on which the name of the drunkard was inscribed. Young and old came here to enjoy the propaganda show of burying a drunken miner.

It was a very interesting sight! A brass band is playing the dead march, accompanying a crowd of people carrying a coffin to the grave. The casket is lowered into the pit, mock speeches are made, then the grave is covered with earth. Everyone will now point their finger at the 'dead' drunkard, who, as a result, stops tippling. His grave is then removed as he is restored to life!

I'm probably influenced too much by propaganda. But that show saved me from a common vice. But the most impressive and convincing 'show' involving alcohol that I saw at the front, was when we took a village by the name of Chervonny Prapor, which contained a distillery.

Afraid of unexpected German 'mousetraps' our infantry and cavalry scouts carefully reconnoitred the ground around the village but found nothing. Through the invisible 'soldiers' telegraph' our battalions learned that the distillery was still working fine, which meant that there was a whole sea of spirit there! Even before the attack the soldiers winked at each other, chuckled and joked: we'll do anything to take this distillery, but please, no artillery preparation! We don't want any unnecessary damage!'

Our staff and political department gave definite instructions to battalion, company, and platoon commanders, as well as to *partorgs* and *komsorgs:* they would be held personally responsible if any soldier was found inebriated. Apart from that, we were warned that the alcohol might be poisoned. Our battalion commanders then received the exact route of march through the village: down one of the main streets, which was farthest from the distillery, the latter being about 2km [about 1¼ miles – editor's note] away. It was dangerous to go round Chervonny Prapor, because its environs were mined. Thus, under the strict control of the officers responsible for the march, we went through it without any incidents. Soon the distillery was left far behind.

We continued our movement, following our advance and flank patrols. We had left the village about 2km behind, when the Germans shelled our vanguard using their six-barrel mortars. We extended, lay low, and began digging in. Night came.

Suddenly, not long before dawn, the bombardment stopped. That was the moment when we should have tried to advance, but grave news began coming in from our companies: the troops are dead drunk. Some are literally dead! We got an order from the regimental HQ: 'The battalion is to attack the not numerous forces of the Hitlerites!' But only a quarter of our infantrymen could rise for the onslaught! At that very instant a staff Willys jeep with the regimental commander appeared near our lines. The major was infuriated, yelling at our battalion commander: 'Well! What's going on?! Where's the battalion?! Everyone's either dead drunk or kicked the bucket! Answer me!' I stood with the *partorg* stood next to our CO. Some of our tipsy sub-machine gunners staggered up from the rear. 'Such a battalion commander deserves to be shot along with the *partorg* and the *komsorg!*' He took a pistol out of his holster and pointed it at me. I thought that the black hole of the barrel was the size of a 45mm gun! It was directly opposite the bridge of my nose. That's it! The end! So be it! Anyway, I'm fed up with this war! With the lice! With this trench life, its hunger, hard work and sleepless nights! I've been in constant action since October 1942! I kept my eye on the manicured hand of the major and see his index finger tremble on the trigger! What will the staff clerks write on my death notice? My mother will read: 'Your son was shot dead as a criminal.'

But the shot never came. Our regimental commander, seeing the infantrymen who stood nearby click the breech mechanisms of their sub-machine guns, decided to stop this show and left in the same direction that he came from. It turned out that during the night our soldiers, unobserved and taking turns, had run back to the distillery, and in the dark filled their flasks and mess tins with anything that smelled like spirit. Our Battalion Commander Kartoshenko was at a loss what to do. We decided to lie low and wait, hoping that the men would sober up the following day. The Germans, perfectly aware of our generous nature and inexhaustible passion for alcohol, had worked out a very reliable plan!

As dusk fell, some tanks and armoured troop carriers, equipped with flame throwers, appeared on the horizon. They were approaching us in two staggered rows. Moving quite slowly, they rode up to our dead drunk soldiers and coolly began to shower them with fire. In one instant our lines and their defenders were ablaze. One could see the men, their figures like live torches, rush about, consumed by flames like butterflies. Even sober, it was difficult to escape from this hell! The German tanks, switching off their flame throwers, used the same corridor to ride back unharmed and soon disappeared beyond the horizon, while our lines blazed all night, until the inflammable mixture burned out.

I don't like to remember that episode. If one is sober, standing firmly on two feet, one can hide or run away. Many excellent, heroic soldiers died in the sticky fire of the flame throwers. The most humiliating thing was that retreating from Chervonny Prapor, the Nazis, it seems, did not have a single doubt that their plan would work.

We are expecting fresh reinforcements, because our units are hugely undermanned: fifteen to twenty soldiers in each company. German gunners keep incessantly shelling us. The bastards fire as if they can see us!

We found out that their artillery is directed by a special plane. We call it the 'hunchback' [the Henschel HS126 was a stout two-seater aircraft, designed for aerial reconnaissance – editor's note] because it really does have a hump. This low-speed machine has only one engine and hovers over our positions to check how accurately the shells are falling . . .

In our mortar company we had an anti-tank rifle, a PTR. As soon as the 'hunchback' appeared in the sky over us, I began firing at it with the PTR. I desperately wanted to destroy that plane and for our chiefs to learn about it. Apart from an order, a shot down plane was rewarded with a period of leave. I confess that at that time I was weary of fighting. Both my body and my mind needed some rest. I couldn't quit the war on my own initiative, I realized that, but if only I could go on leave for ten or twenty days to have some quiet sleep, to drink some fresh milk, to go fishing.

I continued firing at the 'hunchback' until I became deaf and infuriated my whole company. Everyone was fed up with my shooting, including me. The PTR has a very strong recoil, so my shoulder was killing me! Every time you are thrown back for a distance of half a metre. My head almost exploded with the report! But after every miss, I angrily went on. Several times the plane would suddenly dive and disappear without apparent damage, only to return. A week passed, we finally got our reinforcements, dislodged the Nazis from their trenches, and moved farther into their rear. There I saw my 'hunchback' riddled with PTR shots and burned out. I must have hit it a hundred times! I was very glad to know that I did actually destroy it. But how could I prove that the plane's destruction was down to me? Some of my comrades congratulated me: 'Mansur, you're the one who shot it down!' But others cast doubt on my achievement: 'Maybe someone else was also firing at it? How the mortarmen had criticized me for this seemingly aimless shooting! 'We're all deaf thanks to your PTR! If only you could fire it someplace else!' Now these same soldiers looked amazed, seeing the plane riddled with PTR armour-piercing shots.

First in the regiment, and then in the division, our anti-tank gunners were instructed to fire PTRs at enemy planes. Sometimes they were shot down. The only problem was that no one knew who was to be decorated and rewarded with a vacation. Nevertheless, this became a traditional way of fighting German aircraft, even though it was a pretty difficult thing to do. What was most important, however, was o ur collective effort to destroy Nazi planes, bringing Victory Day closer, after which we would all get a 'vacation'.

I did not receive anything for killing the 'hunchback', because it was difficult to prove that I was the one who brought it down. Our Regimental commissar, Vladimir Yegorov, used to tell us: 'For you, battalion *partorgs* and *komsorgs*, the best reward should be the fact that you hold these posts! Be modest and don't think about your decorations. But never forget to recommend for one a private soldier for his heroic deed!' Vladimir himself did not have many orders and medals. However, when we fought at the Kursk Salient, he met me once and commented with some surprise: 'Why, you have only one medal "For Bravery?" Impossible!' I felt ashamed and walked on, while he, nodding his head, continued speaking about me to his companions, who looked in my direction. Some time later a report came from HQ, stating that *Komsorg* M.G. Abdulin had been recommended for the Order of the Red Star. Once again my comrades congratulated me. How many times had I heard it?! I finally got the order after the war, in 1948.

Together with the *partorg* of the battalion (while I was *komsorg* I served with four different men), we tried to stay day and night with our companies and platoons. We appeared at our HQ, personally reporting to our battalion commander Nikolai Kartoshenko, once a day in order to discuss current affairs. Kartoshenko was always alone at the HQ. All his aides and staff were also with the men, following his strict order to keep him informed about their actual position. We had very little sleep and very little food, eating whatever we could find. Company *komsorgs* dropped out very often, and had to be replaced as soon as possible. In the case of our company commander becoming a casualty, it was my duty to substitute for him until a new officer arrived.

Each night it was my job, together with the *partorg*, to visit our outposts, which were located in No Man's Land in front of our lines. I had an additional reason to accompany Lieutenant Peter Vasiliyev, the battalion *partorg* because he was near-sighted. His eldest son Vasily, who was the same age as myself, was also at the front. Lately there had been no letters from him, and Peter was very much afraid his son had been killed.

We creep through the neutral zone, while Nazi flares fall near us, blazing like electric welding, zigzagging on the ground, hissing like snakes. One wrong move and a machine-gun round will riddle you.

Creeping to check our outposts, I always remembered how I once fell asleep in the Stalingrad steppe and how I and Suvorov, without making a move, found ourselves in the German rear.

Once, when it was quiet, Peter and I were delayed in a certain rifle company. During a pause in the fighting, soldiers usually like to have a conversation on different matters: only the war itself is not a popular subject. For instance, if God really exists. Or, as it happened with these riflemen, the origin of Man. The old soldiers were particularly interested. As to the young ones, having spent some years in schools, they were indulgent and inclined to laugh at their older comrades, who had virtually no education. One of the elderly men, I think his name was Afanasi Kudriavtsev, asked the *partorg* a question: 'Why didn't all the monkeys turn into men? Eh? If men come from monkeys, then there wouldn't be a single of those shameless devils left! So why is it that in warm countries there's still a lot of those monkeys living in herds?'

The soldier looks cunningly at the *partorg*, expecting a convincing answer. Everyone waits to see how Peter will deal with this sly question. I know that yet again, the post has brought no news of Vasiliyev's son. He looks haggard. But I can see that he is thinking hard about what say to the aged Afanasi. And everyone knows that the *partorg* will not give an instant answer, so as to end the conversation, but will let the person speak, giving him an opportunity to unburden his mind. Afanasi, looking at Peter, continues his thought: 'Do our scientists and academicians also come from monkeys? These animals are so shameless and impudent. They look for lice and eat them! Well, do I really have in my veins the blood of a monkey?' Some men around us start laughing. 'What's so funny? I'm on your side! I am sorry that such young and smart men should be included by our scientists and academicians among the monkeys! And you believed them! Wow, how stupid we are! All this shame we heap on ourselves! Pooh! I disagree! If it was not for this war, I'd go to Moscow to make a scandal with those academicians! I'd show them! I'm not afraid! Let them say about themselves that they come from monkeys, but don't judge normal folk!' Afanasi, glad that the *partorg* gave him an opportunity to speak up, was now rolling a cigarette and excitedly waiting for Peter's reply.

To the surprise of the young soldiers, Vasiliyev did not answer the question the way it was taught in schools: 'The monkeys existed by themselves for millions of years, just like they are now. And they will still be the same in the coming millions of years. Men also existed millions of years by themselves – scientists agree with that. Only that millions of years ago people lived in the woods, in caves and ate raw food. Then they learned how to cook, how to make stone axes. In fifty or a hundred years men will fly to the moon and to other planets. And the monkeys will stay just as they were millions of years ago.'

Afanasi looked delighted: 'What did I say?' he screamed, and I thought he was ready to embrace Peter, 'Comrade *Partorg*, find me this smart book where this is written, just like you explained it to us now! I don't want any order, just give me this book!' Now the young soldiers became excited, and referring to Darwin and to their school books, demanded an answer: 'Then why did they tell us "from monkeys" at school?' But there was no time for a discussion. We heard a command: 'Company! Action! Tanks!'

In a second we split up, taking our positions in the trench and preparing our grenades.

It turned out that the Germans launched their attack across the whole breadth of our division. The speeding tanks appeared unexpectedly, there was some confusion and our two neighbouring regiments began retreating.

If your comrades to the left and to the right are falling back, it's hard to stop oneself from following them, because you run the risk of being encircled. In such cases some soldiers think the following: 'I can't be the first to retreat. The first man to run will face a tribunal. Let someone else begin, and then I'll see what's going on . . . ' Peter and I decided that one of us should take care of the left flank, and the other the right, so we split up. I did not know it, but it was the last time I would see Peter Vasiliyev alive.

The tanks were now very close. Two of our 45mm guns made a shot each, but missed. Then both of these guns were put out of action by tank fire. Our boys started throwing grenades, but that didn't help either. Two of our soldiers, reacting in haste, flung their grenades, forgetting to pull the pin. In one place our riflemen wavered. I rushed there and got them back into the trenches, otherwise the tanks would crush them. We were now engaged in close combat, setting fire to the German armour with our grenades and using our guns to separate the infantry from the tanks.

The situation got worse by the minute. Our neighbouring regiments continued to fall back, increasing the danger of our being outflanked.

I didn't want to be senselessly encircled! I also knew that we were running pretty low on ammunition. But my sixth sense told me that it was too early to retreat. I yelled in every direction: 'Hold on! Hold on, boys!'

At that moment, one of the company *komsorgs* ran up to me and handed me the field bag and the Party membership card of Senior Lieutenant Peter Vasiliyev. 'One more *partorg* killed! Farewell, Peter!' I remember thinking. Then I asked, 'Where's the battalion commander?' 'They carried him away. He was wounded.' As to the deputy CO, he had perished three days earlier. According to army regulations, the officer in charge of the first rifle company should assume command over the battalion in such a case. But there was no time to find the man! '*komsorg*, take charge! Do something!' Screamed the commander of the second company. At that critical moment there appeared, out of thin air, the gigantic figure of Guards Major Bilaonov, our regimental commander, accompanied by Guards Lieutenant Nikolai Korsunov, his adjutant: 'Boys, no retreat!' Bilaonov's voice thundered through the trenches. Even though I felt relieved that I was no longer responsible for the situation, I was not really happy to see our major. 'That's it, the end,' I thought. 'Now with his "no retreat!" we'll all be either killed or captured!'

Bilaonov was a man of impossible bravery. Even now, decades later, the spirit of the man remains a mystery to me. No one, under any circumstances, could make him fall back! This man would sacrifice himself and us together with him.

I saw him pick up an anti-tank rifle that some soldier had thrown away, and automatically open the breech mechanism to see if it was loaded. Yes! He put a cartridge into the chamber. At that very moment, like a moving target in a shooting gallery, we saw before us a rolling Nazi tank. It stopped, fired its turret cannon and shot several rounds from its machine-gun. One can easily realize how mighty a force it is; beware if it moves against you! Bilaonov could not have found a better position for himself than beside an ancient lichen-covered oak cross. He placed his PTR on one of the arms and aimed at the side of the tank. The distance was not more than 50m [almost 55 yards – editor's note].

Naturally, the Germans noticed a Soviet officer aiming an anti-tank gun at them. Their turret with the cannon and machine-guns began turning in our direction. Together with Nikolai Korsunov I lay near Bilaonov's feet. Strange to say, the moving 'trunk' of the tank's gun, gradually became shorter as it turned, until it was eyeing me with its black pupil hole. I realized that this is death. The 'pupil' is going left and right, up and down, trying to catch sight of us, to 'photograph' us more accurately. If it was not the major, but anyone else standing with the PTR, I would have darted away from this place! But such was the influence of this man, that it was unbearable to imagine that his last thought concerning you might be 'Coward!'

Our battalion commander is still aiming. I was ready to accept death together with my CO and his adjutant. The three of us will be instantly killed. Right now.

The report was so loud that at first I didn't understand who shot whom. Was it the PTR or the tank? But if I'm asking this question, then I'm alive! So are the battalion commander and Nikolai! Bilaonov was faster? The major shoots one more time and here I see that his right arm is wounded. The tank caught fire! Nikolai and I want to take the injured man to a safe place, but he refuses to go, so now we have to bandage him here. The Nazis are trying to escape from the burning tank as fast as they can, but rounds coming from our guns turn them into rag dolls. Yes, the appearance of Bilaonov at this critical moment, his bravery in destroying an enemy tank, made our battalion do the impossible: soon the other five tanks began slowly retreating. The Germans are falling back! The neighbouring regiments also managed to repulse the attack. Our division regained its former positions.

The following day I was invited to a meeting of the regimental polit-buro, where my name was unanimously voted to be included into the regimental book of war heroes. Guards Major Pavel Bilaonov, with his right arm bandaged, was sitting in the presidium and I next to him. After the meeting we saw him off to a hospital. The regiment was temporarily placed under the command of his deputy, Ivan Tukhru.

I'm the longest surviving *komsorg* in our battalion. It's a sort of a record. But how much longer will I last?

That morning things were developing in the following way. Three of our mounted scouts (led by Senior Lieutenant Vlasov), after recon-noitring far ahead of our main forces, reported to our HQ: 'Stanitsin Kazachiok is clear. The village is completely burned down, there's no one in sight!' We got our order: 'The battalion columns are to continue their forward movement, and the scouts should keep watch before the column, staying in sight.' The scouts saluted and drove ahead, while we followed them, going up the highroad. After marching for not more than 2km without any incident, we saw with our own eyes the two horsemen tumble off their frightened horses. A second later the third rider was dismounted by two Fritzes and dragged out of sight. The scared horses ran back to our unit and it took us some time to catch them. We instantly extended and continued our march without meeting any resistance. We entered the burned down village, filled with smoke. It was completely destroyed. Not a soul around. Here was a clear example of 'scorched earth' policy!

The weather was hot and windless. The bitter, choking fumes were covering the sky from view. The sun looked like a large cast iron frying pan. Only the big stoves, covered with soot, their 'mouths' and square 'eyes' wide open, standing like tombstones amidst smouldering piles of wood, reminded us that this was once a village. Around the stoves stood the charred remains of some large trees, resembling groups of miserable people, their branches rising like arms, begging the Almighty for mercy. It seemed they were burned down before help came and are now left petrified in that state, in order to prove that the Almighty never existed!

Near some of the stoves we could also see self-made metal beds, mutilated by the fire, with patterned backs done in open-work. Large and small cast iron and clay pots were scattered around. On the side and front of the stoves, through the soot, one could catch a glimpse of some naive and touching pictures, with inscriptions made in indelible pencil: 'Baskets with Sunflowers', 'Young Peasant with his Girlfriend,' 'Kittens Playing with a Ball,' 'Fighting Roosters' or 'Hen with Chickens.' We slowly moved up the street.

As in many other villages, in the centre of it there was a well. An empty wooden bucket was hanging. We rushed forward hoping to have a drink of fresh, cold water. Before we reached the well, on one side of the street, we found the dead body of Senior Lieutenant Vlasov. His mutilated remains were placed into our staff car and taken out of the village, to be buried nearby. We reached the well and lowered the bucket. It struck something strange. It was definitely not water: perhaps the well had dried out? We brought the bucket back and saw blood inside. It was clear that the Germans had thrown corpses into the well. Not far from the well we saw the dead bodies of naked women and even very small girls. We covered them with our water-proofs and marched on.

In one of the ovens I saw a large, slightly parched grey cat. It was lying on its belly in a traditional posture, paws underneath and hairy tail spread along the body. The ears on its large, smart-looking head were turned a little back and downwards, speaking of some serious grief. The sad eyes of the animal seemed to be indifferent to the outside world. It wasn't paying any attention to me and did not make a move to run away. I doubted whether it was alive. But then I saw large tears in its eyes. It was not dead. I wanted very much to stroke the cat, but I did not dare, because I didn't deserve it. With a feeling of unbearable anguish and burning sorrow I walked away from that oven, from the destroyed house, from its 'owner' the cat, now an orphan, which miraculously survived this disaster.

When we had almost passed through this land of ashes, we saw a ghost-like female figure, which appeared and vanished in the smoke several times. The woman seemed to be waiting for us by the road. We came up and formed a circle around her. We were interested in getting information about what happened here from a live witness. Even though the woman was totally exhausted, she managed to stand erect. Looking at her ashen-grey, thick and wavy hair, hanging loose down to her waist, one could say that she was still young. Her skin was stretched tightly across her skull, her eyes were deep-set, her arms and legs gaunt and feeble. There was but a spark of life left in her body. We were afraid to ask her anything. One of the old infantrymen, who still had a little water in his flask, poured it into a small glass and handed it to her. She took it with her thin, trembling fingers and slowly drank it up. Then she returned the empty glass, pronouncing with a little pause after each word: 'Many thanks, but you are a bit late.' Uttering this sentence she collapsed into the arms of the nearest soldier. Her head with open eyes fell back and her arms sank like empty sleeves. We realized that she was dead.

Hoping that all the horrors were now behind us, we finally reached the end of the village. But the worst was yet to come. All the inhabitants were lying stretched out along the road. All of them shot dead. The infantrymen, taking off their caps, slowly walked past the several hundred shot women, old people and children. We felt ashamed. I sobbed violently, beside myself with anger and rage. I promised myself to avenge these people, to get as many Nazis and our own traitors as I could! And to do it at the first possible instant!

CHAPTER TEN

The Fatal Road

Our 32nd Guards Rifle Corps received a new order: to force a crossing over the River Vorskla from the right bank to the left in order to approach Poltava from the West.

The river is not so wide: not more than 100 or 120m [between 110 and 132 yards – editor's note]. And it's not very deep, so we can wade it. But it's surrounded by marshland no less than 1km wide [just over 1,000 yards – editor's note]. Where and how should we cross it? Our scouts, aided by some of the locals, decided that the best place would be a gravel road with a bridge, the former stretching over the bog. The approaches to the bridge should be seized, so the Nazis could not destroy it. The road runs over an embankment from 5 to 6m high [around 6½ yards – editor's note], with steep slopes. If you fall down, you'll get sucked in by the swamp. We calculated that if these 1,000m were being crossed at a speed of 15km per hour [just over 9 miles per hour – editor's note], then each soldier would need about six or seven minutes. But if we double the speed, this dangerous sector could be left behind in three minutes.

Fate had it that our regiment was chosen to be the first to cross the river and create a bridgehead on the right bank. We started our preparations. From the divisional HQ we received automobiles and two wheel carts led by two horses apiece.

We had some Party and Komsomol meetings in order to discuss the best way to carry out the order with as few casualties as possible. We will have to move under heavy artillery fire: the Nazis, of course, have all their guns aimed at the road and at the bridge. They will surely not spare us any shells, and many of our men are not going to make it to the other side. It was the first time I found myself in such a situation!

Here is the hour when every man will test his fortune. It will be hard to survive under tomorrow's mass barrage, and only the luckiest will survive. Everyone knows that but men go around as usual. Not a single one of my comrades had an air of being doomed.

I felt every live cell of my body. In my mind I rolled the film of my past experience. I was thinking that this might be the last day I breathe. What are the options? You can't jump from the embankment, there's a marsh to both left and right. There's only one way: forward. And how? Through a wall of blasts?

So I decided to move across this dangerous sector in a two-wheel cart. I know of a very important quality of horses: they do not lose their way in the heaviest of snowstorms. Even if it's pitch dark horses will never get lost! And so the horses will never leave the road, whatever the explosions around them. I chose a pair of Mongolian horses with a solid cart. Cart driver Moiseev asks me: 'So, son, you pin your hopes on horses?' And he tapped one animal on the neck. 'Yes, yes,' I reply, 'horses are reliable. I worked as a horse driver in a mine and know them well. You can always rely on them! Horses are the smartest of animals.' Moiseev was happy to hear me say that: he spent all his life with horses.

I must have touched a sensitive chord because he said in a kind and trusting voice: 'You're right, son! Horses are smarter than men, they just can't talk. But they understand things better than we do!' We had enough food in our knapsacks, so we settled down underneath the cart to have a meal. Moiseev suddenly casts an inquiring glance at me and asks: 'Listen, son, have you been to Stalingrad?' 'Yes.' His eyes widened with amazement: 'Your surname is Abdulov?' 'Not Abdulov, but Abdulin.' 'Why, we've served in the same mortar company!' he exclaimed. 'I remember our commander, his name was Buteiko, right? I remember Suvorov, who had a small beard. Because of my age, I was later sent from the mortar company to the salvage team.' Now I remembered: 'Yes, at that time there were four of you, "old men", who were transferred from our company!' Moiseev suddenly looked grave: 'They were killed at the Kursk Salient.' I instantly remembered my seven friends from the Stalingrad days, with whom death had also caught up at the Battle of Kursk. To be frank, I was not glad that mine and Moiseev's paths had crossed right before the deadly thrust over the River Vorskla.

A scout approached us, another old acquaintance of the Stalingrad battle, Gregory Ambartsumiants, an Armenian by birth. It was him, who together with his comrades, went to reconnoitre the marshy banks of the river and could not find any place for a crossing: there were swamps everywhere. Gregory was my age or perhaps two years older. He was a very strong man, even though he was not tall. His large eyes were very expressive. We knew that he served in the Special Department of the Corps staff. When Ambartsumiants visited our battalion, the rear was really in trouble if ammunition or food were not brought to us on time! He didn't ask any questions, but immediately saw all the shortcomings in our units. The military tribunal never became involved, he just reminded men that they should do their duty voluntarily, and do it at any cost. Everybody was happy to see Gregory, especially front line soldiers.

The scout energetically tapped our 'Mongolian' on the withers: 'Oh, my horses, yes, my horses!' he quoted a well-known song. 'And you, Mansur, what do you think? It's better to make the dash on horses, right?' He opened his eyes wide and then slowly winked at me. I proposed that he might join our landing party. He walked around the animals, examined the hoofs, the horseshoes, then had a look at the oak cart. 'All right! I'm with you. And you plan to ride or to run along?' I told him that I personally was going to run, while Moiseev sat in the cart, into which I planned to put my sub-machine gun, knapsack, cartridges, and grenades. I'll run along, holding this rope, with one end wound around my wrist, the other tied to the cart. Gregory listened and said: 'Fine. I'll also run along.'

In this way the three of us, Stalingrad veterans, formed a single team. We would all share the same fate! Could it be that all three of us were going to be cut down by death tomorrow?

We had dinner together and brought some forage for the horses. We left some food for breakfast and gave the rest to the horses. They ate it all: our bread, wheat porridge, and sugar. Our destiny was now entwined with that of the animals from the remote Mongolian steppe. Five live creatures were now facing a great ordeal. During the war I saw wounded horses die many times. They groan like humans and their eyes ask for help or for death. It's a groan that comes from the chest, as with men.

Something like a prayer cycled endlessly round my mind: 'My dear horses, don't let us down tomorrow, run forward as fast as you can! Don't be frightened!' I lay on the ground but was unable to sleep. Moiseev also remained awake all night, wrapped up in his own thoughts. When I sat up next to him, showing that I was awake, he said: 'I'm not concerned about myself. I have lived my life. I have a family. I brought up seven daughters. I've seen a lot, lived through a lot. But you and Gregory are just boys. You have not even experienced men's happiness. You haven't even put your arms around a girl! And how many sons-in-law have been killed, yes?' And the father of seven daughters shook his head . . .

Day is breaking. I approach the horses, which are not harnessed, but tied to the cart. Their heads are hanging, lowered to the ground: maybe they're thinking about their own lives. We harness them. I bring some fresh water from a well and give it to them. Everything's ready. We're waiting for the signal. We know whom we should follow, when the time comes. In front of us is another cart with soldiers. We see some staff officers ride towards the head of the column. We're just a moment away from rushing forward against the enemy, into the unknown. I feel calm. All the pluses and minuses are balanced in my soul.

The carts begin to rumble. Some movement ahead of us. I hear orders and instructions being given. We're still 1 or 2km [approximately 1¼ miles – editor's note] away from the fatal road. We'll try to approach it as quietly as we can, using small side streets and vegetable gardens, taking cover behind bushes. We begin to move, making short stops. I hear some swearing coming from the men ahead.

The three of us are sitting in the cart. Later, when we reach the road of death, Gregory and I are going to jump out and run on both sides of the cart, holding our ropes. Our very first landing parties have already dashed forward. Cars, artillery, horses, and men are irrepressibly gaining speed and force. Now nothing can stop this might, not even death. The Nazis open an avalanche of fire from all their guns. Shells and bombs, with a terrible whizz and roar, smack into the embankment, as if the enemy plan to level it with the marsh. But the movement continues as more and more carts pour forth onto the high road. German shells now begin hitting those who were standing and expecting their turn. Our time has come!

Without pausing to stop, we hit the gravel road. The horses, their short hairy tails high in the air, instantly understand what they have to do and break into a gallop. The cart in front is led by a splendid pair, so we can barely keep pace with them. We know that, just in case, we should maintain a distance of no less than 20m [nearly 22 yards – editor's note].

Moiseev lets go of the reigns and like an insect, clings to the sides of the cart, so as not to be thrown out at full speed. Gregory and I, leaving all our stuff inside, jump out and start running next to the cart. It's easy to run but hard to breathe! There's not enough air. From the sky, as from some gigantic hatch, earth, sand, and swamp algae are falling on our heads. My nose is full of dirt and dust and my lungs are bitten by smoke and marsh gas, which is rising from the depths of the bog.

The blasts follow one another with such speed that whatever rises from the ground does not have the time to fall back: new explosions throw it up again and again. Shell holes are everywhere, and the cart is leaping up and down. It might break into pieces any moment. I suddenly think that we should have tied our ropes to the traces. If the cart falls apart, the horses will run off on their own and we'll be doomed!

Our horses are going faster and faster. In the dust and thick smoke I can only see their glimmering hooves. The horses are so overstrained and frightened that they keep defecating and blowing wind, so we are covered with shit from head to foot! I run with my eyes closed, I don't want to be blinded by all the dust and smoke. I open them from time to time in order to catch a glimpse of what is going on. Some scenes flash before me: bits of automobiles, guns, and carts fall down the slopes. There falls a torn-off horse's head with open mouth, which tumbles into the green-black slush of the swamp. Flying past me – oh God! – someone's half-naked bloody body without head or arms . . .

The cart in front of us vanishes, and our horses, darting after it into a cloud of smoke, also disappear. Could it be that the cart is hit? But the rope, its end tightly wound round my fist, is still pulling me forward and I go on running into the unknown. The choking smoke of half-burned TNT is scorching my lungs. It's nitric oxide – very poisonous gas. My mouth is full of earth and sand. I still try to protect my eyes, opening them as little as possible. In any case, I can't see a thing! Thank God, our horses are still safe and speeding like mad, as if driven by the devil himself.

Most important is not to fall down! I should watch for those shell holes! One of my feet keeps sinking into one pit or another, but I'm experienced with this danger and am now concentrating as never before. What if something blocks the road ahead and the horses will leap over it? Will I make it as well? My body is like a steel spring, I think I can jump over anything.

We run, skip and gallop, but the embankment is still under our feet. At last! The sound of the bridge planking! We're about to hit the right bank! Well, my beauties, one more gallop! Will we make it? 'Moiseev!' I scream. 'Grab the reigns!' We should also take care not to ride straight into enemy lines! We must turn to the left or to the right, as soon as the bridge ends. Moiseev takes the reigns and almost falling off, pulls the left one as hard as he can. Somehow, we manage to turn from the road towards the bank.

Without stopping, Gregory and I take our guns and knapsacks from the cart. Our fists let go of the ropes and we fall into thick grass, pressing ourselves against the cool earth for a few seconds. I can't help taking a look at how our boys are pushing through behind us. The whole road is thickly covered with plumes of smoke and flames coming from endless explosions. Along it one can see black pillars rising and falling from the swamp. The bog is moaning, banging, thumping, plopping. The great medley of cars, men, horses, and cannon rolls ahead. This mass flows onto our right bank, splitting to the left and to the right, dissolving into the grass, the corn, and the wheat.

Not having the time to say goodbye to each other, or to Moiseev, or indeed, to the dear horses that saved our lives (the cart raced away further along the bank), Gregory and I run in different directions to take our places. I see Guards Major Ivan Tukhru: he seems to be under a spell, neither a bullet nor a shell can get him! Captain Nikolai Kartoshenko, our battalion commander, also manages to break through with his staff!

I am happy to see anyone who, after going up the road of death, appears on this bank. I am bewildered: 'How did they survive?' My own successful crossing had struck me as something so unique and miraculous!

There, Allah be praised, is Yanson! Bending low under the mortar barrel, our 'Academician' rushes ahead, with someone carrying the gun carriage right behind him. There's Sergei Lopunov with the base-plate. Vasili Shamrai! Nikolai Kobylin! And with their Maxims! They sneak through and are now ready to open machine-gun fire. There's a nurse I know! Isn't that Tonia? There's Ania and Galia! Even the girls made it! Our signaller Vladimir Semionov is already unwinding his coil. But I don't see many other people. Guards Captain Vladimir Yegorov, our regimental commissar is also alive: not even a scratch! He is also a 'Stalingrad' man. And it was a great joy to see our gunners

Leonid Nochovny and Ivan Yemelianov turn their 76mm cannon, preparing their first shot. But where are our other guns? The bridge has now collapsed, but our troops continue their movement along a new embankment made of upturned cars, cannon, carts, horses, men . . .

In half an hour there came a signal to attack. Our loud 'hurra-a-a-h!' rolled from one flank to the other, and our regiment began the onslaught to build up a bridgehead on the right bank of the Vorskla! Our Guards corps energetically continued its advance. We forded the Vorskla once more, at the place where Peter I crossed it with his troops during the Great Northern War, and passed the granite cross, erected in memory of the victory of the Russians over the Swedes at the Battle of Poltava in 1709. We entered that town on 23 September.

Women and old people greeted us. They were all emaciated: just skin and bones. But they were happy. Our men found a ruined mill with flour, ready to be evacuated to Germany, and used their mess tins to distribute it among the inhabitants. In an hour they treated us liberators with *galushki*. [traditional Ukrainian boiled flour rolls – editor's note.]

CHAPTER ELEVEN

How Long Will This War Last?

Left-bank Ukraine [the Ukrainian lands that lie on the east bank of the River Dnieper – editor's note]. Even though we tried hard to press the Germans westward as fast as we could, they still had an opportunity to burn down many towns, villages and farms. Ashes, coals, smoke, everywhere. Only the ovens stand in place of the houses. Charred trees. Total destruction. The Ukrainian people will have to make a gigantic effort to revive this land. The war has left only ashes behind it.

We entered Kremenchug on 29 September 1943. We liberated a POW camp, where the Germans tortured and executed several thousand Soviet soldiers. Captured partisans were also kept here. The Nazis invented the most savage methods to torment their prisoners. For example, the gallows here was quite unusual: the Germans used metal hooks to hang people by a rib, a leg, an arm, the jaw. Vlasov's men were the executioners. Around 100 victims were suspended in this way. We managed to take down about a dozen of them alive.

I later saw with my own eyes a scene which I will never forget. Peasant women, armed with axes, pitchforks, pokers, sticks, were leading several Germans and traitors down the street. The women were terribly excited, screaming loud in Ukrainian. Then they stopped near a pit and started pushing their prisoners into it. One Nazi, trying to resist, shrieked: 'Mein in Haus drei Kinder!' But the women responded: 'And what about us? We have puppies, you think? Throw him down there!' There was not a force in the world that would make me stop this just punishment of the Nazi butchers.

In Kremenchug the Germans mined anything that could attract attention. In one instance, the *partorg* of the neighbouring battalion picked up a *balalaika* from the ground: the explosion killed him and seventeen others who were standing around him. In a side street I saw a new bicycle placed against a wicker fence. I always had a boyish desire to have a good bicycle ride, which had never been quite satisfied, so I headed straight for it. I quicken my pace, but then I see a senior lieutenant heading in the same direction, trying to beat me to it. I feel disappointed, but nevertheless assume a disinterested air. Well, I don't really need it. I make a U-turn and walk back to the street. Suddenly I hear an explosion! I turn round: there is nothing left of the officer or of the bike, just a large hole where the wicker fence was.

The inhabitants of Kremenchug, leaving their hiding places, were hurrying back to their town, to their houses, and everywhere around we could hear mines going off in one place or another. Children, women, soldiers, all were blasted to bits . . .

'Right-bank Ukraine is Expecting us!' 'Give us the Dnieper!' 'Forward Beyond the Dnieper!' Everywhere we see such slogans. In every newspaper and leaflet we read these calls of our Motherland. And now we stand on the bank of the enormous river! Eleven hundred metres wide [just over 1,000 yards – editor's note]. How will we cross it? We'll use sheaves of straw: little by little, swimming across the Dnieper! It'll take us three hours of bobbing, until we reach the other bank. Under fire? Well, Mansur, will you tempt fate once more? Eh? That's fine, if you haven't wasted all your good luck. But what if there's none left? How many times did you come face to face with death? Is there still gold left in the treasury of your destiny?

On the night of 5 October 1943, near the Village Vlasovka, not far upstream from Kremenchug, our 32nd Guards Rifle Corps, including my 66th Guards Division, began a crossing with the object of landing on the island of Peschanny. The island's code name was 'Helmet.' It is quite big – 5 square kilometres – absolutely flat, and practically the same level as the surface of the water. Not a blade of grass. Not a bush. Fine grey sand . . .

The day before, when I was looking at that sand from the left bank, I remembered, for some reason, the time when I walked into a small stone church in Kremenchug. The Nazis had tried to destroy it several times. They made an attempt to blow it up and to set fire to it. Inside, everything made of wood was burned, but the building stood intact. In the churchyard I met an old man: 'Who are you, father?' 'I'm a priest.' We sat down and had a chat. I already mentioned that I'm very curious and like talking to different people. The priest was not wearing a vestment but an old quilted sweater and did not look at all like a clergyman. But what should we talk about? As a kid I heard that the Bible tells us what is going to happen in the world, and that everything that was and will be, is foretold in the Scripture. It's just a question of understanding the words: 'If everything is foretold in the Bible,' I begin, 'then this war must surely be mentioned, right?' 'Yes, yes, my son.' I was surprised that he did not try to puzzle me with theological talk, so I laid before him the question that interested me most: 'How long will this war last?' I was sure that instead of answering he would shrug his shoulders. He thought for a moment, as if counting or remembering, and responded: 'Around forty-eight months.' Where did the priest get this figure from? Definitely not from the Bible, I realized that. Most probably it was simply his intuition. Now, sitting on the left bank of the Dnieper and thinking about these 'forty-eight months' I calculated that if the figure was correct, this must be the middle of the war!

For five days, from 29 September to 4 October, our division had been preparing a forced crossing of the Dnieper. Every riflemen was supposed to make for himself a special device to keep him afloat: sheaves of straw were placed into a waterproof and sewed up with string. It looked like a large pillow. We tested it in water and saw that one really could hold onto it and not drown. Some men also sewed up their knapsacks and tried them in the water. I was always a very experienced swimmer. I grew up in the Cheliabinsk Region, on the bank of the River Miass. There were also lots of lakes around. I bathed in them all and on a bet would swim very far, or would compete with other boys. But I too needed a float, because we were supposed to cross with full combat equipment.

On the night of 5 October 1943, near the Village Vlasovka, we began crossing the Dnieper, our objective being the 'neutral' Island Peschanny. On my feet I'm wearing close-fitting canvas boots. When wet they become especially tight. I also have my SMG, two cartridge-drums, two grenades and a TT pistol. My knapsack will serve as a float. I filled it with fresh, dry straw, carefully sewed it up and greased it with a piece of American fat.

This island divides the Dnieper in two. Our left channel, is 700m [some 765 yards – editor's note] wide, and the right one, from the German side, is 300-400, and is not only narrower but also shallower.

The Nazis crossed it easily and prepared to meet us, making well-protected trenches disguised with sand-coloured camouflage. But we did not know that at the time . . .

Taking into account the speed of the current, all our units quietly went into the water upstream from the island. The enemy was silent. I was among the last to cross. I saw all my battalion comrades begin their crossing. When I was left practically alone on the bank, I also walked into the cold water of the Dnieper. It was black. The night was pitch dark. Not a star in the sky. Ideal weather for us.

I begin to swim. It's difficult, but I can manage. Seven hundred metres and another 400 drifting downstream. It's all right, I'll make it. I swim on. I calculate that I have covered more than half the distance. At that moment, the sky burst and I heard the familiar sounds of bombs and shells coming from the right bank. Now the surface of the river is a medley of things: splinters, flinders, rags, boards, sticks. Straw, like duckweed, is everywhere around, coming from the floats ripped open by explosions. The water keeps tossing me back and forth, like I'm in a heavy gale. It's the shell blasts sending waves in every direction. A pillar of water rockets me upwards: then I fall, go under, and my eardrums are suddenly pierced by the sound of a dozen explosions. There's no escape either on the surface, or beneath it! I remembered how I used to fish with dynamite. Now I, myself, am like one of those unfortunate fish.

I try to move my hands and feet faster and faster, so as to reach the island, but the waves whirl me to and fro. Suddenly I see myself swimming back to the left bank, but terrified by it, I again turn to the right. I am less afraid of the island, though I still don't know that the Fritzes are there. I feel, somehow, attracted to the right bank, even though hundreds of enemy guns are shooting from that direction. I dread drowning men that might get hold of me. A drowning man is like an octopus, ambushing its victim, and in no way can you free yourself from his embrace. That's really horrible! I swim alone amidst the raving chaos.

I see one soldier whose head often sinks beneath the surface and who's gasping for breath. It seems he desperately tries to go on but is out of strength. How can I help the poor man? I carefully swim up to him and touch his arm with my float. His hands tightly clasp the knapsack, while I begin to support him a little from the back. He is moaning and breathing heavily. Unblinking eyes gaze around, as if he sees the world for the first time. What a horrible expression that was!

He seemed to recover his breath and to begin to understand what was going on. I swim next to him, slightly pushing him forward. Very slowly he tells me: 'Thanks, friend!' I felt relieved that he is no longer dangerous and put one of my hands on the knapsack. I'm swimming on my back.

My new acquaintance weakened his grip and began holding the float with his left hand, while rowing with the right. How strangely and beautifully man is made! Even in this hell one can experience moments of pure joy. I'm so glad that I found a new friend and that I saved his life. We move on, looking happily at each other.

At last we feel the bottom beneath our feet. It is flat. Flashes of explosions light the figures of our soldiers, running from the bank towards the centre of the island. A blast! Another blast! A cloud of sand engulfs me. Chunks of something warm and wet fall from the sky with the sand: these are bits of human bodies.

My new friend rushes along by my side and screams to those running or lying on the ground: 'Where's the 13th ? Where's the 13th?' While we were crossing the Dnieper, all the regiments and divisions got mixed up, so no one can find his unit. 'Where are my men? Where's the CO?' I keep asking myself. Out of nowhere there pops a stupid answer: 'Look in the sand! Look in the sand!' Everywhere around in the sand I see soldiers. Are they dead or alive? I see only their raised heads, like water melons in a garden.

I'm covered with sand. It's also in my mouth. It grazes my face like emery. It beats and lashes, trying to bury me underneath. The blasts of air cut me down. I twist and turn, sinking into the damp sand like a crab. A mixture of sand, water and silt envelops my broken, exhausted body. I simply want to lie without moving. But if I'm wounded, I won't be able to get out. I was so sucked in that I barely managed crawl out! My comrade from the 13th Guards Division was looking for his men, but unable to find them, he fell by my side and shouted in my ear: 'My name is Alex, Alex Kolesnikov. Let's stick together. OK? If anything happens, we'll help each other out. Agreed?' 'Agreed!' I yell.

The Nazis are battering hell out of the island. The fire never ceases. What can we do? Our sub-machine guns won't work: every hole is clogged with sand. Same with grenades. I can see Maxim barrels half-buried in the sand. Only the entrenching shovels glitter, the single weapon we have that can't be damaged by sand. But where is the enemy we are supposed to fight? The German artillery on the other bank of the Dnieper? The bank from which we are divided by a second channel! Alex and I decided to move further towards the centre of the island, in the direction of the right bank of the Dnieper. It's quieter there, no blasts: the 'dead zone'.

We run forward, jumping over people, stranded like seals. Stop! There's no one else ahead. But what's that ? We meet with machine-gun fire! We can see the flaming-red tongues coming from the barrels! The Nazis are on the island? This is why there are no explosions in front: the enemy gunners are shooting over the heads of their infantry! That's it! The Germans are on the island! We should really stay alert but we're deafened by blasts. We should be on the lookout for trouble but the damned sand blinds us. It's bad. Very bad.

Daybreak. The fire is even more intense. From the high right bank the enemy can see both our men and their own units against the light background of the sand. They shoot unmolested. There's not a single plane in the sky. Where is our airforce? And our guns are silent on the left bank! I have the impression that we are left to the mercy of Fate.

But no one leaves the island. Hiding in the sand, our men wait for their hour to act. One soldier, with a typical Cossack face, is crouching on all fours. His walrus moustache is hanging down to his chin. He keeps wagging his head, trying to shake off his deafness. The bursts dance around, while he, rocking in every direction, butts the air. I hadn't the nerve to keep on looking at him. But when I glanced again several minutes later, I saw only his shoe heels sticking out of the sand.

Nazi shells keep raining again and again, but some of us are still alive. Enemy guns pause for about five minutes, then continue their barrage. Twenty minutes of battering and then again a five-minute break. In my head I roll once more, the 'film' of my war experience: the Vorskla crossing, Chervonny Prapor, Dragunsk, Prokhorovka. No, none of those scenes were as bad as this! I thought I had left behind me the most horrifying engagements: at Stalingrad, Kletskaia, Kalach-on-Don, the Kursk Salient. But this! The Dnieper island! An island-grave! It was so fearsome, senseless and over-whelmingly hopeless that this battle eclipsed everything else from the Volga to the Dnieper. We were unarmed, deafened, half-blinded, shell-shocked, isolated from each other! We had no choice but to die in this hail of enemy fire! These were my thoughts and I could not, however I tried, force them away: someone had made an irreparable strategic mistake.

By nightfall, the Nazis stopped firing. Alex and I began looking for our comrades once more. We were joined by other soldiers who were still able to move. They hoped to find their battalions or regiments. As for the divisional staff, they had remained behind on the left bank of the Dnieper. Some boys still had a little bread and shared it with us. But what next?

Hoping to be evacuated to the left bank, lots of wounded soldiers crawled up to the water. If someone could inform our command about them! Alex proposed that I should swim back and find our HQ. He's right but I'm afraid. They might think that I'm a coward and that I deliberately escaped from the island, using the wounded as an excuse. They could even accuse me of being a panic-monger. So I came up with an alternative plan, which to me, at least, seemed less frightening. I told Alex and his eyes sparkled when he heard what I had in mind.

The plan was as follows. We should give up looking for 'our' men – everyone here is a fellow-soldier – and form a 500-strong assault group. Then, at sunrise, we should attack the Nazi positions on the opposite bank of the island. There, at least, we would be safe from artillery fire. But how could we attack without sub-machine guns, without grenades? Our sub-machine guns will be the blinding sun, shining into the faces of the Germans! Our grenades will be the element of surprise and swiftness! We will fall on the heads of the Fritzes sitting in their trenches! We will trample them with our boots and tear them with our teeth! We'll grab their machine-guns and SMGs and put up an all-round defence! And there's food over there!

I explained my plan to many other soldiers. Some thought it unrealistic but everyone agreed to participate. Here, on the island, any kind of action was good: the only other option being death. And it's better to die fighting than lying on the wet sand.

We quickly rallied the men. More than 500! We quietly advanced as close as possible to the German lines and camouflaged ourselves, digging into the sand. The signal for the attack will be my group standing up.

It was still dark, only a little grey in the east. The Fritzes opened fire once more. At first they ploughed far behind us, where the wounded were lying, then moved to the centre of the island, to where we were. A powerful blow struck the back of my head: it must have been no less than a ton of sand! It knocked my face to the ground and I didn't even have time to shut my eyelids. I was crushed against the sand with my eyes open! My ears are ringing, my eyes stinging, it's dark and I feel myself lying under a gigantic press. My whole body makes an upward lurch, in order to throw it off. My head rises easily, and only then do I realize that there's nothing over me. But I can't hear or see a thing. Blinded, I dig a small hole before my face. Some water gathers. Grabbing handfuls of liquid mixed with silt and sand, I try to rinse my open eyes. I simply have to see! I wipe my raw and stinging eyes with this slush and eventually see a dull, bloody, gleam of light. At first it is dark red but then becomes brighter and brighter.

Alex digs up some sand and scooping some relatively clear water, helps me rinse my eyes. I try to blink. It hurts! I do it again and again. I seem to be getting better. The dead silence exists only for me. Shells still go off everywhere around: but I barely see them, and cannot hear them. Every time we need to duck, Alex pushes my head into the sand. When the danger passes, he lifts me up again, taking me by the collar. Oh Alex, Alex, what would I do without you? Help me out, my friend! I can't hear a sound. I follow the movements of other soldiers: they press their heads against the ground and I do the same. 'I'm finished, finished,' I keep thinking, 'that's it. The end.'

I look to the east and see the sun rising over the horizon. Alex sticks out his thumb right under my nose, then his two fingers 'run' over the sand: time to attack. I nod approvingly.

I rise, happy to find that my legs can still carry me! We stand up, some ten or fifteen of us at the same time, just as planned. We barely make the first three steps when an avalanche of men emerge from the sand right after us: a black tidal wave consisting of 500 desperadoes that dashed towards the Nazi trenches. I see gaping mouths scream. I also cry out, even though I can't hear myself. Maybe I've lost my voice. My throat smarts.

Slipping in the sand, I run towards the panic-stricken Germans. No wonder they're terrified: we appeared out of nowhere, from under the sand, and now threaten to crush them. Some reload their sub-machine guns hastily, but the majority are completely stupefied. It seems that our very appearance has made them shudder. It is strange, but I myself feel frightened, realizing that I am the cause of this horror. It's hard to explain. I see a man staring at us, paralysed with horror, this horror affects me and grows stronger, doubled by a return glance. Unable to snap this eye contact, I run faster and faster, in order to put an end to this unbearably growing feeling. Kill him!

I will be forever repeating: 'Accursed war!' Many of those running next to me fall to the ground. But the sun-blinded Germans can't aim properly. I see a Fritz who is trying to escape, climbing up the far side of the trench. An officer is yelling at him, his mouth wide open. He fires his pistol and the lifeless form of the soldier falls back. But he can't shoot them all: other Nazis have already crawled out and keep running away. We jump down on the shoulders of the most desperate or simply horror-struck Germans. Trample and crush them with our heels and fingers, taking away their SMGs.

There's one of our boys sitting on the shoulders of a Fritz, riding on him back and forth. I use my jammed gun as a club. Finally, I rip an SMG off a dead Nazi and am ready to face the devil himself. I begin firing at the running Germans. We all grab guns from the Fritzes and clear a small area for ourselves. Like a pack of mad dogs, the Germans throw themselves at us from the right and the left flanks: but now we have grenades and machine-guns.

Finally the exhausted Nazis stop their onslaught. We throw the dead bodies out of the trenches and begin dressing each other's wounds. Alex brings me some clear water in his mess tin and I try to rinse my eyes again. I could see better but still couldn't hear a thing.

The boys are chewing and carefully listening to what's going on. We're keeping up an all-round defence. The only thing we're not afraid of is artillery fire. The Fritzes are on both sides of us, so German cannon will not be shelling us here. Alex sticks his thumb upwards: 'situation normal!' He looks into my ears and gestures: 'There's nothing there.' He casts a questioning glance at me: 'I don't see why you can't hear?' But I feel as if wooden corks are clogging my ears.

For five full days we defended these trenches, while eating all the German supplies we could find. Then, on the morning of 12 October, I saw something strange happening to the boys. They turned their heads around, poking them out of the trench in curiosity. Alex signalled to me: 'It's quiet. There's no bombardment!' The minute he made his gesture, my deafness disappeared. It seemed that my ears desperately wanted to hear this silence!

There's no enemy movement on our flanks. Alex, myself, and several other men crept out and carefully examined the space around our positions. The Nazi trenches are empty! Maybe it's some ruse? Maybe the Germans left so that their artillery could shell us here? We tried to stay close to our lines, in order to take immediate cover if something goes wrong. Across the island I saw other groups of our soldiers. Their heads were popping up here and there, turning inquisitively, as if the men were asking: 'What's going on? Why aren't the Germans opening fire?'

The island looked like a lunar landscape, being everywhere cratered with shell holes. Inside these craters, thick bloody liquid and corpses, corpses, corpses. Yes, Nazi guns did a good job here, Goddamn them! The putrid smell of decomposing bodies makes us sick. Do they still need us here? No, it seems. Small groups of survivors hurry on to the bank of the Dnieper. Farewell, island-grave!

We were not given any specific orders to leave the island, but together with Alex I also went into the water and swam in the direction of our right bank. The river was quiet. No one was firing. Silence everywhere. When we reached the other side, we took off our clothes, carefully washed them in the Dnieper, and then slowly wrung them out. Then we started a fire and dried ourselves. No one spoke. It was as if we were meeting after a funeral. There is no honour or glory for us in this mess: we were not ordered to leave the island.

'Let's go. We must find our command and report.' We walked in single file, some fifteen or twenty men. Then we saw some of our soldiers crowding around a field kitchen: well-cooked wheat porridge with sunflower oil! We were treated to some. It smelled wonderful and we gobbled it with relish. I can't believe it: 'How did I manage to stay alive?' If I survive this war, I will write about this island-grave. Well, no, not a grave – an island of death.

The HQ of my 193rd Regiment turned out to be the closest. The first man I met there was Captain Bondarenko, chief of staff. 'Was there an order to evacuate the island?' Bondarenko consoled me: 'The order was given as early as 10 October.' I saw other survivors enter the HQ and each of them began with the same burning question: 'Was there an order?' Bondarenko tried to comfort everyone: 'The order to evacuate was given on 10 October.' Only now could my comrades relax and allow themselves to experience their great relief.

A little later, our boys were approached by war correspondents in officers' uniforms. 'Tell us about it . . .' But we had no strength to speak. I informed some of the soldiers of what Bondarenko told me. Since we were really ordered to leave the island, each one of us now wanted to find his division, regiment, battalion and company as quickly as possible: 'Otherwise, we would have had to swim back!' we thought.

Some thirty years later I learned that our corps successfully carried out an order to stage a 'false crossing'. While the enemy guns were busy firing at us, other troops managed to cross the Dnieper safely both upstream and downstream. Sixty kilometres downstream from Kremenchug, near the villages of Deriyevka and Kutsevolovka, our engineers succeeded in constructing a pontoon bridge and more survivors crossed over from our island. They approached their comrades and anxiously asked: 'Was there an order?' Only after receiving a positive answer did the guardsmen go and find some wheat porridge.

These are some of my regimental comrades who survived the operation: machine-gunner Vasili Shamrai (he managed not to lose his Maxim even in this mess); two other machine-gunners, one, a brave man called Timonin, I knew personally; mortar man Aleksei Yanson, our 'Academician'; scouts Kim Dobkin and Gregory Ambartsumiants; and our regimental commissar Vladimir Yegorov. He was the last to leave the island. He always acted this way: in an attack, he was the first, in a retreat, he was the last. I have named only those I was acquainted with. Our battalion commanders Nikolai Kartoshenko and Feodor Gridasov also survived by some miracle.

But an even greater wonder is what happened to the 145th Guards Regiment of our 66th Division. Guards Lieutenant-Colonel Aleksei Dmitriyev, commander of the regiment, succeeded in forming a group from his surviving men, fording the right channel, and digging in on the enemy bank. Dmitriyev's guardsmen were aided by an underground Komsomol group called 'Tocsin', headed by Vasili Us. These partisans operated in the region of the villages Beletskovka and Malamovka. For his heroism Lieutenant-Colonel Dmitriyev was awarded the rank of Hero of the Soviet Union.

CHAPTER TWELVE

My Last Shot

I have been the battalion *komsorg* for four months already. How many attacks! And I'm still alive. Some might say that I am too lucky! After the war I never won any lottery, except only one rouble once, but on the battlefield neither a bullet nor a bayonet could get me. Am I really a fortunate man? I think I am.

The true feelings of a soldier fighting in the Great Patriotic War [official name of the USSR's war with Nazi Germany and its allies in Soviet historiography – editor's note] is an interesting thing to look at. If any of us veterans begin speaking really frankly, some of the things we confess might seem naive, even silly. For my part, I was seriously afraid that if I died, our Motherland would perish as well. When, on 28 November 1943, after we had crossed the Dnieper, I was hit near Znamenka, I became really terrified: 'How will things go on without me? Who will go on fighting, if I'm seriously wounded?' Of course it was naive. But it was this childish fear that I could not get rid off for some time to come. And only later, when our boys liberated our country without me, when they entered Berlin, I laughed at myself for being so presumptuous. Nevertheless, even now I believe it was the right way of thinking. Each man had to hold himself responsible for the fate of his country. Only in this way could we have won our decisive victory.

After the 'Island of Death' operation, around 20 October 1943, our 66th Guards Division (which consisted of not more than two companies) crossed the pontoon bridge over the Dnieper without any incidents, near the villages of Kutsevolovka and Deriyevka. On the right bank our troops had already built up an enormous bridgehead in order to continue their Ukrainian offensive.

As we moved on in the direction of Kirovograd, we entered the large village of Deriyevka, which had escaped destruction. Its inhabitants were just returning from the woods and cornfields, where they had been hiding from Nazi punitive units. That same day some local volunteers joined our regiment. Our recruits were dressed in civilian clothes, so at that time, having a great shortage of uniforms, we looked like a large partisan detachment. In jest we nicknamed our greenhorns 'corn men'. Being treated with *galushki* and *varenniki* [a sort of ravioli with different fillings – editor's note] by the locals, our columns marched on.

Another village which we entered without a fight was Kutsevolovka, where we were met by partisans from the 'Tocsin' group. These men prevented the Nazis from looting the village and sending its inhabitants to do forced labour in Germany. They, as well as certain peasants, also joined our regiment. The partisans got some information that the enemy was preparing to ambush us as we would approach the next hamlet, called Dacha. Naturally, they showed us how to bypass the German positions: so the Nazis retreated to their reserve line, the Village Uspenskoye, which we had to storm.

Our guns and planes pounded the enemy for an hour and seemed to clear the way for our attack. But the Fritzes, firmly established in their second defensive line, met us with a hurricane of fire. Our tanks were burned by thermite shells or exploded on anti-tank mines. Then the Germans counter-attacked. In one sector, near Znamenka, we had to dislodge the enemy from the same positions twice in a single day!

When our first onslaught had succeeded, we found in one of the trenches a very young Fritz. Almost a boy, red-haired, and wearing enormously thick glasses (probably due to myopia, as it was no less than minus six). He was sitting with a sadly lowered head. He had thin arms and delicate fingers. Our lads, seeing this tiny Fritz, felt pity and gave him some bread and a piece of lard. The boy guzzled this and kept mumbling something in German. I could catch only one word I understood: 'Musik . . . ich bin Musik . . .' And with his delicate fingers he began playing an imaginary violin. So he was a violinist, a musician . . .

Meanwhile, the enemy counter-attacked. Even though we fired a hail of bullets at them from our automatic weapons, eventually we had to retreat to our former positions. But we completely forgot about our new prisoner!

One can imagine our surprise when, retaking the trenches, we saw the little Fritz sitting in the same place! We said: 'Guten Morgen!' 'Guten Tag!' he answered. And mutters: 'Hitler Kaputt! Stalin gut! Russ Kamerad gut!' This time the little Fritz looked happy and was very active. Making rapid gestures with his hands, he kept on insisting: 'Mein kommen Russ general . . . Schnell, schnell . . . Mein kommen Russ general!' So he wants to speak to our chief! We hurriedly sent him to our HQ. In the evening seven brand new T-34s drove up to our engagement line, and once again we saw our little Fritz, sitting on the leading machine. The tank men did not have the chance to chat with us, and our prisoner only waved from a distance. When it got dark our armour drove off into the enemy rear.

All night long we carefully listened and waited. Finally, at daybreak we heard the noise of moving tracks and soon saw all our seven tanks, safe and sound, swarming with strange-looking German soldiers. They had no weapons in their hands but cases with musical instruments. When I came close up to our T-34s, I shrank back from a sickening sight: between the tracks, mixed with mud and bits of telephone line, one could see human hair, cockades with swastikas, shoulder straps.

The German soldiers, some eight or ten men jumping from each tank, started playing our Katiusha on their mouth organs. What an amazing spectacle! Now, I'm not writing a book of fiction, where I can invent things: I'm simply trying to describe accurately what I saw at the front with my own eyes. One has to remember that my outlook was limited – 'a view from a trench' – and I can only guess that it was a military band, which the Nazis, in the days of heavy fighting, ordered to go into action and defend their positions.

On 7 November the enemy decided to 'congratulate' us on the occasion of the 26th Anniversary of the October Revolution. At six in the morning our front line suddenly found itself under a torrent of mortar and artillery shells, as well as aviation bombs. Black pillars of steppe soil rocketed up into the sky, which new explosions kept suspended in the air. It seemed that night had swiftly returned. For two hours black and fiery monsters continued their deadly, diabolical dance over our heads. I was choking with acrid smoke, my deafened ears were bleeding and the blasts made my lungs vibrate inside my chest like two birds in a wire cage. In the dark I saw red bursts of fire rising from the shell holes.

When the German artillery ceased firing and their planes finally left, it felt as if an earthquake had ended. I peeped out of my hole and saw a lunar landscape: fuming craters everywhere. At first I was terrified by the thought that I might be the only one left alive. Then I began to feel envy for the dead. A minute later however, I saw some of my comrades moving about. I was ready to kiss each one of them, as if they were my close, dear relations. But there was no time for embraces. The Fritzes began their assault, ordering some Romanians, Hungarians, Bulgarians and Yugoslavs to advance before their own men. Once again, we opened fire from all our automatic weapons and rifles. The first rows of the attackers lay down and began creeping backwards. There were two more assaults before night came, but we held on. Most of our infantrymen perished that day, not even getting a chance to make a single shot from their rifles. But those who survived took their revenge: through my periscope I saw No Man's Land dotted with numerous enemy corpses.

The town of Znamenka was some 20km away [almost 12½ miles – editor's note] and the Nazis did everything in their power to slow down our offensive. Our attacks were repelled one after another. We had very heavy losses, but we still couldn't approach the town of Znamenka. Among the casualties in our battalion were several company commanders. Each new day I, as a *komsorg*, had to take their place, while an officer was dispatched to us from the regimental reserve.

The war brutally and mercilessly devoured people. If, from mid-October till early November 1943, recruits from the Poltava region prevailed in our division, by late November there were only a handful of these 'corn men' left in our units. Each company had only fifteen to twenty men instead of the standard 100–120. Reinforcements came almost every night but by noon the next day every unit was under-manned again. In this situation, you really begin to feel that you are the only one alive ...

It may seem strange, but on 28 November 1943, I knew this would be the day I'd get wounded. Early in the morning I began preparing myself. I picked up a knapsack, lost by some Nazi soldier, and took from it ('I'll need it in the hospital!') a razor kit packed in a small, fine-looking plastic box, a thick batch of writing paper, and a 'life-time' pen which, when turned upside down, revealed the figure of a naked woman.

We attacked twice but were both times thrown back. While I was running in short bursts, I was caught under machine-gun fire. The gun emplacement was so close that I could catch a glimpse of the malicious face of the Fritz. I fell down, feeling that my left heel had received some kind of a strong blow, after which it instantly became numb. 'Wounded! I should climb down this shell hole and wait.' I took off my boot. It's back was torn to pieces but my heel was all right! I put the boot back on and rushed out to catch up with my comrades! By midday only about seven men armed with rifles and SMGs remained in each company. The Nazis noticed how few we were and decided to counter-attack. But only after some artillery bombardment. They aimed well. I saw with my own eyes how an explosion tore the breastwork off our battalion command point. I was sure that Guards Captain Nikolai Kartoshenko, our CO, was killed by the blast and rushed towards the place. I was happy to see him alive but he couldn't hear a thing because of shell-shock.

From the elevation of the CP one obviously has a much better view of our position than from inside a trench. The captain continues to yell to the signaller, who shouts into the phone and then listens to the orders from the regimental staff, while I get a chance to observe the battlefield. Suddenly I notice a group of Nazi soldiers with sub-machine guns, who, covered by their artillery, advance in short rushes towards our trenches, clearly intending to surprise us with their attack as soon as the bombardment ends. Meanwhile, our boys, threatened by the hurricane of fire, cannot even stick their noses out and spot the enemy. I drew the CO's attention to the German unit and rushed along the trenches to warn our men.

We opened fire at the enemy and threw some grenades. The Nazis were forced to fling themselves to the ground. I sent a message to the battalion commander that we need fresh ammunition immediately, because we're running out of cartridges and grenades. The signaller told me on the phone that reinforcements and ammunition were already on their way to us, but we must hold on for another twenty or thirty minutes. On that day everyone in the regimental staff was mobilized to help us out: each person from the HQ was ordered to carry boxes of cartridges and grenades.

Twenty or thirty minutes? So long! It seems it was the first time in my life that I wished an enemy artillery preparation to go on.

The Nazi infantrymen moved forward a little. Now they were on the very edge of the area bombarded by their guns. We had run out of bullets. My eyes searched for at least one cartridge, to cut down an officer who emerged from a shell hole, waving on his soldiers, urging them forwards. Behind the trench I saw a rifle with an open breech mechanism and with a cartridge in the magazine. I was ready to jump out but then I noticed Lieutenant Ivan Yakovlev creeping towards the gun. He would definitely get there first. I turned away and saw the German officer in the next shell hole, even closer to us. If I only had something to shoot! Once more I cast a glance in the direction of the rifle: the lieutenant lay dead. I darted out of the trench, grabbed the gun and rolled back under cover. Now that I was armed, I popped out again. The officer continued to wave his men forward. I aimed and fired. His figure suddenly sank and disappeared in the shell hole, while his soldiers changed their minds and decided to stay put.

It turned out that there was one more cartridge in the rifle: 'This is surely my last one.' Another German, his back turned towards me, is looming in the corn ahead. He is bending on one knee, shaking his head, and gesticulating nervously. He is surely no rank and file. For such a man I won't spare even my last bullet. I adjust my sight and fire. The black figure of the Nazi staggered and fell prostrate to the ground, crushing the dry corn stalks.

I was not aware that this would be my last shot in the war. I was not aware that for me, a mortar man, my battles on four different fronts of the Great Patriotic War would fit between two shots – the first, near Kletskaia on 6 November 1942, and the last, near Znamenka, on 28 November 1943 – fired not from a mortar, but from an autoloading SVT.

The bombardment will end any moment now and the Germans will dash towards our trenches. To sit here unarmed is suicide. Where is the reinforcement? Here it comes. I see our staff clerk, Sergeant Major Nosov, running in my direction with a box on his shoulder! Nosov always accompanied Commissar Yegorov. A regular officer, he could, if needed, easily handle a machine- or anti-tank gun. He had a great knowledge of different military equipment. Apart from that, the Sergeant Major had a master's degree in law and had held posts in the Communist Party. He was really great at paperwork! It was Nosov whom the commissar had charged with explaining the duties of a *komsorg* to me some four months ago. Right on time! I wave to him but he does not notice me. I jump out and dash towards him through the open, hoping to get some ammunition for myself. At that instant a deafening burst thunders behind me. I can feel myself lifted from the ground and thrown to one side, while my left leg flies in a different direction! I assume that my leg must have been torn off at the very top, near the crotch, together with one of my buttocks. As I was falling down several separate thoughts flashed through my mind: 'You can't even use a tourniquet. Not a bit of your leg left. You'll bleed to death and that's it. Even my entrails won't hold. I'd be better off dead. Oh, Mansur, Mansur, you can't even be wounded the right way!' As I crashed down, I immediately felt for my leg! It's there! My hip is slippery, covered with blood, but it's there! What the hell, why can't I move my leg?

It turned out that a shell splinter had cut my left sciatic nerve. I learned this much later, when I got to a hospital. People have these sciatic nerves, and if they're injured, then your leg just hangs there like a rag.

But at present I'm lying on the ground near a giant fuming shell hole, big enough to hide an entire field kitchen. Only one thought bothers me at the moment: if this enemy attack succeeds, I may find myself in the German rear. And so I began crawling, dragging the dead leg, my left boot full of blood. It was heavy. I could not help remembering the soldier near Stalingrad, who cut off his own leg, as if it was some unnecessary load. But now I'm not so much in pain as terrified that I may be captured by the Germans.

I was fortunate enough to see my friend, Lieutenant Aleksei Tarasov running past me, both his legs apparently in good shape. I cried out to him, and he fell flat beside me. A shell splinter hit his left hand. 'Yes? Where? Your leg? Get up. Three legs will be enough for the two of us! We must get out of here fast while we're still alive!' So we ran onwards together, blasts still thundering around us. I lost my left boot without even noticing when and where. My leg was absolutely numb. We finally reached the 'dead zone' and after a little rest, rushed on towards the road: 'Some automobile or cart will pick us there.'

My left trouser leg is sticky and soaked. I should try to stop the blood with a tourniquet but that's impossible because there is only my stomach above the buttock wound. If I don't get to a sanitary unit fast, I'll be terribly weakened by loss of blood. Here is the road. I lay down while Tarasov stood next to me. No one in sight. We almost lost hope.

The lieutenant tried to console me: 'Don't worry. I won't leave you.' At last we heard snorting horses and squeaking wheels. A loaded cart. It stopped and the sound of a familiar voice reached my ears: the driver turned out to be Moiseev, my friend from the Vorskla crossing.

He also recognized me and we embraced each other like close family. It seemed unbelievable that I chanced to meet this man again and that once again, a horse is saving my life. Moiseev unloaded his cart, threw some wheat straw into it, so that it formed something like a thick mattress, and together with Tarasov I lay on this 'bed', while our cart dashed towards the Dnieper.

When we reached the river it was already dark. The pontoon bridge was only for traffic going from the left bank to the right. The wounded were moved in the opposite direction in different boats. Here I said good bye to Moiseev and I never saw him again. Some lorries waited for us on the left bank, their floors covered with straw. The drivers were impatiently waiting to load and leave before sunrise, so as to get as far away from the Dnieper as possible. During the day the Nazis were bombing our rear.

Finally the lorry drove up to the road and rushed eastward. The road was in a terrible state, rutted and crated from shells, but we moved ahead at top speed. The driver tried to cover as many kilometres as he could, in an attempt to escape the bombings, the war. We jumbled like a pile of logs but we had to put up with it. We were no longer afraid of this wild jolting, we simply wanted to get to the sanitary battalion as quickly as possible. The driver made a short stop and checked how we were doing: 'Hold on, brothers! I know it's difficult in the back, but we have to cover some 150km [just over 93 miles – editor's note] before daybreak. You'll have to bear it. It's for your own safety.' And the lorry rushed ahead once more, rocking and zigzagging. We reached the sanitary battalion. Near an enormous tent one could see hundreds of wounded men, sitting or lying while waiting for an operation. We were placed on stretchers and put down on the ground. The driver said goodbye: now he had to load his vehicle with cartridges and shells and return to the Dnieper.

A nurse quickly examined me and ordered a few fat-faced orderlies to carry my stretcher to the operating table. Inside the tent, wounded men screamed so loud. The surgeon declared that there will be no anaesthetic. Everyone will have to go through some pain. The surgeon stands in his white coat, which is spattered with blood. There is blood on his cap, on his mask, and on his chest. His strong hands looked like those of a miner or a gunner. I am put facedown on a table and my hands and feet are quickly bound to it with bandages. The surgeon tries to comfort me by saying that the buttock on which he is going to operate, does not require much precision from the doctor. It can be cut without any danger to the patient's life whatsoever: 'It will hurt, but you'll survive. Just lie still and let me do my job! Understand?' I lay there thinking that the surgeon was right: what's so special about a buttock? Just a soft spot in the human body. Meanwhile I bury my head in a heap of cotton wool as deep as possible. If I scream, it will muffle the sound.

It seemed that the doctor was not cutting but tearing and chopping my body to pieces, trying to remove the splinter deep inside. I yelled very loud. I yelled until my voice became hoarse, as happened hundreds of times when we rushed to the attack. Then we screamed in order to overcome our own fear and to terrify the Fritzes. When you're shouting at the top of your lungs, you feel yourself braver and more frightening for the enemy. But now I was yelling in order to suppress the terrible pain in my body, which the surgeon was ripping apart with his knife. The doctor did nothing to stop my yelling. It was more important for him that I didn't jerk. My deafening roars were not a problem. At war people understand each other without words.

The burning pain became more even and general. I heard the clatter of the splinter as it fell into a basin. Then came the mosquito bites of a needle, and my wound was dressed with a broad bandage. This was no longer the surgeon. All the nerves of my tormented body felt the hands of a young girl, the kindly touch of a stranger's fingers. Only my imagination created a picture: a heavenly image of a blonde beauty. I could not see her because I was lying with my face down. I was put on a stretcher in the same position so I could not catch a glimpse of the girl, who had first touched my heart. In the morning we were again loaded on lorries and driven to a field hospital, situated in a local administrative centre: the Village Novye Sanzhary.

I don't remember the number of the hospital, in this village located between Poltava and Kremenchug, but I can still recall my first visit to a *bania*. It was organized with the help of the locals – old people, women and children. All the inhabitants who could work came to help complete this difficult and painstaking job of washing the wounded front line soldiers. All the men who arrived here were very dirty with dishevelled beards and hair. They were washed clean and received a haircut and a shave, so that each soldier now looked like a baby: tidy, well-cared for, and full-fed.

It is not actually a *bania*, but some kind of office or school. People keep bringing more and more water. Where from? From the Vorskla?

Those that are young and strong carry the buckets using shoulder-yokes: they move like a string of ants. In the yard, enormous fires warm the water in large kettles and iron barrels. It is then brought inside, where iron ovens heat the air. Everywhere in the room one can see tables, benches, and beds, covered with white sheets, the wounded soldiers lying stark naked on them.

There are women, old people, and young girls busying themselves near the men: they shamelessly soap the bodies with large pieces of bast and go on rubbing and rubbing. And the soldier just lies there in perfect bliss, even though his wound hurts, even though there is only a stump which remains of his leg. The soldier does not know what he should react to – the pain of his wound or the tickling touch of the bast and female hands. The women are in a hurry: washing, cleaning, soaping. They want to finish the work as soon as possible, but the soldiers keep asking with tears in their eyes to be soaped a little longer. Their bodies really miss the soap, the water, the *bania*. This is sheer happiness! Even if he lost a leg, the soldier is overjoyed, like a small kid.

The men are staring at the women around them. Some soldiers have not seen a female face for a couple of years! The women begin with soaping the heads of the wounded, so they would not be looking at them with those begging, eager eyes. But through the acrid, smelly suds the men are still admiring the female figures. The women again splash their faces with soapy water: 'Don't you look!' But the soldier jerks his head, throws off the suds and keeps on staring.

My dear women, how beautiful and sweet you seemed to us in that *bania* in Novye Sanzhary! There was not a single one among you that was not pretty! Everyone was good-looking! Every single one! You wore white hospital gowns. Through the thin, wet fabric, one could admire your beautiful bodies. I have never seen such beauty, neither before nor after. I can state with authority: the prettiest women lived – and live – in Novye Sanzhary! And you were covering our eyes with soap, so we wouldn't look!

I was lying on a bench facedown, so all I could see was bare feet. But I admired them all the same, my imagination completing what was out of sight. Here are the feet of a young woman. They look like they belong to a child. Here is another pair, already slightly affected by walking. This woman must be around thirty. But what is she like? Probably a very good person. Here's a girl of about my age. If I could only have a glance at her! But lying on my stomach I can't see her. All my life I'm so unlucky! I couldn't even be wounded the right way! All I can do is stare at the floor boards.

There is a soldier lying on his back not far from me. He feels great! He had a chance to have a good look at all the women and is now smiling, totally satisfied! Even the soap could not make him close his eyes. He says that he's not afraid of the suds, that soap doesn't affect him. For some reason only old women are around the soldier. The girls and young women ran away. They ran away with shrill and joyous laughs! The soldier is smiling from ear to ear. He's a handsome man under forty. One of his legs is gone and his arm is bandaged. But he's happy to be alive, happy that the women ran away from him. And the old ladies? The old ladies are happy to see that God really exists: He saved this strong man so he could have handsome and healthy children. 'Our dear fellow! Our fine, sweet soldier!' they keep mumbling, like a sort of a joyous prayer. The soldier does not worry that the girls went away: 'They're running now! But wait till my wounds heal! They'll be right back! I won't even have to call.' The soldier is smiling. Life goes on! I lie there and think . . .

They cleaned and washed me. Put on fresh underwear, shirt, underpants. Then I was carried to the hospital, to the officers' ward, because I was recently promoted junior lieutenant. After the *bania* I fell dead asleep, sinking into a sensation of bliss, which I never again experienced. I slept for twenty-four hours. Hunger awakened me. I ate and went to sleep again. For the first two weeks I only slept and did not even see any dreams. When I had enough sleep, I began practising walking on crutches. I also started visiting other wards and hospital buildings, hoping to find some of the boys from my regiment and battalion.

Our machine-gunner Vasili Shamrai was the first to spot me. He shouted gaily: '*komsorg!* Our *komsorg!* Look here, boys, that's our *komsorg!* By God, it's our *komsorg!*' He had pinned his three medals on his undershirt and was showing off, turning round in his bed. He looked emaciated but sounded very energetic. I visited my friend Vasili every day. He had lost a leg. Pointing at me, Shamrai used to say to his neighbours, speaking in Ukrainian: 'Ask our *komsorg* about the "Island of Death!" He'll tell you, if you don't believe me.'

Vasili was sad only about one thing: he regretted that there wasn't a writer who would describe what really happened on the 'Island of Death'. I could only console him by saying that someone after the war would surely write about our island, as well as about our other bloody battles.

Thirty-five years after Victory Day I will again meet Vasili Shamrai and he will ask me: 'Did anyone write about the "Island of Death?"' 'No, no one did.' I myself would wait for a long time, hoping that one of our comrades-in-arms would do it. I knew one mortar man from the battalion who could have written a book about all of us. His name was Edward Bartashevich and he came from Omsk. But he was killed. I also thought: if only some writer could be in my place! Such a wealth of material! I saw around me lots of amazing things both good and bad, I saw a lot of marvellous beauty. I lived through and experienced both the war and the mine. I tried everything. I loved and was loved! Impressions, which no one knows about except me, overwhelm my spirit. I would like to hand them over to a real writer, so he would tell our story. But working before and after the war at various mines, I never met any writer: someone I could have a private chat with and know that he is interested to learn about my past, beginning with that first shot near Kletskaia and ending with my hospitals, which were also an integral part of war.

My friend Vasili Shamrai, during our next meeting in Kremenchug in December 1981, asked me again: 'Has anyone written yet?' I understood what he meant. But I did not dare disclose my secret: I had begun to write a book about us guardsmen. I wasn't sure what the result would be. A cat with a little bell will not be able to catch even the stupidest mouse. I was afraid of premature 'ringing', afraid of scaring away my dream, putting a jinx on it. I had already waited too long. I was in a hurry. My memory was still strong. By the way, our memory is a strange thing. It's so choosy! I can remember every detail of some scene, recall the sounds, the smell, and most interesting of all, my thoughts at that precise moment. But I can't remember the name of the place! Or I mispronounce it. Or the date is wrong. Then you have to scrutinize a detailed map, or write to friends so they can remind you. Finally, you succeed in restoring everything, exactly when and where it happened. I managed that. But everything you describe, you relive once again: thus my heart began to ache anew. Will I have enough time to finish this book? Will Vasili Shamrai have enough time to read it? He also kept complaining about heart trouble: 'As if an awl is going right through it!'

I did not spent a lot of time in the field hospital at Novye Sanzhary. A month only. My sciatic nerve could not be revived, and my leg remained motionless. A train took me to a stationary hospital in Pavlovo-on-Oka.

Pavlovo-on-Oka was located deep in our hinterland. I was brought to a ward with seventeen beds. One of them was waiting for me. Its last occupant died in the course of a serious operation. Even though I had my superstitions, this time I told myself: 'Two shells do not hit the same spot one after another.' I was also sure that it was impossible to die of such a wound as I had. Well, not unless you try desperately!

My bed was standing in a corner. Next to me there was lying an Azerbaijanian named Yaroliyev, who was wounded in the knee. There were two men in the ward from my division, but I was not acquainted with them. Another fellow served in the 13th Division of our 32nd Corps. But he was hit before the 'Island of Death' operation, so he did not know my friend Alex Kolesnikov. I told the story of that island several times, after which my roommates would remain silent for some minutes.

We lived like a united family and helped each other in any way we could. We would help someone feed himself, fetch someone a bedpan, even teach someone to walk again. We spent a lot of time remembering things. And not only the war. Sometimes, hearing all the noise we made, the frightened nurses would rush into our ward. My wound was regularly dressed by a girl named Alla. She had fiery-red hair and large blue eyes with lashes like butterflies. Golden freckles covered her snow-white face. Her hands were white, smooth and also freckled. She knew that my bandage kept slipping all the time. In the morning and in the evening, she came to my bedside and removed the blanket. With the back of my head I could feel her beautiful face turned towards me, and I was afraid that she might notice my excitement and leave without giving me help. I lay motionless, but my heart was thumping loudly, like a heavy hammer. Alla, as if she noticed nothing, slowly proceeded with dressing my wound. Then she would cover me again and quietly depart.

After this treatment I remain there motionless, not being able to lift my heavy, feverish head. In half an hour I turn and lie on my side. I can see Yaroliyev, who whispers to me: 'In your place Mansur, I would have instantly died. But you're alive. How come you're so sturdy? She is the most beautiful and tender girl. She loves you!'

Everyone in the ward was envious that Alla paid more attention to me than to others. But I didn't dare to look her in the eyes. It was all because of the place of my wound. I wished I had been hit in the arm, in the leg or even in the head. Of course I felt ashamed that I was so touchy. I was afraid of girls' eyes but at the same time I was so much attracted to them that I cried with despair. How many secret tears did I shed in that ward, hiding my face in my pillow!

Then there was a new problem. My wound began to bleed again. It turned out there was one more splinter. Several days later Alla rolled me to the operating theatre. The surgeon cast a glance at my miner's figure and ordered: 'Prepare him for spinal anaesthetic!' The nurses asked me to bend down as low as possible. Lower, lower! I doubled over, it was the best I could do. They used bandages to tie me up in this position and also pressed their bodies against mine, blandly asking me not to twitch. It was difficult for me to sit that way, I wished I could straighten myself, if only for a short time, but these women were cunning! Their tender voices – 'Patience, my dear, it's for your own sake' – really did comfort me and I was ready to go through anything. Alla was also nearby. I saw the edge of her gown and her hand, which I held as tight as I could. Poor thing, she had to suffer as well! I heard some crunching sound as they stuck a large needle between my two separated dorsal vertebrae and the lower part of my body became numb.

I remembered how in the sanitary battalion they removed a splinter from my buttock without any anaesthetic. I didn't know which was worse: then or now? Then I no longer felt pain. But the spinal injection itself hurt terribly. In the sanitary unit I had not seen the first splinter. As to this one, it looked pretty small. Maybe that was why it penetrated so deep. I had a close look at it: a little piece of metal called a 'shell'. What a strange thing: it was invented and produced on some plant for the simple purpose of piercing human flesh. Smart, civilized men pondered over it: what should be the best design, so it could penetrate deeper? Yes, millions of years ago, we humans, lived in caves and ate the raw meat of wild animals. We're now a lot different from those men. In another million years we'll change just as much. This was what Guards Senior Lieutenant Peter Vasiliyev, our battalion partorg, was telling the soldiers on the final day of his life. He probably believed that in the future we would become better. He died with this faith, killed by a similar piece of iron, specially created by human hands to murder others.

The women and children of Pavlovo-on-Oka visited us once a week, so we would not feel lonely. They told us about some of the happy things in their lives, as well as about their many problems and misfortunes. Their fathers, husbands or sons were being killed at the front, or like us, were lying wounded in hospitals. We tried to comfort them as best as we could. They usually brought us something to eat, knowing that their men would be similarly visited by the locals in some other place. They even organized concerts for us. Some of our soldiers, who were dismissed from the service for reasons of health, decided to stay in Pavlovo-on-Oka. It was a small, cosy, and clean town. There was lots of work for everyone. Many boys got married and lived happily there.

Once I saw a young girl among the visitors. I felt my heart sink and trembled all over. While she stayed in the ward, she glanced at me several times. I was looking at her and telling her with my eyes that she was the one I was searching for all my life. It seemed she understood me and felt something similar. I was sure that – if not, perhaps, on that day – she would definitely approach me next time.

In the evening there was quite a hot discussion between the boys. It turned out that this girl with flaxen hair aroused everyone's curiosity. My roommates said that her blue eyes were even deeper than Alla's, adding that her skin was amazingly white and smooth: not shiny, but opaque and soft. I lay there silent and felt envy hearing those words. There were two faces in my imagination: Alla and this visitor. Whom should I choose? I love them both! My heart beat violently and was about to burst out of my chest. I was so miserable! I felt a bit calmer when I reminded myself that I had not yet spoken to them about my love. Maybe they don't like me at all, and here I am choosing which one! 'You're a fool, Mansur!' I told myself. But nevertheless I fell asleep only at daybreak.

Alla looked gloomy when she entered our ward in the morning. She checked everyone's temperature, wrote it down and left, without even looking at me. Then she came once more and fixed my bandage. She was about to leave but couldn't help telling me that one girl from among the visitors asked who I was, where from, and whether I was married. Alla glanced me straight in the eyes. It seemed that she wanted to ask something. But I looked away. She left quietly. I felt so sick. What have I done to deserve all this suffering, here, in the hinterland, lying on a clean bed? I felt something burning inside me. It's worse than the front! Why did I first meet Alla and then that other girl? Why didn't she appear sooner? She would have been my only true love and I wouldn't have needed anyone else.

A week passed and it was visiting day again. The locals brought us some pickled mushrooms and cranberries. As soon as the girl with the flaxen hair entered, she fixed her eyes on me. I did not know what to do. I can't leave Alla! That evening she was not on duty, but for me she was present right there. The new girl seemed to softly move Alla to one side and came up to me. The image of Alla melted in the air and disappeared: 'Hi, Mansur! My name is Liudmila. Are you happy to see me? I thought about you the whole week.' She seemed nervous as she was talking to me. I could not believe my ears! I only listened and kept blinking stupidly. In a low voice Liudmila told me about herself, about the town and the river. My head was spinning. I learned that the girl worked in the hospital, in the commissary department. She had written ten applications to be sent to the front, but she had to finish a nursing course first. Her graduation was still three months away. I did not want her to leave. From that moment onwards I was afraid to lose Liudmila! My roommates quieted down after they saw what happened. No one had thought I stood a chance with that girl.

The doctors decided to operate me for a third time. The head physician explained: 'We must tie up your sciatic nerve, which has been cut by the splinter. It's not going to work right away, but it's necessary.' Once more I was taken to the operating theatre. Both Alla and Liudmila helped move me there. Liudmila had to remain in the corridor. Saying goodbye, she winked at me and smiled. Alla was by my side all the time. Again I felt the pain in my chest: 'Whom do I love?' Once more they tied me up and pressed me with their bodies. At first they couldn't make an injection in the right place, so they kept sticking the needle into my back several times, before the lower part of my body became numb. Some time later the effect of the drug passed, but the operation continued. I couldn't scream: Alla was standing at the head of the table, Liudmila was waiting behind the doors, so this time it was really difficult for me. The surgeon put in some fifty stitches. After they finished with me, I saw Liudmila in the corridor. I still had enough strength left to wink at her and raise my thumb: everything is all right.

She visited me every day and I helped her practice. She would bandage my arm, my leg, my head or my chest. She laughed and joked, while I was ready to play patient twenty-four hours a day.

There was a little less warmth between me and my roommates. 'I don't see anything special about Liudmila!' 'She won't make a good housewife or a mother. She's too pretty' 'You're wasting your time on Liudmila, Mansur. She should be a general's wife. And who are you? A green junior lieutenant.' This was what all of them said, except my neighbour from Azerbaijan. Yaroliyev envied me, but at the same time he was happy and proud of me. He would put his thumb against the end of his aquiline nose and rapidly move all his other fingers back and forth, teasing the rest of the boys.

One old officer, who usually kept silent listening to these discussions, finally said: 'I knew that Liudmila and Mansur would become close friends. Women like modest and honest men. And who do you think you are? Dive-bombers! You're just looking for an affair!' We all laughed at his moralising tone. By that time I already realized that the boys are simply trying to forget the horrors of the front. That the stories the 'dive-bombers' told were more or less invented and that each of them only dreamed about meeting his true love. In some mysterious way I knew that my true love was waiting for me at home. I did not know her name. I did not know the colour of her eyes. But I was sure that she was somewhere there. The only girl I truly needed was one I would instantly recognize.

It was April 1944. During the five months that I had spent in hospitals, our troops completely freed Right-bank Ukraine. We were now on the offensive to liberate the remaining part of our lands. We're pressing the Nazis and will soon fight them in Germany itself! 'Who is our battalion *komsorg* now?' I wondered with envy. 'Who was the next to hear the terrifying words of the commissar: "On average a *komsorg*'s life lasts from one to two-three attacks." Is the commissar himself alive? Who else survived among our boys?'

The wound on my buttock healed and the medical board decreed that I was fit for active service. But I, a former volunteer, no longer had any desire to return to the battlefield. 'I'm fed up and sick of fighting!' They brought me my uniform. 'Hurry up! There's a train leaving for the front in half an hour!' But then something unbelievable happened: one of my roommates, also listed as 'fit', invited a major (a member of the medical board) to our ward and declared: 'The junior lieutenant's left sciatic nerve is cut. He cannot go into active service. Please, look for yourself.' The major ordered me to undress and confirmed that my leg was hanging like a rag, useless and numb. This was how an unknown medical officer saved me from inevitable death. Essentially my leg was good for nothing, it couldn't even hold a boot.

Later, when the USSR declared war on Japan, I, as an officer with fighting experience, was again listed 'fit for active service.' I felt ashamed to insist that even though my leg was intact, it was actually dead. I was afraid that I, a Communist, might be accused of cowardice. But an old woman, a neuropathologist, announced before the board: 'I will not allow you to send this invalid to the front with a numb leg!' Thus I was saved from death one more time.

Almost two years have passed since the day that Nikolai Koniayev, Ivan Vanshin, Victor Karpov and I, being exempt from service, nevertheless managed to enlist and enter training. Almost two years since I left Brichmulla for the Tashkent Infantry School. Only two? It seems that I lived an entire life! Fought on four different fronts: Stalingrad, the Kursk Salient, the battle for the Dnieper, the Ukraine.

I often remembered the day when I joined the Communist Party. This was in the freezing November of 1942, when under constant snowstorms the Stalingrad steppe became the arena where the turning point of the war was decided. In the trenches, soldiers kept telling each other the amazing news: a group of party officials had come to our sector of the front, so now people had the opportunity of joining the VKP(b). In my mind all the best and most honourable things in life were connected with the Communist Party. In my imagination, the procedure of becoming a Communist was linked with an image of some magnificent building, bathed in sunshine. While here, at the front, there were just muddy burrows at the bottom of the trenches, where we hid ourselves during the short pauses in fighting. I must confess I felt sorry that my dream was about to come true in such unromantic surroundings. It turned out, however, that our political departments were aware of such feelings. A group of three or four people from the staff, including a clerk and a photographer – armed like the rest of us with grenades, SMGs and pistols and ready for action at any moment – did everything it could to create a festive, cheerful atmosphere for the front line soldiers. Clean-shaven, neatly dressed, these men emphasized with their very appearance the fact that however unpleasant life in the trenches might be, the day we joined the Party should be remembered as something exceptional. In their briefcases and bags they carried all the necessary things, so the paperwork could be done right there, on the spot. They would busily fill in our forms and hand out a blank sheet of paper, so we could write our applications. 'How should it look?' we asked, feeling sure that there must be some standard. But the people from the political department say: 'Write as your heart tells you.' So each man, turning away from the others, begins to think it over. Our heart tells us a lot of things: hate for the invaders, pain after yesterday's battle, where you lost a friend, desire to fight for the liberation of our Motherland. And if you're destined to die, then you want to die a Communist! One also passionately wishes a better future for our Soviet people. So in the end, the soldier just writes a few almost sacred words: 'I want to join the ranks of the VKP(b) . . .' This was how millions of front line applications were written. To the men who put down those words, they seemed to express all his thoughts and feelings.

In my case there was one other thing, which bothered and troubled me all my life: a very acute (or should I call it unhealthy?) sense of conscience. I even felt remorse that I survived on the 'Island of Death' on the Dnieper, while almost all of my comrades perished. And one other thing. By intuition I knew even then that whatever the future had in store for me, whoever I may meet, I would never find such close friends as I made on the front, under fire.

Many years after the war, I was driving a car with my wife, hurrying to get to a certain place. In a desolate spot we saw a cow that had just calved. The calf was still wet and there wasn't a soul in sight. Naturally we drove back to the cattle farm to tell what had happened. It turned out that the cow had been lost and everyone thanked us very warmly. One of the men said: 'You can see that the fellow is driving a *Zaporozhets* [the cheapest kind of car produced by Soviet automobile industry – editor's note]. He's surely a front line veteran. If he had a *Lada* [much more expensive brand – editor's note], he wouldn't have bothered to drive 25km [about 15½ miles – editor's note] because of some cow.' I felt very proud (especially since my wife was present) that after so many years, people still thought so highly of us veterans.

This opinion is justified. As I see it, those who fought at the front managed to preserve a certain special quality for the rest of their life. It is an ability to understand other people's needs, to help others because of a certain brotherly feeling.

Somehow, I felt that the most fortunate men among us would be those who served till the very end of the war, till Victory Day. Not those who fell behind halfway in sanitary battalions and hospitals . . .

Upon leaving the hospital, I asked for a railroad ticket via Moscow. There were April puddles everywhere in the capital, but my own spring was waiting for me back home. I rushed to Kazan Station so as to be in time for the Tashkent train. But it was cancelled, so I had to take another one. For the time being, therefore, my destination was Kuibyshev. I reached that Volga city in a little over twenty-four hours. It was very crowded in the station. I saw many children, all of them going around hungry. I untied my knapsack: the kids surrounded me like pigeons. They were all very thin, just skin and bones. Large eyes. I was surprised to see so many of them patiently waiting to get their share. And so I got into the Tashkent train with an empty pack, without a single food card, and if it was not for other passengers who shared with me their meagre supplies, the three days of my journey would have been very difficult.

In Tashkent I entrained one more time, in order to reach the town of Chirchik, after which I planned to hitchhike to the village Brichmulla, situated on the bank of the Upper Chatkal, close to the mountains. Our family moved there from the Altai not long before the war. My father told us that he was taking us there because he wanted to 'fill us with apples and grapes.' The place is situated near a mine of arsenic ore. Upstream, in the mountain mine of Sargadon, they also extracted tungsten ore. I left my family living in that area. Now my mother and two small brothers were waiting for me, the youngest one being only five. I could already imagine how happy he would be: his elder brother came back from the war! How he would tell other boys in the street in the Russian, Uzbek, Tartar, and Tadzhik languages that his Mansur is a hero, that Mansur 'killed a hundred or a thousand Nazis.'

I climbed onto a lorry, which was already crammed with Uzbek and Tadzhik women. They cleared a place for me near the cab. I was looking at my fellow travellers, they at me. The women were curious to know about me, where I was heading, into which family a brother or a son is returning from the war. 'To Brichmulla!' I shout my favourite word and begin speaking Uzbek and Tartar. Their black eyebrows fly up with amazement. 'Hey! It's Mansur!' The Uzbek and the Tadzhik women began chattering like magpies, remembering myself, Nikolai Koniayev, Victor Karpov and Ivan Vanshin, the four friends who two years ago volunteered to join the army. After endless talking, the girls finally informed me that Nikolai Koniayev was on leave, that General Cherniakhovski had personally given him a month's holiday for carrying out some important order, and that Nikolai is now at home in Brichmulla. I was so overjoyed to hear this news, even thinking that it was too good to be true. Is it possible that after two years of so much adventure, destiny would grant us such a meeting? It didn't.

The lorry was speeding forward, rising behind it an endless cloud of dust. We already passed Khodzhikent, then Charvak. We were driving now across some smooth terrain. Over there, down below, the waters of Chatkal were boiling furiously. I saw another lorry rushing ahead in the opposite direction. It was also crammed with women in brightly-coloured dresses and among them I noticed a figure in summer uniform. My God, it's Nikolai! As both automobiles passed each other, I had a second to cry out: 'Nikolai! It's me, Mansur!' He also recognized me and shouted something. The lorries were quickly taking us away from each other: myself to Brichmulla, and Nikolai back to war. Even though we could not see properly because of the dust, we kept waving for some time. He had his peak-cap in his hand, I my field cap.

I will never see him again. In May 1944, when I was already working in the mine, the Koniayevs got an official notice that their son had perished. However, I will find in my friend's family the one and only girl, about whom I had a premonition: my Nadezhda. But this is a different story.

Meanwhile, I showed up at the very same Bostandykski Military Registration Bureau, where almost two years ago I was beating my fist against a table, demanding to be sent to the front. It seemed that now I was sitting on the same chair. The same Major Galkin was opposite me. For some time he silently looked at me with an expression of great curiosity and finally said: 'Well, tell me what happened!'

Epilogue

Soon afterwards, without taking time to rest, I was happy to return to the mine and receive my bread card again. Life was very difficult and there was always a shortage of food. Then I decided to go back to Siberia. I had no relatives or friends left there, but I was sure I could survive, even if just on potatoes, mushrooms and nuts.

I reached the town of Kansk in the Krasnoyarsk Region and asked the local Party secretary there to send me to work 'as far away into the forestland as possible.' He was happy to offer a job in the Tarakstroi Mine, where they had recently begun extracting monazite, a rare mineral, which contained up to 20 per cent of radioactive thorium.

As a front line veteran and a Communist, I got the necessary character reference from the local Party committee and soon arrived at the mine. Apart from other things, my new job was to conduct drilling and blasting operations: 'to keep my pants from falling,' as people said in those days, they gave me 50kg [almost 8 stone – editor's note] of potatoes and a cask of pickled mushrooms. They also found a small room in a barrack for me.

I had to do a lot of blasting. It was a dangerous affair. One had to be on the alert and very careful all the time. Once, as the working day was coming to an end, I was supposed to go down a prospecting shaft in a bucket. The problem was that in one of the twenty blast-holes there was a malfunction of the explosive device. I quickly found it. It turned out that a neighbouring detonation had cut off part of the safety fuse. Automatically, I lit a match and set fire to the remaining piece of the fuse. But in an instant, I realized that I had forgotten to give the signal to the men on the surface to lift me up! I pulled the wire, which was connected to the signal hammer on the surface, but it snapped somewhere in the middle and fell to my feet: the signal never got through! The horizontal blast-hole was only 5m long [almost 5½ yards – editor's note]. The explosion would surely kill me! If only I had enough time to climb some 3m [roughly 3¼ yards –

editor's note] above the blast-hole, then I might survive! I decided to use an 8mm [almost ⅓ of an inch – editor's note] cable, which was hanging down, to cover these 3m, but my hands kept slipping. If only it had been rope! Meanwhile, the fuse was burning at a rate of 1cm per second, and the distance to the detonator was only 30 or 40cm! [Between 12–16 inches – editor's note.]

'Oh God!' I thought. 'I survived the war, but now I'll be killed here at home, in Siberia!' I was barely able to breathe because of the thick, suffocating smoke of the burning powder and asphalt. Suddenly, the bucket in which I was standing, began moving upwards. My first thought was: 'Why so slow?!' But as the distance from the blast-hole increased, so did my hopes of surviving the coming blast. The bucket kept ascending, and I cursed myself for being so absent-minded, my eyes filled with tears of joy. With the exit only 1.5m away [almost 60 inches – editor's note], I heard the sound of the explosion. The shock wave rocketed me from the shaft like a shell from a mortar barrel!

When I came to my senses, I asked the men – who seemed even more terrified than me – 'Why on earth did you lift the bucket?' 'We thought we heard you cry out "Vira-a-ah!" so we ran up and started lifting you . . .' I remembered perfectly well that I didn't yell 'virah' when I was down there, 20m [almost 22 yards – editor's note] below ground-level, because I knew that the other miners were sitting in the instrument hut, sheltering from a minus thirty frost, and would never hear me.

Next morning, I asked a colleague, who was removing rock from the shaft, to scream 'virah' as loud as he could. He yelled until his voice became hoarse, but I, being near the hut or inside it, did not hear a thing! Nor did the other miners . . .

At that time the mine where I worked was run by the NKVD [Soviet security service, predecessor of the KGB – editor's note]. The digging was done by convicts. Being the section foreman, I never had any trouble with them. Once, when the working day had just begun, I was told by some of the miners that I was in mortal danger. My life had apparently been 'lost' in a game of cards [the convicts played for a person's life, the loser being the one who had to commit the murder – editor's note]. Now it was no longer safe for me to enter the working zone. I felt somewhat frightened and offended: 'What had I ever done to them?' Now I had a choice to make: I either have to avoid going into the area where the convicts work, which actually means quitting my job, or continue as usual, disregarding the threats and hiding my fear. I knew that the convicts liked to have 'fun' with their free bosses, trying to frighten them with different horrors, including this fatal card 'losing'. However, we could never say for certain when they were serious, or when it was simply a joke. As a front line veteran, what I feared most of all was becoming an object of mockery or that someone might take me for a coward. I invited Sergeant Kozlov, the senior NKVD security guard, to my office and told him that the convicts had threatened me, explaining that I still had to go on with my job and supervise their digging. I asked him to inform all his men, armed with SMGs, to keep me in sight when I was among the convicts.

An hour later I was busy checking their work. Every one of these men, sentenced to twenty-five years, was holding a pick, a sledge-hammer, a crowbar or an axe. I kept glancing at the guards in the corners, ready to open fire any second from four different directions. When I walked out of the zone, my back was soaked in sweat but I was alive. Just as I sat down in my office, I heard the loud clank of a piece of suspended rail, which meant a state of alarm. I ran out and saw a convict trying to escape. It was the man who was supposed to kill me. I ran after the guard, who was ready to open fire and finish him off. I stopped him and quickly asked for his gun. I aimed low. A short burst and the man fell to the ground. We approached him and I helped tie a tourniquet above his knee. We exchanged thanks for saving each other's lives.

After eighteen years of working in such conditions, a heart disease forced me to leave the post of the chief of an ore-mining and processing site. In 1963 I underwent a cardiac operation and then, until the year of my retirement, I had several jobs involving only light work. It is astonishing that with my serious wound and a heart operation, after which I was partly disabled, I lived to celebrate my eighty-first birthday, while many of my more healthy acquaintances and colleagues had already died.

In 1946 I married a sister of my close friend Nikolai Koniayev, with whom I had volunteered to go to the front and who had been killed in action. We had three children, who are now themselves grand-mothers and grandfathers. Together with Nadezhda I have five grandchildren and five great-grandchildren.

Looking back at my life, a large part of it filled with so much poverty, famine and war, I regret nothing. However difficult it was, whatever the losses, I can say that I did my duty well. Fate had it that I survived the war, when so many comrades and childhood friends perished in battle. Memories of them will always remain in my heart and in this book, which you have before you.

The 293rd Rifle Division

Unlike the warriors of ancient times, the majority of soldiers in both World Wars went into combat protected only by the fabric of their battledress and greatcoats. This did not mean, however, that on the march or on the battlefield they did not have to carry many kilos of metal. Instead of chain-mail or plate armour there were now collective arms, some of which even had to be disassembled for transportation. The most well-known example of such a weapon was the heavy machine-gun. The men had to carry both the bulky mount and the gun itself, often with a massive hydro-cooling jacket for the barrel. Without water, a dismounted Maxim machine-gun, the standard weapon of the Red Army, weighed 20.3kg [over 3 stone – editor's note]. But the real weightlifting specialists were battalion mortar detachments.

Just like the tank, the modern mortar appeared during World War I. The mortar was created by a man who had little connection with military affairs, Wilfred Stokes, who was CEO of a company manufacturing pumps, valves and gas equipment. The first shells for them were simple grenades, produced without any concern for aerodynamics. But between the two great wars the mortar improved greatly. The bombs were given stabilisers, a tear-shaped form, and special detonators. They became an important weapon for World War II infantry.

Between 1942-43 the Red Army mainly used three types of mortar: company, battalion, and regimental. The latter (120mm) was a highly successful weapon, which the Germans copied in 1943. Even when taken apart, it was too heavy to be carried around by hand: this is why wheels were attached, so it could be moved by car or horse. The company mortar (50mm) was the lightest of all, weighing some 14kg [almost 2¼ stone – editor's note]. However, this weapon was not very effective, its shell weighing only 922gm [just over 2lbs – editor's note] and carrying 90gm [just over 3oz – editor's note] of explosives. An intermediate model, combining a relatively powerful shell with transportability by hand, was the battalion mortar (82mm), beside which Mansur Abdulin served as a gun-layer. It was constructed in the USSR on the pattern of a Stokes' weapon (81mm), which had been captured in a border incident with China in 1929. Its shell was 3.31kg [about 7¼lbs – editor's note] with 400gm [just over 14oz – editor's note] of explosives. The detonation produced some 400-600 splinters, capable of striking anyone within 6m [just over 19½ft – editor's note]. The maximum range of fire was 1,100m [almost 1,203 yards – editor's note]. This mortar was especially effective when assaulting infantry met with unexpected machine-gun fire. Automatic weapons proved to be so successful that each infantry section had one light machine-gun (the Wehrmacht tank and motorised infantry units had two). One such gun could stop an attack of a company or even a battalion. But an 82mm mortar bomb, blasting nearby, could easily silence its clatter. During defensive operations this mortar could strike enemy infantry hiding in hollows or behind the folds of the earth, which otherwise could not be reached by machine-gun fire.

Light as it was compared with cannon, the weight of the mortar was still substantial for those supposed to carry it. The Soviet 82mm (model 1937) in a combat-ready state weighed 56kg [almost 9 stone – editor's note] and when carried around, would be divided into three parts: the barrel, the base plate and the bipod. The load of the first was 19kg [almost 3 stone – editor's note], the second 22kg [almost 3½ stone – editor's note] and the third 20kg [under 3¼ stone – editor's note]. Apart from the weapon itself, the soldiers also had to the carry ammunition. A box with three shells weighed 12kg [almost 2 stone – editor's note]. One should also keep in mind that all this was additional cargo, apart from the standard kit of each soldier: personal belongings, food, gas mask, small arms and ammunition for them. In winter frost or summer heat the mortarmen carried their heavy loads, often marching dozens of kilometres a day. We must remember that the bulk of both the German and Soviet armies was formed not by tank or motorised units, but by the infantry that had to move on foot. One such infantry formation was the 293rd Rifle Division in which Abdullin served.

The history of the 293rd Rifle Division began in 1941, in the town of Sumy, and its first engagement took place in the Ukraine, during the disastrous days of September 1941, when Kiev was threatened by Guderian's tanks. The 40th Army, to which the 293rd Rifle Division belonged, tried unsuccessfully to hinder the advance of the Nazi armour and the division was lucky not to be trapped in a large pocket created by the German thrusts. Successfully evading encirclement, it retreated via its native Sumy, and in November passed the Kursk Region, marching unhindered through the Prokhorovka area, which in 1943 would become the scene of fierce tank battles.

In the winter of 1941–42 the division was quartered close to Kursk, taking practically no part in the major Soviet offensives launched near Leningrad, Moscow and Kharkov. In the spring of 1942 the division was attached to the 21st Army, to which it belonged for almost a year, receiving an élite 'Guards' rank. When the catastrophe near Kharkov broke out in May 1942, the division was protecting a relatively quiet sector of the front. On 30 June, after the Germans launched 'Operation Blau' – its objective being the Caucasus and the Volga – the 21st Army was engaged in heavy fighting. As a result, formations belonging to four of its divisions were surrounded. However, the 293rd miraculously escaped encirclement and destruction yet again. The Army subsequently crossed the Don and continued its retreat eastwards. It was then transferred from the Stalingrad Front to the rear in order to be rehabilitated and remanned. The division was reorganised in Buzuluk, a large railroad junction in the South Urals.

How did the division look before being thrown into one of the most decisive operations of World War II, the Battle of Stalingrad? During its three-months leave the 293rd division was practically fully manned with new rank and file, NCOs, and officers. When on 24 October 1942, the reorganisation was completed, out of the 10,868 men officially required, 10,420 were present. The nationality of the personnel reflected the heterogeneous demography of the Soviet Union. Russians proper formed less than a half (some 4,523 individuals). The Slavs (Russians, Ukrainians and Byelorussians) amounted to 5,748. There were also 269 Jews, three men from the Baltic republics and one Chechen. The rest were people from Central Asia: the most numerous among them being the Kazakhs, at 2,280 individuals. Only one-third of the rank and file and officers were younger than twenty-three. The largest group – almost half of the personnel – were men between the ages of twenty-five and forty. The influence of the Communists was not as strong as is usually believed. If two-thirds of the officers of the 293rd Division were members of the VKP(b) or the Komsomol, among soldiers this number was less than 20 per cent.

In 1942 the standard fighting equipment of a Red Army division was quite different from its German counterpart. As early as July 1941, Soviet rifle divisions were made 'lighter', so as to simplify their management. The artillery of such a formation consisted of one artillery regiment, which had only twelve light howitzers (122mm) and twenty divisional cannon (76.2mm). For comparison, a German infantry division had thirty-six light (105mm) and twelve heavy (150mm) howitzers. The difference here might be explained by the fact that the primary principle of Soviet military strategy was to concentrate heavy artillery (from 152mm onwards) in the hands of the supreme command, so as to use it in the direction of decisive blows. In order to fight enemy tanks the division also included the 331st anti-tank battalion, armed with twelve anti-tank guns (45mm) and thirty-six anti-tank rifles (14.5mm). The principal transport of the formation was horses, but there was a shortage of them. The official number required was 1,800 but in reality, the division only mustered 1,016. There was also less than 100 automobiles.

The main striking force of a Soviet rifle division was the three rifle regiments. It was in one of these that Mansur Abdulin went into combat. On 10 November 1942, in the roll of his 1034th Rifle Regiment there were listed 2,130 men: somewhat less than the officially required 2,532. The regiment had the following arms: 1,655 rifles, 222 PPSh SMGs (Pistolet-pulemiot of the Shpagin design; 7.62 mm, with 71-round drum magazine), fifty-two light machine-guns, twenty heavy 'Maxim' (7.62mm) machine-guns, two large-calibre AA machine-guns (12.7mm), fifty-four anti-tank rifles (14.5mm), four regimental guns (76.2mm), six anti-tank guns (45mm), six devices for throwing inflammable mixture (against tanks), six regimental (120mm), twenty-seven company (50mm) and twenty-seven battalion mortars (82mm). Abdulin belonged to one of the crews of the latter. By the time of the engagement the regiment was practically up to its full strength.

The 293rd Rifle Division had its first encounter sometime in early November 1942. The most dramatic day of fighting was 14 November, when the formation was ordered to go on the offensive. M. Abdulin describes the terribly fierce fighting of the day, but we must bear in mind that this was an impression of a young soldier lacking combat experience. According to divisional reports, casualty figures for the 1034th Regiment on 14 November were as follows: eight officers were killed or died as a result of their wounds, twenty-seven NCOs, and seventy-one soldiers. Another fifteen, thirty-nine, and 223, respectively, were wounded or shell-shocked [TsAMO RF F.1197. Op.1. D.52. L.83]. The overall casualties, both killed and wounded, of the regiment were about 20 per cent of its initial roll. The division in general lost 1,183 men in the period between 10–20 November. On 10 November the personnel list numbered 9,274 men, on 20 November it was 8,069 (Ibid., L.86).

According to the operational plans of the supreme command, the division, along with the rest of the 21st Army, was assigned the unenviable mission of forming an internal front within the encirclement ring, so as to prevent German troops from breaking out. Engaged in heavy fighting with enemy formations, among which there were such Eastern Front veterans as the 14th and 16th Tank Divisions, the ranks of the 293rd dwindled, receiving practically no reinforcements. On 1 December 1942, the roll included 6,113 men; on 10 December 4,142; on 20 December (after receiving some 500 new men) 3,797. Some two-thirds of the officers and rank and file were either killed or wounded. The gravest was the period between 1–10 December, when the Germans attempted a breakout. The 21st Army, deployed on the western side of the pocket, closest to the outer line of encirclement, took the strongest blow. During these ten days the 293rd Rifle Division lost, both killed and wounded, almost one-third of its personnel (2,102 men): sixty officers, 140 NCOs, and 315 were either killed or died of serious wounds; eight NCOs and thirty-nine rank and file were reported missing in action.

In the Stalingrad area the Soviet chiefs were successful for the first time in its attempt to organise a large-scale encirclement of enemy forces. The 21st Army in general, and the 293rd Rifle Division in particular, played an important role in this operation, pushing back German motorised units. The heroism of the division was fully acknowledged by the central authorities: after the Battle of Stalingrad it received the 'Guards' rank, thus joining the élite of the Soviet forces. Russian Guards formations had an independent system of numbering, so the division was reappointed the 66th Guards Rifle Division. Its units were also renamed: Abdulin's 1034th Regiment became 193rd Guards Regiment. In terms of appearance the Guards differed from other units, having special badges, resembling an order, attached to their uniforms. The same sign would be painted on various machines and equipment. In this way the men felt themselves to be the cream of the Red Army. In practical terms, being a Guards formation meant getting better matériel and having one's own personnel, as well as having more weapons. For instance, an artillery regiment of a Guards rifle division had twenty-four 76.2mm guns instead of the usual twenty. The standard roll of a Guards rifle regiment was 2,713 men, armed with 1,006 rifles, 788 autoloading rifles and 344 SMGs.

During an operational pause in the spring and early summer of 1943, when both sides did not conduct any large-scale offensives and were preparing themselves for another series of crucial battles, the 293rd Rifle Division was reformed. By 10 July 1943, when Abdulin's 193rd Guards Regiment engaged the enemy, it was practically fully manned and equipped. One exception were autoloading rifles: instead of 788 there were only 295. An autoloading rifle was difficult to produce, being an expensive weapon, which the USSR could ill-afford at the height of a total war. The lack of these arms was compensated by the use of PPSh SMGs. Instead of the standard 344, the 193rd Guards Regiment had 680 of them. There were also 161 light and fifty-three heavy machine-guns. The main infantry weapon of both world wars, the rifle, was also in short supply, outnumbered by SMGs: only 610 in place of the required 1,006. The shortage of this type of weapon was in direct proportion to the lack of personnel on the rank and file level. For if the regiment's officers exceeded the prescribed number, the NCOs were understrength at 701 men instead of the prescribed 770; and so too were the rank and file at 1,321 men instead of the prescribed 1,748 [TsAMO RF F.1197. Op.1. D.55. L.2].

The Artillery of the regiment, however, mostly remained the same: four regimental guns (76.2mm), twelve 45mm guns, eight heavy mortars (120mm), twenty-seven 82mm mortars and eighteen 50mm mortars. We shouldn't imagine, however, that being elevated to the 'Guards' rank meant that the regiment instantly switched to Studebaker trucks. Horses remained the prime means of transportation. The unit had only six lorries and 234 horses (instead of the standard 363). The automobiles were generally used for moving the 120mm mortars. Heavy weapons, such as the 45mm and 76mm guns were transported by four horses each. The two smaller types of mortars were carried by their crews.

At the beginning of the Battle of the Kursk Salient the 66th Guards Division was a unit of the 5th Guards Army of the Steppe Front, which in the course of this important operation was a large reserve force. By that time the Red Army had returned to the corps formation, abolished in 1941: a corps – such as the 32nd Guards Rifle Corps – being an intermediate step in the chain of command, between a division and an army.

During the defensive stage of the Kursk Battle the 32nd Guards Rifle Corps was deployed in a relatively quiet sector of the front, at the junction of the XXXXVIII SS Panzer Corps and the II SS Panzer Corps. When the 66th Guards Rifle Division finally went into action, the German chiefs had already revised its plan to break through towards Kursk along the shortest line, i.e. via Oboyan, concentrating its blows on the flanks instead, primarily against Prokhorovka. Consequently, the losses of the 66th Guards Division, protecting the Oboyan sector, were not too heavy. On 10 July there were 8,744 officers, NCOs and soldiers listed in the division, on 20 July 6,931. Reinforcements at this period were rare: sixty-two men arrived after being treated in hospitals, seventeen (including ten officers) were dispatched from the corps and the army. But there was also a movement in the opposite direction: four officers were sent to the army's personnel department, and for various offences two officers, two NCOs, and five soldiers were escorted to a penal battalion. The losses in killed, wounded, and missing, amounted to 1,879 men [TsAMO RF F.1197 Op.1 D.55 L.11].

The defensive stage of the Battle of the Kursk Salient was followed by an offensive operation, which led to liberating left-bank Ukraine, i.e. the lands of this Soviet Republic situated on the left bank of the Dnieper. After an exhausting 350km [217½ miles – editor's note] march, accompanied by fierce clashes with battered but still combat-effective units of the Wehrmacht, the 5th Guards Army reached the Dnieper. The 66th Guards Rifle Division, although sustaining heavy losses after ten weeks of continuous fighting, remained battle-worthy, but its ranks were very much depleted. Less than 4,000 men, instead of the almost 7,000 that survived the Battle of Kursk, made it to the river bank.

The forced crossing of this river, one of the largest in Europe, was a very difficult operation. The western bank was high and steep: from it one could easily observe any movement on the eastern bank. Nevertheless, Soviet troops captured about two dozen bridgeheads, not all of which, however, were later used. Of all the armies of the Second Ukrainian Front (this was the new name of the Steppe Front as its forces reached the Dnieper) only the 37th Army managed to build up a bridgehead that could be later expanded. The bridgeheads near Kremenchug, created by the efforts of the 4th and 5th Guards Armies and by the 52nd Army of the Front, were considered as having no prospects. The losses of the 66th Guards Rifle Division during the forced crossing of the Dnieper were not particularly heavy in terms of figures, but were quite substantial if we take the percentage from the total divisional roll. On 29 September 1943 the division numbered 3,965 men and on 19 October 4,160. The number increased because during this 20-day period, reinforcements amounting to 1,041 men joined the ranks of the formation. During the same time span the toll of dead and wounded was 821. During the three weeks of fighting the 193rd Guards Rifle Regiment had three officers, five NCOs and thirty rank and file killed; as well as eighteen, forty-one, and 220 wounded respectively. Two officers and four soldiers were listed as 'missing' [TsAMO RF F.1197 Op.1 D.55 L.176]. Meanwhile, the Dnieper bridgehead was expanded and reached a depth of 90km [almost 56 miles – editor's note]. Estimating the results, we should keep in mind that the Soviet forces, including the army in question to which the 66th Guards belonged, were mainly opposed by the Wehrmacht's tank corps. This bridgehead played a substantial role in the winter of 1944, when one of the two thrusts aimed at encircling the enemy near Korsun-Shevchenkovski was launched from here.

During the crucial period of the Dnieper Battle, on 9 October 1943, the division had only 3,756 men, instead of the officially fixed 10,596. The 193rd Guards Rifle Regiment numbered just 609, instead of the prescribed 2,713 men. In fact, the regiment turned into a battalion, half of which consisted of officers and NCOs: for of the total 609 effectives, 141 were officers, 172 sergeants, and 296 rank and file. The predominant weapon of this 'officer and sergeant' unit was the SMG. There were 240 rifles, 259 PPShs, twenty-six autoloading rifles, seven light and four heavy machine-guns. The artillery consisted of four regimental guns (76.2mm), four 45mm guns, seven 120mm mortars and three 82mm mortars [TsAMO RF F.1197 Op.1. D.55. L.134]. As we can see, the artillery, deployed on the engagement line alongside the infantry, lost a substantial amount of its matériel. It is also worth noting that the divisional artillery regiment remained almost intact. On 9 October 1943, it was armed with eleven howitzers

(122mm) and seventeen guns (76.2mm). For comparison, in the Kursk area on 10 July, the artillery regiment had twelve howitzers and twenty-four guns. The gunners were also much better off in terms of staff numbers. If rifle regiments preserved only some 20 per cent of their personnel, for the artillery regiment this figure was more than 65 per cent. The formation still largely relied on horses: there were 703 of them as opposed to seven cars, 114 lorries and four specialised vehicles (mobile communication stations). The 193rd Guards Rifle Regiment had 202 horses and eight lorries.

The 66th Guards Rifle Division was a typical unit of the Red Army between 1943 and 1945. Usually, Soviet divisions were hopelessly undermanned, while the amount of heavy guns was very near the standard requirements. If we examine a typical 1943 division, we can see a compact (some one-third of the prescribed strength) formation, well-qualified for combat owing to a high share of officers and NCOs, equipped with a large number of automatic weapons and supported by a strong artillery fist. The majority of NCOs came from resourceful and resolute soldiers, so a sergeant's rank usually meant an extremely able private. The division achieved victory not by sending forward endless human waves, which drowned the enemy in their blood, but by the highly professional actions of well-prepared officers and NCOs, with solid artillery support. Such was the division that pushed forward, along with other formations of the 5th Guards Army. Its progress was relatively high, taking into consideration that it was moving on foot, storming large towns, such as Poltava and Kremenchug, and forcing the crossing of such rivers as the Vorskla and Psel. During the 28 days of September the 5th Guards Army covered almost 200km [over 124 miles – editor's note], fording rivers and repelling the endless counter-attacks of German infantry and armour.

Rifle divisions formed up to 80 per cent of the Red Army. However, during the final phase of the war, when Soviet forces launched a whole series of offensives, leading eventually to the destruction of Nazi Germany, the high reputation of the infantry was somewhat eclipsed by the armoured formations. It was the rifle divisions, however, which created the basis for the successful attacks of the tank corps and armies. Their task was to destroy the enemy 'pockets' entrapped by Soviet armour. The author of these memoirs traversed an enormous distance in the ranks of the 'Queen of the Fields' (as front line veterans termed the infantry), stretching from the Volga to the lands beyond the Dnieper. On many occasions his battalion had to face the formidable strength of German armour. It was a cross that the infantry had to bear: to tie down enemy tanks so that the Soviet armoured corps and armies could break into the rear of the Wehrmacht and surround its formations. Fierce fighting led to heavy casualties: essentially, the division was completely remanned several times. However, the number of losses was somewhat different from that described by Abdulin. The most breathtaking episodes of these historic events might well have imprinted themselves with terrible clarity on the memory of their active participant, forcing him to project his impression of casualties on the whole period of active service. The author also seems to exaggerate the numbers and frequency of reinforcements. However, these small deficiencies, inevitable for human memory, in no way undermine the significance of this text, a priceless testimony of a simple soldier who faced death almost every day of his frontline existence, and who survived the crucial battles of World War II.

Stalingrad, Kursk, and the Dnieper

Stalingrad and Kursk are cities widely known outside Russia. They are associated with two battles that proved to be turning points in the course of World War II. Their names strongly echoed in the hearts of both Soviet and German people, strengthening the hope for victory in the former, and filling the latter with an uncomfortable sense of alarm for the future.

German troops appeared near Stalingrad owing to a radical change in Hitler's plans. If, in 1941, his main target was the Soviet capital, the objective of the summer campaign of 1942 was the oil of the Caucasus and the major thoroughfare of Russia: the River Volga. Stalingrad was connected with the south of Russia by many roads and it was a natural objective for an army advancing towards the Caspian Sea. It was also the most convenient way to reach the Volga. Apart from that, the city was an important industrial centre, producing matériel for the Red Army. The Stalingrad Tractor Factory was the only plant in the country which was equipped to make T-34 Tanks, even before the war, and which did not have to pass through the chaos of evacuation. There was also an artillery factory, one of the oldest in Russia. In the Soviet era it was renamed 'Barricades' and was producing field-guns of up to 203–280mm in size. Apart from economic and strategic significance, the fight over Stalingrad had an important symbolic meaning. The city was named in honour of the all-powerful head of the USSR, and its capture would have had a strong psychological effect, discouraging millions of Soviet citizens. Stalin would lose face if he retreated from the city that bore his name. It was also the place where he himself had fought during the Russian Civil War. 'The Defence of Tsaritsin' (as the city was called in 1919) was one of the legends of the new regime: movies were made about it, articles and books written, all of them praising the role of the 'Chief'.

However, Soviet troops could not save the city from death and destruction. By the time German planes started bombing Stalingrad and the first shots of street fighting sounded, the population had still not been evacuated. The factories continued to produce machines and equipment, right up to the moment that war entered their workshops. The last T-34s went into combat only several minutes after being assembled by the workers of the Tractor Factory. Reinforcements for the city's garrison had to cross the largest river in Europe on barges and boats, under enemy artillery fire and air force attacks, and go into battle straight upon landing.

While fierce clashes erupted in and around Stalingrad itself, the Soviet chiefs worked out an operation to surround the units of the 6th Field and 4th Tank armies, tied up in street fighting. The front of the enemy advance towards the Volga stretched out over a vast distance of almost 800km [almost 500 miles – editor's note]. A shortage of Wehrmacht divisions forced the Nazi commanders to cover the flanks of their offensive with Romanian and Italian armies, which had much less experience and training than German troops. This created favourable conditions for using armoured thrusts to cut off and encircle the enemy formations in and around Stalingrad. The Soviet chiefs were about to challenge the Wehrmacht, resorting to a strategy which constituted one of the cornerstones of German military thought. In the steppes of the Don and the Volga, the Russians were to make an effort to re-enact the historic Battle of Cannae: an encircling manoeuvre with decisive goals, which had been a trademark of the blitzkrieg. Until then only Soviet armies had fallen victim to the 'Cannae strategy' [Hannibal's victory of a superior Roman force at Cannae in 216 BC remains a classic example of envelopment, and the idea of using the bulk of one's own army against isolated fractions of the enemy's – editor's note] ending up in numerous pockets near such towns and cities as Minsk, Kiev, Viazma, Briansk and Kharkov. The operation was to be conducted by the forces of three fronts: the South-Western, the Don, and the Stalingrad. On the eve of the offensive these included the following: seventy-one rifle divisions, fifteen rifle brigades, three motorised rifle brigades, eight cavalry divisions forming three cavalry corps, four tank corps, fourteen tank brigades and four tank regiments. Some 1,808 aircraft were to provide the air support (only 1,349 were combat-ready initially). However, one cannot say that Soviet superiority was overwhelming. Red Army forces exceeded the enemy by a factor of 1.2 in personnel, 1.3 in tanks, and 1.3 in aircraft. Only the artillery was almost twice as strong. A.M. Vasiliyevski, one of the best Soviet military leaders, worked out the whole operation. His plan was elegant and in its own way beautiful. The tank corps were to link up near the town of Kalach-on-Don. The cavalry, a sort of a counterpart of the Wehrmacht's motorised infantry, was to make deep penetrating thrusts in order to create the outer encirclement ring as far away as possible from the two trapped armies, so they could not be saved by a strike from the outside. Finally, the rifle divisions were to build up the inside front of the pocket, so the Germans could not manage a breakout to their main forces. This was also the objective of the 21st army, the parent formation of M.G. Abdulin's battalion.

The operation, which was launched on 19 November with an eighty-minute artillery bombardment, developed successfully. As early as 23 November the 4th Mechanised Corps of the Stalingrad Front established communications with the 4th and 26th tank corps of the South-Western Front and almost 330,000 enemy soldiers were sealed up in the pocket. Efforts to bring supplies by air and later to break the blockade with an outside strike failed. By 2 February 1943, Field-Marshal von Paulus's 6th army had capitulated, while its commander was taken prisoner with 91,000 of his men. The Stalingrad catastrophe led to the collapse of the Caucasus offensive. For many it became clear that Germany was losing the war. Nevertheless, the Wehrmacht still maintained its ability for striking painful blows. The Soviet advances winter 1942 and spring of 1943 were stopped near Kharkov by a counter-offensive by the freshly-formed II SS Panzer Corps. After that the front was for some time relatively quiet.

After the Stalingrad defeat the German high command decided to have its revenge and conduct a large-scale operation to surround the Soviet troops in the Kursk salient, which appeared as a result of successful fighting in the winter of 1943. The plan was to use the tank corps of Army Groups Centre and South to surround the bulge from the north and the south and cut off substantial forces of the Soviet Voronezh and Central Fronts. The operation was given the code name 'Citadel'. However, by that time the Wehrmacht was already worn out by two years of heavy fighting on the Eastern Front without respite. Walter Model's 9th Army, it's objective being the northern edge of the salient, was particularly exhausted. It was this field marshal's formations that for a year had successfully defended the Rzhev bulge in the direction of Moscow, repelling massive Soviet attacks. In May 1943 Model convinced Hitler to postpone the operation until July, using the time to bring his divisions to full strength. Another argument for a later start to the offensive was the arrival of new types of armour: heavy Tiger and medium Panther tanks. For the latter, the coming offensive meant a baptism of fire.

The Soviet chiefs, having fairly accurate reconnaissance information about German plans, and taking into account the recent Kharkov failure, made a decision to meet the German blow on prearranged positions, to wear out Nazi armoured formations and then to go on the offensive. For several months there was calm on the Soviet-German front, broken mostly by separate skirmishes involving reconnaissance, as well as air force attacks aimed at disrupting communications and supply traffic. On both sides of the salient, the Red Army leadership prepared a defensive line several echelons deep, and built up large reserves to parry any surprise thrusts. There was not enough information concerning the exact direction of the advance against the southern edge of the bulge, so in this area, for which the Voronezh Front HQ was responsible, the defence had to be equally spread between three armies: the 40th, the 6th Guards, and the 7th Guards. This was due to the fact that to the south of Kursk the terrain was quite open and 67 per cent of the frontage, some 164km [just over 100 miles – editor's note] made good operating ground for armoured combat vehicles. Later, a sector where one of these armies – the 6th Guards – was deployed, witnessed the main blow of Hoth's 4th Tank Army. Part of the 7th Guards, meanwhile, had to resist the auxiliary forces of Army Group 'Kempf'. But the 40th Army (the strongest) was not attacked at all.

'Operation Citadel' commenced on 4 July, in the afternoon, when the Germans seized several vantage points on the southern edge of the salient, from which they could direct artillery fire. On the morning of 5 July, a massive tank attack with substantial air support was launched against the Central and Voronezh Fronts. Since the forces of the latter were deployed less densely, the defensive line of the 6th Guards Division was pierced and the Front's HQ had to throw its reserves into the battle: the 1st Tank Army and units of the 40th Army. Soon the deep penetration of the German XXXXVIII Panzer

Corps and II SS Panzer Corps forced the Soviet generals to use their strategic reserve: the 5th Guards Army and the 5th Tank Guards Army, all in all about 100,000 men. They were ordered to stop the advance of the II SS Panzer Corps in the direction of Prokhorovka and Oboyan. In the former sector, the 5th Guards Tank Army counter-attacked the 1st SS Panzer Grenadier Leibstandarte Adolf Hitler Division, where a tank battle of unprecedented proportions took place. The 5th Guards Army went into action at the junction between the II SS Panzer Corps and the XXXXVIII Panzer Corps. Near a bend of the River Psel, the left flank of the army, having no armour itself, engaged the SS 'Totenkopf' Division, which had thirteen Tiger tanks. The right flank of the 5th Guards Army, to which the 32nd Guards Rifle Corps pertained, was in a more fortunate position. Its units, together with the machines of the 1st Guards Tank Army, counter-attacked XXXXVIII Panzer Corps, which by that time had lost almost all its Tigers and Panthers. It was in the 66th Guards Rifle Division of the 32nd Corps that M.G. Abdulin fought.

The strong reserves which joined the battle, the beginning of the offensive on the River Mius in the south of the Eastern Front and the Allied landings in Italy forced the German chiefs to put a stop to 'Operation Citadel'. The main striking force of the 4th Tank Army – the II SS Panzer Corps – was moved to the Mius River; the élite 'Gross Deutschland' Division was dispatched to the Oriol salient to help out Model's troops. However, the German generals could not contain the Red Army's several simultaneous offensives. In early August, re-formed and remanned after the bloody defensive battles, the forces of the Voronezh Front joined these, along with its 5th Guards Army. In the course of the Belgorod-Kharkov advance the latter city, which in May 1942 and in the winter of 1943 had cost the Russian troops so much, was at last captured. This time Kharkov was seized with relative ease and the Red Army could begin liberating Left-bank Ukraine.

By the end of September 1943, the extended Soviet armies approached the Dnieper. It is one of the largest rivers in Europe, its width in some places reaching 4km [almost 2½ miles – editor's note]. Its right, western bank is steep and high, which made it a formidable barrier and prevented the Soviets from seeing German defensive positions. One element that could aid the advancing troops was the presence of various small islands, which gave the opportunity to cross in two stages. The Soviet chiefs took the decision to attempt a large number of forced crossings straight from the march, with whatever available means, in order to capture as many bridgeheads as possible. This plan had its advantages: the German commanders would be disoriented, unable to establish which sector would eventually serve as the base for an important advance. It also gave the opportunity to find out the enemy's weakest points, enabling large Soviet forces to be sent against them at a later date. There were also more prosaic reasons for choosing this novel strategy: we should remember that Red Army units, most of them infantry regiments moving on foot, advanced towards the Dnieper at high speed. The formations of the Steppe Front, for example, covered an average of 9km per day [about 5½ miles]. It was a march across 'scorched earth', the invaders leaving behind devastated roads, bridges, etc. and making the supply of Russian troops an extremely difficult business. The engineering equipment also fell behind, especially the bulky pontoons. It was a regular situation for a whole army, ready to launch a forced crossing, had only three pontoons: not enough material to make a single normal bridge, only a fragment of one.

By 30 September 1943, the Soviet troops had captured twenty-three bridgeheads on the Dnieper itself and two on its tributary, the River Pripiat. In the Steppe Front sector, where Abdulin's 66th Guards Division was deployed, the most promising bridgehead was created by the 37th Army south of Kremenchug. By 10 October it was expanded to a width of 35km [almost 22 miles – editor's note] and to a depth of 6–12km [between 3½ and 7½ miles – editor's note], its supplies going through two pontoon bridges and four ferry crossings. It was decided that the bridgeheads held by other armies should be abandoned, while the main forces were moved to the one south of Kremenchug. Consequently, the 5th Guards Army, including the 66th Guards Rifle Division, was transferred to the right bank and participated in the fighting to enlarge this bridgehead, from which an offensive was expected to be launched in the winter of 1944. Thus German efforts to halt Soviet troops, using this formidable river barrier, proved unsuccessful.

Chronology of Major Events

1939

1 September	Germany invades Poland thus igniting the Second World War
3 September	Britain, France, Australia and New Zealand declare war on Germany
17 September	USSR invades Poland
27 September	Warsaw falls
29 September	Germany and the Soviet Union agree to partition Poland with the signing of the German-Soviet Boundary and Friendship Treaty
30 November	USSR invades Finland

1940

12 March	Finland sues for peace
9 April	Germany invades Norway and Denmark
10 May	Germany invades Low Countries, while in Britain, Prime Minister Chamberlain resigns and is replaced by Winston Churchill
12 May	German forces enter France
26 May	British troops begin their evacuation of France at Dunkirk
5 June	German forces begin the Battle of France in earnest
10 June	Italy declares war on Britain and France
13 June	Paris falls

15 June	USSR occupies the Baltic States of Latvia, Lithuania, Estonia
21 June	France sues for peace
26 June	USSR occupies Bessarabia and Bukovina
10 July	Battle of Britain begins
7 September	London 'Blitz' begins
5 November	Roosevelt is elected US President for a third term
18 December	Hitler authorizes 'Operation Barbarossa', the invasion of the USSR

1941

5 April	Germany (aided by Italy and Hungary) invades Yugoslavia and Greece
12 April	Belgrade falls
13 April	USSR and Japan sign non-aggression treaty
17 April	Yugoslavia capitulates
23 April	Greece capitulates
22 June	Germany invades the USSR
24 June	German troops capture Vilnius and Kaunas
27 June	Hungary declares war on the USSR
28 June	German forces capture Minsk, trapping some 200,000 Soviet troops in pockets west of the city
29 June	German troops capture Lvov
30 June	Soviet State Committee of Defense (GKO) is formed with Stalin as its chairman
2 July	German troops capture Riga
3 July	Stalin addresses the Soviet people after 10 days of silence, warning that the war will be long and hard, and referring to the conflict as the Great Patriotic War for the first time
8 July	German forces capture Pskov and drive north-east on Novgorod and Leningrad
10 July	Battle for Smolensk begins
11 July	German tanks advance to within 10 miles of Kiev

12 July	Anglo-Soviet pact is signed, stating that both countries will 'render each other assistance and support of all kinds in the present war against Hitlerite Germany' and declaring that 'they will neither negotiate nor conclude an armistice or treaty of peace except by mutual agreement'
22 July	First German bombing raid on Moscow
5 August	German forces eliminate Soviet resistance around Smolensk
8 August	First Soviet bombing raid on Berlin
14 August	President Roosevelt and Prime Minister Churchill sign the Atlantic Charter on board H.M.S. *Prince of Wales*
17 August	German troops capture Novgorod
21 August	Battles for Leningrad and Kiev begin
25 August	USSR and Britain occupy Iran
27 August	German troops capture Tallinn
30 August	Soviet troops launch an offensive north of Gomel
31 August	First convoy of Allied war materials arrives in Archangelsk
15 September	German troops complete their investment of Leningrad
19 September	Kiev falls
2 October	German forces launch 'Operation Typhoon', the assault on Moscow
3 October	Hitler announces that Russia has been broken and 'will never rise again'
12 October	German forces encircle Red Army units near Viasma, capturing some 650,000 prisoners
14 October	German forces capture Viasma and Kalinin
16 October	German and Romanian troops capture Odessa
19 October	Stalin announces a state of siege in Moscow
23 October	German forces advance on Kharkov
30 October	President Roosevelt upholds the decision to provide $1 billion in financial and material help to the

	USSR on a 'lend-lease' basis, meanwhile the Siege of Sevastopol begins
31 October	Luftwaffe launches forty-five separate sorties on Moscow
3 November	Kursk falls
6 November	In Moscow, the 24th Anniversary of the October Revolution is celebrated in the Mayakovsky underground railway station
7 November	Arrival of Russian winter temporarily holds up German advances
15 November	Germans renew drive on Moscow
20 November	Germans capture Rostov, while stalemate ensues at Leningrad
27 November	Soviet forces launch a counter-attack on the Southern Front
29 November	Red Army troops liberate Rostov
5 December	Soviet forces counter-attack on the Moscow Front
7 December	Japanese forces launch a surprise attack on the US naval base at Pearl Harbor
8 December	US declares war on Japan
11 December	Germany and Italy declare war on the US
16 December	Soviet High Command reports good progress on all fronts as Russian advances continue and Red Army troops liberate Kalinin
19 December	Hitler takes personal control of the German Army
25 December	Hong Kong surrenders to Japanese forces

1942

1 January	United Nations Declaration is signed in Washington
27 January	British withdraw from the Malay Peninsula to Singapore
15 February	Singapore falls to Japanese forces
7 March	Japanese forces invade New Guinea, while British troops evacuate Rangoon

12 May	Soviet forces launch the Kharkov offensive
17 May	Battle for Kharkov begins in earnest
20 May	Japan completes its conquest of Burma
28 May	German forces are victorious at Kharkov
30 May	RAF launches 1,000-bomber raid on Cologne
3 June	US carrier fleet defeats Japanese carrier fleet in the Battle of Midway
9 June	Japan completes its conquest of the Philippines
28 June	German forces in Russia launch offensives on all fronts
1 July	First battle of El-Alamein begins
4 July	German troops capture Sevastopol after a 250-day siege
7 July	German troops cross the Don and capture Voronezh
9 July	Germans begin drive on Rostov and Stalingrad
24 July	German troops capture Rostov
27 July	Stalin issues Order 227 declaring 'No retreat!'
12 August	Prime Minister Churchill visits Moscow
24 August	Siege of Stalingrad begins
16 September	German troops close in on suburbs of Stalingrad
23 October	Second battle of El-Alamein begins
8 November	Allied forces launch 'Operation Torch', the seaborne invasion of North-West Africa
13 November	British troops capture Tobruk
14 November	Heavy fighting continues at Stalingrad
19 November	Soviet forces unleash 'Operation Uranus', the counter-offensive at Stalingrad
23 November	Soviet troops complete the encirclement of the German Sixth Army at Stalingrad as five Romanian divisions surrender
12 December	German forces under Manstein unsuccessfully attempt to relieve the embattled Sixth Army at Stalingrad

1943

12 January	Siege of Leningrad is broken with the launching of 'Operation Spark' and the subsequent opening of a narrow corridor south of Lake Ladoga, through which supplies are fed into the city
14 January	Allied conference at Casablanca begins
16 January	Soviet forces continue to pressurize German troops inside the Stalingrad pocket and in some places, Red Army units are just 6 miles from the city centre
24 January	Von Paulus, the German commander at Stalingrad, asks Hitler for permission to surrender: he is told that 'The Sixth Army will hold its positions to the last man and the last round'
26 January	Soviet forces begin the destruction of German troops trapped at Stalingrad
2 February	German forces surrender at Stalingrad
14 February	Red Army troops liberate Rostov and Voroshilovgrad
16 February	Red Army troops capture Kharkov
10 March	German forces retake Kharkov
19 April	Warsaw ghetto uprising
9 May	Axis forces in North-East Tunisia surrender
16 May	German forces complete their destruction of the Warsaw ghetto
10 June	Hitler demands the launching of 'Operation Citadel', the destruction of Soviet forces within the Kursk salient
5 July	Battle of Kursk begins on a 200-mile front
10 July	Allied troops invade Sicily
12 July	Red Army troops of the Western and Briansk Fronts launch 'Operation Kutuzov', a major offensive from Smolensk in the north to the Black Sea in the south
16 July	German forces begin their withdrawal from the Kursk salient
	Mussolini resigns

3 August	Red Army troops of the Voronezh and Steppe Fronts launch the Belgorod-Kharkov Offensive
5 August	Red Army troops liberate Orel and Belgorod
23 August	Red Army troops liberate Kharkov
2 September	Soviet forces push towards the River Dnieper
8 September	Italy surrenders
12 September	Soviet forces advance on all fronts, liberating some 240 villages and towns
25 September	Stalin announces the recapture of Smolensk
13 October	Italy declares war on Germany
7 November	Red Army troops liberate Kiev
28 November	Roosevelt, Churchill and Stalin meet at Tehran in Persia
1 December	Allies begin assault on 'Winter Line' in Italy
3 December	Allied conference at Cairo begins

1944

8 January	Red Army troops liberate Kirovograd
15 January 16 January	Soviet forces launch offensives on the Novgorod and Leningrad fronts
22 January	Eisenhower becomes Supreme Commander of the Allied Expeditionary Force
23 January	Allied landings at Anzio begin. Meanwhile, the Soviet High Command announces that bad weather is holding up operations in the Vitebsk area
24 January	Red Army begins the Korsun-Shevchenko offensive, which results in the encirclement of more than 50,000 German troops
27 January	Soviets announce the complete raising of the Siege of Leningrad, during which some 1 million citizens have perished
3 February	Red Army troops of the 1st and 2nd Ukrainian Fronts trap two German corps at Korsun
9 February	Soviet forces begin the annihilation of the German 8th Army in the Kirovograd region, west of the River Dnieper

13 February	Allied chiefs authorize intensive bomber offensive against Germany
6 March	Japanese 15th Army advances on the Indian frontier
15 March	Red Army troops of the Ukrainian Front reach the pre-war Soviet frontier
20 March	German troops occupy Hungary
23 March	Red Army troops of the Ukrainian Front break through German positions south-east of Lvov
4 April	Soviet troops enter Czechoslovakia
10 April	Red Army troops recapture Odessa
9 May	Red Army troops liberate Sevastopol
11 May	Allied campaign to take Rome opens with an attack on the Gustav Line
17 May	Monte Cassino falls to Polish troops
4 June	US troops enter Rome
6 June	Allied forces launch 'Operation Overlord', the invasion Normandy
13 June	Red Army troops capture Vilnius
22 June	Soviet forces launch 'Operation Bagration' on the Central Front, resulting in over 500,000 German losses, while the Japanese Indian offensive is halted at Imphal
20 July	An attempt by several high-ranking German officers to assassinate Hitler fails
27 July	Red Army troops liberate Lvov
1 August	Warsaw uprising begins
15 August	Allied troops invade the South of France
20 August	Soviet forces launch the Yassy-Kishinev Offensive
23 August	Anti-German uprising in Romania begins
24 August	Romania declares war on Germany
25 August	Allied troops liberate Paris
3 September	Allied troops liberate Brussels
10 October	Soviet forces reach the River Nieman, trapping German Army Group North in Courland

11 October	Bulgaria declares war on Germany
13 October	Red Army troops capture Riga
15 October	Allies take the offensive in Burma
20 October	Red Army troops of the 2nd Ukrainian Front, aided by Yugoslav partisans, liberate Belgrade
3 December	Civil war breaks out in Athens
16 December	German forces counter-attack in the Ardennes, beginning the so-called Battle of the Bulge

1945

12 January	Soviet forces launch a major winter offensive
17 January	Red Army troops capture Warsaw
19 January	Red Army troops of the Ukrainian Front reach the German frontier
20 January	Hungary signs an armistice with the Allies
4 February	Allied conference at Yalta begins
13 February	Red Army troops capture Budapest, while RAF raids destroy Dresden
19 February	US troops invade the island of Iwo Jima
3 March	Finland declares war on Germany
7 March	US troops cross the Rhine at Remagen
23 March	British troops cross the Rhine at Rees
30 March	Red Army troops capture Danzig (Gdansk)
1 April	US troops invade Okinawa
9 April	Soviet troops capture Königsberg
12 April	Roosevelt dies and is replaced as US President by Harry S. Truman
13 April	Soviet troops capture Vienna
16 April	Soviet forces launch the final Berlin offensive
21 April	Allied troops capture Bologna
25 April	At Torgau on the River Elbe, the first contact is made between Soviet and US troops
30 April	Hitler commits suicide
2 May	Red Army troops complete their capture of Berlin

3 May	British troops capture Rangoon
5 May	Prague uprising begins
7 May	All German forces surrender unconditionally
13 May	German resistance ends in Czechoslovakia thus ending the war in Europe
22 June	US troops complete their capture of Okinawa
16 July	Allied conference at Potsdam begins
25 July	Japanese resistance ends in the Philippines
26 July	Churchill resigns as British Prime Minister and is replaced by Clement Atlee
6 August	US drops an atomic bomb on Hiroshima
8 August	USSR declares war on Japan
9 August	US drops an atomic bomb on Nagasaki
14 August	Japan surrenders unconditionally thus ending the Second World War

Index

INDEX